OUR HOPE

THE RETURN OF THE MESSIAH

THE
KINGDOM

AND OUR RESURRECTION

KEN
STEWART

WESTBOW®
PRESS
A DIVISION OF THOMAS NELSON
& ZONDERVAN

The Greek text and words in parentheses are the taken from Nestle-Aland Greek New Testament Aland, B., Aland, K., Black, M., Martini, C. M., Metzger, B. M., & Wikgren, A. (1993). The Greek New Testament (4th ed.). Federal Republic of Germany: United Bible Societies. Copies of words were through the use of Logos 5 Software 2013 Logos Research Systems.

Scripture quotations taken from the New American Standard Bible®, Copyright © 1960, 1962, 1963, 1968, 1971, 1972, 1973, 1975, 1977, 1995 by The Lockman Foundation. Used by permission. (www.Lockman.org)

For other reference works used or cited, please see the bibliography at the end of this book

WestBow Press books may be ordered through booksellers or by contacting:

WestBow Press
A Division of Thomas Nelson & Zondervan
1663 Liberty Drive
Bloomington, IN 47403
www.westbowpress.com
1 (866) 928-1240

ISBN: 978-1-4908-3397-2 (sc)
ISBN: 978-1-4908-3398-9 (hc)
ISBN: 978-1-4908-3396-5 (e)

Library of Congress Control Number: 2014906973

Printed in the United States of America.

WestBow Press rev. date: 5/21/2014

CONTENTS

Maps and Figures

DEDICATION

It is with fond remembrances that I dedicate this book to Fred and Nadine Kenison, who introduced me to the Kingdom of God and further instructed me on God's grace. Fred taught me how to study the Word. Every day while I lived in Iola, Kansas, they took me to coffee and we spent hours discussing these topics. Fred was the most knowledgeable and studied theologian I have ever met. I truly sat at a master's feet while God inspired Fred to teach and demonstrate how much God loved me.

I also dedicate this book to my beloved wife of over 35 years, Sallie, and my two sons, Jason and Matthew, who have had to tolerate me their entire lives. I could not be a more proud parent than I am of these men and Sallie deserves all of the credit for that.

I thank God for placing these wonderful people in my life.

Author's Note

If you happen to be a skeptic or do not claim to be a Christian, I hope that you find in this book some truth that makes a relationship with God and Jesus Christ seem more appealing to you.

I first became a Christian because a classmate, Ken Curl, and his wife Joni were kind enough to share their faith with me. In their car in front of my college dorm late one night, they told me that God had forgiven me and had a wonderful plan for my life. I was skeptical. I did not want to quit drinking beer, and that proved to be my biggest hurdle. I had never touched beer before college, but Kansas's drinking age of 18 allowed me to try it for the first time. I ended up really liking it, as well as the good times in the bar that came with it. Ken and Joni explained that if I turned my life over to God and He wanted me to quit drinking, He would take care of that.

As I went to my room, I decided to challenge what they were saying. I told God that if He really did exist and what they told me was true, to prove His existence to me. I went to sleep. What happened may sound like a fairy tale, and you have to take me at my word: the next morning when I woke up, I realized and believed God was real and that He loved and forgave me for all of my sins. The whole world seemed to take on a new meaning, and I was so happy to no longer have a guilty conscience.

That was over 40 years ago, and I still drink an occasional beer. I have been up and down in my life and have done things that I would rather not share. If people knew the things I have done, they would think I was a hypocrite for calling myself a Christian. I have strayed from God many times and did whatever *I* wanted. Somehow, I have always come back and found Him waiting with open arms, ready to start the relationship from where we left off. God never left; I am ashamed to say I left Him. I am no doubt a hypocrite, but most people don't understand that a Christian is not someone who claims to be a good person. We don't claim we don't commit sin; we only claim to know we have received God's forgiveness and unconditional love.

Know this—you have been forgiven for all of your sins, past, present and future. All I challenge you to do is ask God to help you to believe it. Meet Jesus Christ face to face, and open your mind so you can fall in love with Him for what He did for you. Let Him prove His existence and love for you.

Ken Stewart
December 14, 2013

PREFACE

Fred Kenison introduced the doctrine of the Kingdom to me in the fall of 1969. Having been raised in a Christian home, I (involuntarily) attended Sunday school during my entire childhood. I became a believer through the ministry of Campus Crusade, but I had never heard anything about this doctrine before I met Fred. I found it very interesting, and it just seemed to ring true. I spent many hours studying with Fred and others, and the more I learned, the more I was convinced. My friend helped me work through a lot of my questions but also encouraged me to learn to study on my own. I found this doctrine of the Kingdom to be a basic tenant of the Christian faith, yet no one I talked to seemed to understand it or place the emphasis on it I felt it deserved. This good news is too important not to be understood by your average layperson. Christians need to have a solid grasp of the subject.

I have been trying to write a book about the Kingdom for over 44 years. This is not just a book of my ideas, but what I have been taught and learned from many years of research. That is why you will find I have extensively quoted other authors who expressed spiritual truths and ideas more concisely and with far more eloquence than I ever could. I have included scriptural verses for convenience, but I encourage the reader to read the verses in context to be sure I am not taking them out of context. My aspiration is that this book would be used in a group Bible study.

You might not consider me a likely candidate to write a meaningful book regarding the Christian faith. I am not what most people would think of as a religious person. Those who know me are well aware I have lived a carnal life. I have strayed about as far away from God as one can stray. For reasons known only to God, He has allowed His Grace, and His Creation, to stir my soul to return to Him and His unconditional Love.

I am now experiencing a wonderful relationship with Christ. As you will learn if you continue with this book, He is not concerned as much about my sin as with my realization that He paid for all of those sins. We are all free to boldly come to the Throne of Grace. I am not advocating that we continue a life of sin. However, if we concentrate on Grace, we will no longer desire to live a sinful life but a life that glorifies God. He has much more work to do in my life, but He is not finished with me yet. I am not what I want to be, but, thank God, I am not what I used to be.

Lastly, I want to express my appreciation to those who have acted as a sounding board for ideas about this book. Dr. Ron Tarlton, Donnie Robertson, and Mindy Roeske have been great about helping me see things from a different perspective. I was surprised to find not everyone looks at things the same way I do. I also want to thank Callie Revell, my godson Sam's wife, who edited this so well, I almost sound like I know what I'm doing.

My prayer is that you find the topic of this study as inspirational as I have.

1

INTRODUCTION

Do you know where you are going to go after you die? You might say the funeral home, or the grave, but what is it you really believe about the ultimate destiny of your soul or spirit: heaven, hell, purgatory, reincarnation, or oblivion? The majority of the world's population expects that they will have eternal life; even those who do not claim to have any relationship with God still imagine that they will end up in some kind of heaven after they die.

Vast majorities of Americans believe in heaven and think they're headed there. But elbow room won't be a problem: About eight in 10 believers envision heaven as a place where people exist only spiritually, not physically.

Eighty-nine percent in this ABC News poll believe in heaven, which is consistent with data going back 30 years. Among believers, 85 percent think they'll personally go there—mainly in spirit, since 78 percent say it's a place where people exist only spiritually.

Who gets in is another matter. Among people who believe in heaven, one in four thinks access is limited to Christians. More than a third of Protestants feel that way, and this view peaks at 55 percent among Protestants who describe themselves as very religious.

Among all adults, 79 percent are Christians, 14 percent have no religion, and the rest, 5 percent, are non-Christians. Among Christian groups, Catholics account for 21 percent of adults; evangelical Protestants, 19 percent; and non-evangelical Protestants, 13 percent.

There are fewer differences among religious groups on the question of whether heaven is a physical or spiritual place. Belief that it's a physical place peaks at 22 percent among Protestants who describe themselves as very religious.

As noted, people without a religion are the least likely to believe in heaven (51 percent do, 46 percent don't), followed by people who describe themselves as not religious (72 percent of them do believe, 26 percent don't). Non-religious people who do believe in heaven are slightly less likely than others to think they'll personally go there, but it's a still high 77 percent.[1]

The conviction a heaven exists implies an afterlife exists, and that implies if you live a good life, you will be rewarded with eternal life in heaven. Very few people could define what heaven is or what it will be like, but, whatever it is, they believe it will be a pleasant place to spend eternity.

However, should you live a selfish life and live to fulfill your own carnal desires (a life of sin), the majority of religions teach that you are then destined for some kind of hell or an afterlife of suffering. One theme they all seem to endorse is that it doesn't matter how good you are, if you do not believe the "right way" (the way they themselves believe), you will go to hell anyway. I have seen many people have a tendency to exclude people who are not like them or don't think as they do. It's very easy to think of "those people" as destined to hell.

---

[1] (Sussman, 2005)

2

In 1988, Gallup asked Americans who said there is a heaven where people who had led good lives are eternally rewarded and what their chances were of going there themselves. Seventy-seven percent rated their chances as "good" or "excellent," while 19% rated them as "only fair" or "poor." That same year, Americans who said there was a hell where people who led bad lives without being sorry are eternally damned were quite optimistic that they would not be going there themselves. Only 6% said their chances of going there were good or excellent, and 79% said their chances were poor.[2]

What do most people imagine hell is like? Many have been indirectly influenced by Dante's *Divine Comedy*. Dante's poem is divided into three parts: *Inferno* (Hell), *Purgatorio* (Purgatory), and *Paradiso* (Heaven). It has had more of an influence on Christian doctrine regarding the afterlife than any other Christian document. Dante's hell is described with horrific details about eternal suffering, extreme torture, and pain. Most of the paintings and descriptions of hell come from Dante and not from the Bible.

Even with terrifying imaginations, the threat of hell does not seem to deter anyone from living an ungodly life. Fear is not strong enough to keep them from selfish or evil actions. They think it doesn't apply to them because they aren't as bad as other people. If the afterlife is going to happen, they don't have much confidence they can influence their path in either case, so why worry about it?

That fact that hell is not a deterrent is so obvious that it is difficult to understand why so many preachers and fundamental denominations preach "hell fire and brimstone." People who respond to the fear of hell only end up in a works-based relationship, trying to *EARN* their salvation and forgiveness. The message of salvation is one of love and forgiveness, not works.

---

[2] (Albert L. Winseman, 2004)

Most Christians, however, trust that heaven is where they will spend eternity, and they believe it will be with the Lord. Can they explain what heaven will be like? Is it floating in the clouds with angels, playing harps, walking streets paved with gold, living in mansions? When we die, do we travel into the bright light and then see God and our loved ones? What judgment takes place to decide where you go if that is what happens? It seems everyone would need their own judgment as soon as they die.

Heaven is where God is, and we would all like to be there to be blessed by His presence. The Bible says that Jesus Christ is now seated at His right hand. The Bible also teaches that Christ is going to return to earth in a physical body, and at that time we all will be resurrected. Then, for a thousand years, Christ will rule the earth from His throne in Jerusalem in the Kingdom of God.

> "The Kingdom of God" has never been lost to the church; only obscured, often, by misinterpretation. If we may judge by His own words (Luke 4:43), the most holy necessity laid upon Jesus was "the preaching of the Kingdom of God;" and if "handling aright the word of God," means the conformity of teaching and preaching to the plan and points of Bible emphasis, then "the Kingdom of God" should never fail to hold the first place in the thought and instruction of Christendom. If Prophet and Apostle are to be accepted as our inspired guides, theocracy—or God on the throne—is the scarlet thread in the Old and New Testament teaching. **The Pentateuch presents no other plan; the Psalms sound no other note; the Major and Minor Prophets see no other vision; the Forerunner of Jesus framed no other philosophy, while the most matchless exponent of "the Kingdom of God" was the Master himself.**[3]

---

[3]   (Riley, 1913)

4

Contrary to popular belief, the Bible does not teach that heaven is the hope for eternal life, nor does it teach us to strive for or look forward to heaven. Is it a hope that would empower you to endure extreme torture as the early Christians did? What enabled them to sing God's praises as they burned alive while impaled on posts set up to light Nero's parties? What empowered them to suffer and still praise God? I am convinced they had a strong, tangible belief they would be ***physically resurrected here on earth***, in the presence of Jesus in the Kingdom of God. They knew they would see their loved ones again and be forever in the presence of Jesus Christ and the Lord God.

The great American evangelist D.L. Moody (1837–1899) published a book called *Heaven: Where It Is, Its Inhabitants, and How to Get There*. The very first chapter is titled, "Its Hope: The Home of the Soul". Later, he discusses the resurrection of the body but still places this in heaven, not on earth. In his book, he never really says where heaven is, except to say that it is up and beyond the firmament. This is a typical thought pattern of many Christians that spiritualizes our hope and places it on an imaginary plane, not a tangible reality.

The difference is like telling your kids that someday you might take them to Disneyland. They may smile and say, "When, daddy, when? Tell us when," but if you don't give them any more details, that hope soon fades away. The promise has no physical reality and it just becomes an imaginary dream. Now, if you tell them, "Get in the car, we are heading to Disneyland," you can imagine how they will react. What a difference it makes to those children. The Hope is now tangible.

Close your eyes and imagine heaven, and your spirit being there with your loved ones spirits. Can you see it? Does it seem real? Do these thoughts produce emotions, excitement, motivation to change the way you live? Now imagine that next week you are getting on a plane for Israel. That night you will attend a formal dinner with Jesus and Abraham. Your entire family and your friends will be there as

5

well. Which vision inspires you more? A physical resurrection and a geographical location inspire a more passionate hope than something we cannot identify with. This is why it is important to understand the Kingdom as our Hope.

The Kingdom is a real place. I will show you the land where it will be located. The hope of the Kingdom includes our physical resurrection and ruling and reigning with Christ, who we will see as He really is: a King and the Messiah.

There are three specific themes that set Christianity apart from other religions:

1. Total cleansing and forgiveness of sins through the blood of Christ, once and for all without any actions required on our part.
2. The concept of submitting to the Holy Spirit to empower us to live the Christian life.
3. The actual physical resurrection of the dead and the promise to be in the presence of the Messiah here on earth.

Let's look at each of these in more detail:

1. Total cleansing and forgiveness of sins through the blood of Christ, once and for all without any actions required on our part.

Other religions offer forgiveness of sins if you are contrite and seek forgiveness with a repentant heart. Islam says that one must repent, believe, and do righteous deeds. If one incurs difficulties, sickness, and suffering and is patient while going through these trials, that can earn forgiveness, too.

> When the time for a prescribed prayer comes, if any believer performs ablution [a ritual cleansing of parts of the body with water] well and offers his prayer with

humility and bowing, it will be an expiation for his past sins, so long as he has not committed a major sin; and this applies for all times.[4]

… if he performs ablution completely and then goes to the mosque with the sole intention of performing the prayer, and nothing urges him to proceed to the mosque except the prayer, then, on every step which he takes towards the mosque, he will be raised one degree or one of his sins will be forgiven…[5]

Whoever fasted the month of Ramadan out of sincere Faith (i.e. belief) hoping for a reward from God, then all his past sins will be forgiven. [6]

I always wondered why Muslims pray so faithfully, go to the mosque, and observe Ramadan. It appears they have no assurance of being forgiven; in fact, the Quran teaches that no one will know until the judgment day. So, they believe they should do these things to attain forgiveness. This doesn't seem far from what many people who attend Christian churches believe.

Many Christians are still trying to earn God's love and forgiveness. The New Testament, however, clearly states we cannot earn favor with God through our own efforts or works. We must keep in mind that our actions do not change God or His Love for us. People try to place God in a box to make Him fit into their perception of what God is or what He should be. He is not a puppet that reacts by us pulling His strings. Our actions do not change Him or His attitudes; our actions should only be a *response to believing* in God's ultimate Love.

---

[4]   (Stacey, 2012)
[5]   (Stacey, 2012)
[6]   (Stacey, 2012)

Romans 4:4–5
4 *Now <u>to the one who works, his wage is not credited</u>* <u>*as a favor, but as what is due*</u>.
5 *But to the one who does not work, but believes in Him who justifies the ungodly, his* <u>*faith is credited as*</u> <u>*righteousness*</u>...

Why not works? Pride is an unattractive component of our human nature. If we think we are doing something good, we tend to have prideful thoughts and think God should appreciate our work. The real downside of this pride is that we mentally pat ourselves on the back and condemn those who aren't doing as well. When people quit smoking, swearing, drinking, or even when they lose a lot of weight, they tend to see others and think, "What is wrong with that person? Don't they have any self-control?" or "I am better than they are; God must love me more."

I have actually had Christians tell me that God has to love them more than a drunkard lying in a ditch. They really think they've earned it. Is that attitude really demonstrating the love of Christ? Faith in Christ is faith that He took your place on the cross and paid the price for your sin. If you are trying to earn it, then you are demonstrating that you have more faith in your abilities than in God changing your life.

Ephesians 2:8–9
8 *"For by grace you have been saved through faith; and that not of yourselves, it is the gift of God;*
9 *not as a result of works, <u>so that no one may boast</u>."*

Christianity teaches that all sins were forgiven at the cross. This is the Grace of God, a free gift that we do not have to pay for or earn. Believing this will change your life and your relationship with God. You will no longer fear God because of a guilty conscience, but when you meet Christ in a "face to face" experience, you will desire to know Him more.

Romans 5:6–12

6 *"For while we were still helpless, at the right time Christ died for the ungodly.*

7 *For one will hardly die for a righteous man; though perhaps for the good man someone would dare even to die.*

8 *But God demonstrates His own love toward us, in that **while we were yet sinners, Christ died for us.***

9 *Much more then, having now been justified by His blood, we shall be saved from the wrath of God through Him.*

10 *For if while we were enemies we were reconciled to God through the death of His Son, much more, having been reconciled, we shall be saved by His life."*

2. **The concept of submitting to the Holy Spirit to empower us to live the Christian life.**

Jesus said that the Holy Spirit would be sent to us to teach us and remind us what He taught.

John 14:26

26 *"But the Helper, the Holy Spirit, whom the Father will send in My name, He will teach you all things, and bring to your remembrance all that I said to you."*

As I mentioned earlier, Christianity is the only religion that provides a way to live the life that God wants us to live by submitting to, and being led by, the Holy Spirit. This action provides us adoption as children of God.

Romans 8:13–16

13 *...for if you are living according to the flesh, you must die; but if by the Spirit you are putting to death the deeds of the body, you will live.*

14 *For all who are being led by the Spirit of God, these are sons of God.*
15 *For you have not received a spirit of slavery leading to fear again, but you have received a spirit of adoption as sons by which we cry out, "Abba! Father!"*
16 *The Spirit Himself testifies with our spirit that we are children of God...*

Living the disciplined, obedient, loving life that the law teaches and our conscious expects is humanly impossible! The only way we can live that life is to die to self and let the Holy Spirit live in us and control our actions and desires. Dying to self consists of total self-denial and submitting to God through faith. It does not mean denying yourself things, but denying that you are in charge of your life; becoming a slave to Christ, a servant to all.

Acts 2:17

17 *"And it shall be in the last days," God says, "That I will pour forth of My Spirit on all mankind..."*

In the Greek, the last sentence above is ἐκχεῶ ἀπὸ τοῦ πνεύματός μου ἐπὶ πᾶσαν σάρκα The Greek English Interlinear shows the words used in this verse.

POUR	FORTH	OF	MY	SPIRIT	ON	ALL	MANKIND
ἐκχεῶ$_{10}$	←	ἀπò$_{11}$	μου$_{14}$	τοῦ$_{12}$ πνεύματός$_{13}$	ἐπì$_{15}$	πᾶσαν$_{16}$	σάρκα$_{17}$
ekcheō		apo	mou	tou pneumatos	epi	pasan	sarka

In the table above, the Greek words *tou pneumatos* are translated as "spirit," but it should be noted that it has the definite article *tou* (the) with "spirit," designating that it is *"the* Spirit." *Epi* means "upon," and *pasan* translated as "all" means "the totality of any object, mass, collective, or extension—'all, every, each, whole.'"[7] The word *sarka* means "human kind." The King James translates *sarka* as "flesh."

---

[7] (Louw, 1996)

10

The Holy Spirit was poured out upon all humankind. Jesus called the Holy Spirit a Helper.

> **John 14:16–17**
> **16** *"I will ask the Father, and He will give you another* **_Helper_***, that He may be with you forever;*
> **17** *that is the Spirit of truth, whom the world cannot receive, because it does not see Him or know Him, but you know Him because He abides with you and will be in you."*

Even though the Holy Spirit was poured out upon all mankind, the world cannot receive Him. "Receive" in this scripture is the verb *aorist*, active, infinitive of the Greek root word *lambano*.

> The original etymological meaning is 'to grasp,' 'to seize.'
> It develops in two directions. 1 to take, 2 to acquire.[8]

Louw Nida says, "The focus of attention in the transfer is upon the receiver."[9]

The Holy Spirit being poured out on all flesh is always available to anyone who wants to take it. The wonderful thing about this is since the Holy Spirit has been poured out upon all flesh, the Holy Spirit draws us to Christ without any action, works, or faith on my part. My faith is a response to the leading of the Holy Spirit, not something I do on my own.

> **John 6:44**
> **44** *No one can come to Me unless the Father who sent Me draws him; and I will raise him up on the last day.*

---

[8]   (Kittel G. B., 1964)
[9]   (Louw, 1996)

We can allow Him to abide with us and be in us by yielding to Him as a conscious act of will. This is how we conquer the desires and weaknesses of the flesh, by walking by the power of the Holy Spirit.

> **Titus 3:3–7**
>
> **3** *For we also once were foolish ourselves, disobedient, deceived, enslaved to various lusts and pleasures, spending our life in malice and envy, hateful, hating one another.*
>
> **4** *But when the kindness of God our Savior and His love for mankind appeared,*
>
> **5** <u>*He saved us, not on the basis of deeds which we have done in righteousness, but according to His mercy, by the washing of regeneration and renewing by the Holy Spirit,*</u>
>
> **6** *whom He poured out upon us richly through Jesus Christ our Savior,*
>
> **7** *so that being justified by His grace we would be made heirs according to the hope of eternal life.*
>
> If stewards will be obedient to the call of Christ and follow in love the direction of the Holy Spirit, no one can tell how far love will lead them nor yet how high love will lift the world.[10]

Living the Christian life is not difficult—not nearly as difficult as it would be if you were trying to use self-control or discipline to conquer your weaknesses. It is done by focusing on Christ and the Father and submitting to the Holy Spirit as described in Ephesians 6.

> **Ephesians 6:14–18**
>
> **14** *Stand firm therefore, HAVING GIRDED YOUR LOINS WITH TRUTH, and HAVING PUT ON THE BREASTPLATE OF RIGHTEOUSNESS,*

---

[10] (Fallon, 1967)

15 *and having shod* YOUR FEET WITH THE PREPARATION OF THE GOSPEL OF PEACE;

16 *in addition to all, taking up the shield of faith with which you will be able to extinguish all the flaming arrows of the evil one.*

17 *And take* THE HELMET OF SALVATION, *and the sword of the Spirit, which is the word of God.*

18 *With all prayer and petition pray at all times in the Spirit, and with this in view, be on the alert with all perseverance and petition for all the saints.*

The hard part of living the Christian life is always remembering to turn to God and yielding to His Spirit. The truth is, God loves you unconditionally and you are judicially free from all sin, past, present and future. Faith is understanding where you stand with God and trusting Him to take control of your situation, your time, your thoughts, your temper, your wallet, and your life. This kind of faith will build a shield around you to protect from attacks from spirits, your carnal nature, and your evil conscience.

Galatians 5:22–25

22 *But the fruit of the Spirit is love, joy, peace, patience, kindness, goodness, faithfulness,*

23 *gentleness, self-control; against such things there is no law.*

24 *Now those who belong to Christ Jesus have crucified the flesh with its passions and desires.*

25 *If we live by the Spirit, let us also walk by the Spirit.*

The Christian's life-walk, which consists in the constant renouncing of the works of darkness, in the mortification of the flesh and sin, in turning away from the godless; ways of this world, and in the denial of all lusts, desires, and vanities, is an earnest preparation for the resurrection.

Hence Christians prefer the Cross of Christ, and all the shame, and persecution, and contempt which may be heaped upon them daily by the children of unbelief, to all the treasures, and honors, and enjoyments, and friendships of this present life. And this they could not certainly do, if they believed in no resurrection.[11]

John 14:16–17

16 *"I will ask the Father, and He will give you another Helper, that He may be with you forever;*
17 *that is the Spirit of truth, whom the world cannot receive, because it does not see Him or know Him, but you know Him because He abides with you and will be in you."*

The individual is filled by the Spirit when he yields his life to the Spirit's direction and power. If you wish to be filled with the Holy Spirit, you must yield your body, your total self, to Him that He might work in and through you.[12]

The Spirit is not only resident in the believer in the sense of position in him, but He is actively at home in him, living in him as His home. **He has a ministry to perform in him, namely, to give him victory over sin and produce His own fruit.** This, together with the presence of the imparted divine nature in him, and the fact that **God has broken the power of the evil nature**, puts that person out of the sphere of the evil nature and within the sphere of the Holy Spirit. The saved person is therefore not in the grip of the evil nature but under the control of the Holy Spirit **as he yields himself to Him**.[13]

---

[11] (Lange J. P., 2008)
[12] (Hobbs, 1990)
[13] (Wuest, 1997, c1984)

The "power of the evil nature" is the conscience. When you are tempted by sin, that thought should remind you to pray for strength and to refocus on the Lord. I find two things help me focus on God, temptation, and creation. Lustful thoughts remind me that I need the power of the Holy Spirit. When I see trees, fields, mountains, water, and flowers, I am in awe of His Creation. He made the beauty of the earth for us to enjoy and it brings me to my knees spiritually.

3. **The actual physical resurrection of the dead and the promise to be in the presence of the Messiah here on earth.**

The only religions that believe in a bodily resurrection are Islam, Judaism, and Christianity. Interestingly, these religions all stem from Abraham and are the only ones that believe in only one God. What they believe about life after the resurrection is not at all similar. We are told that Islam teaches that men will be served by virgins in Paradise. Does the Quran address the eternal life of women?

Old Testament Judaism and New Testament Christianity teach that the dead will be resurrected, and the following is a good description of this hope:

> **Isaiah 35:5–6**
> **5** *Then the eyes of the blind will be opened*
> *And the ears of the deaf will be unstopped.*
> **6** *Then the lame will leap like a deer,*
> *And the tongue of the mute will shout for joy.*
> *For waters will break forth in the wilderness*
> *And streams in the Arabah.*

> **Ezekiel 37:1–14**
> **1** *"The hand of the Lord was upon me, and He brought*
> *me out by the Spirit of the Lord and set me down in the*
> *middle of the valley; and it was full of bones.*

2 *He caused me to pass among them round about, and behold, there were very many on the surface of the valley; and lo, they were very dry.*

3 *He said to me, "Son of man, can these bones live?" And I answered, "O Lord God, You know."*

4 *Again He said to me, "Prophesy over these bones and say to them, 'O dry bones, hear the word of the Lord.'*

5 *Thus says the Lord God to these bones, 'Behold, I will cause breath to enter you that you may come to life.*

6 *I will put sinews* (tendons) *on you, make flesh grow back on you, cover you with skin and put breath in you that you may come alive; and you will know that I am the Lord.'"*

7 *So I prophesied as I was commanded; and as I prophesied, there was a noise, and behold, a rattling; and the bones came together, bone to its bone.*

8 *And I looked, and behold, sinews were on them, and flesh grew and skin covered them; but there was no breath in them.*

9 *Then He said to me, "Prophesy to the breath, prophesy, son of man, and say to the breath, 'Thus says the Lord God, "Come from the four winds, O breath, and breathe on these slain, that they come to life."'"*

10 *So I prophesied as He commanded me, and the breath came into them, and they came to life and stood on their feet, an exceedingly great army.*

11 *Then He said to me, "Son of man, these bones are the whole house of Israel; behold, they say, 'Our bones are dried up and our hope has perished. We are completely cut off.'*

12 *Therefore prophesy and say to them, 'Thus says the Lord God, "__Behold, I will open your graves and cause you to come up out of your graves, My people; and I will bring you into the land of Israel__.*
13 *__Then you will know that I am the Lord, when I have opened your graves and caused you to come up out of your graves, My people__.*
14 *I will put My Spirit within you and you will come to life, and I will place you on your own land. Then you will know that I, the Lord, have spoken and done it," declares the Lord.'"*

2nd Timothy 1:8–13

8 *Therefore do not be ashamed of the testimony of our Lord or of me His prisoner, but join with me in suffering for the gospel according to the power of God,*
9 *who has saved us and called us with a holy calling, __not according to our works,__ but according to His own purpose and grace which was granted us in Christ Jesus from all eternity,*
10 *but now has been revealed by the appearing of our Savior Christ Jesus, __who abolished death and brought life and immortality to light__ through the gospel,*
11 *for which I was appointed a preacher and an apostle and a teacher.*
12 *For this reason I also suffer these things, but I am not ashamed; for I know whom I have believed and I am convinced that He is able to guard what I have entrusted to Him until that day.*
13 *Retain the standard of sound words which you have heard from me, in the faith and love which are in Christ Jesus.*

Romans 6:4–5

4 Therefore we have been buried with Him through baptism into death, so that as Christ was raised from the dead through the glory of the Father, so we too might walk in newness of life.

5 For if we have become united with Him in the likeness of His death, certainly we shall also be in the likeness of His resurrection...

When Jesus was resurrected, He had a resurrected body, one of flesh and bone (no mention of blood). It was a body designed for the spirit because He was raised with a spiritual body. Jesus could appear and disappear, yet his body was still flesh and bone.

Luke 24:30–31

30 When He had reclined at the table with them, He took the bread and blessed it, and breaking it, He began giving it to them.

*31 Then their eyes were opened and they recognized Him; <u>**and He vanished from their sight**</u>.*

Luke 24:36–37

36 While they were telling these things, He Himself stood in their midst and said to them, "Peace be to you."

37 But they were startled and frightened and thought that they were seeing a spirit.

Luke 24:39–40

*39 <u>**"See My hands and My feet, that it is I Myself; touch Me and see, for a spirit does not have flesh and bones as you see that I have**</u>."*

40 *And when He had said this, He showed them His hands and His feet.*

Jesus being raised from the dead is critical to the faith of Christians. It is proof that He defeated Death and we will also be resurrected. Adam's sin brought about death; Christ's resurrection brought about the defeat of death.

1st Corinthians 15:12–23

12 *Now if Christ is preached, that He has been raised from the dead, how do some among you say that there is no resurrection of the dead?*

13 *But **if there is no resurrection of the dead, not even Christ has been raised**;*

14 *and if Christ has not been raised, then our preaching is vain, your faith also is vain.*

15 *Moreover we are even found to be false witnesses of God, because we testified against God that He raised Christ, whom He did not raise, if in fact the dead are not raised.*

16 *For if the dead are not raised, not even Christ has been raised;*

17 *and if Christ has not been raised, your faith is worthless; you are still in your sins.*

18 *Then those also who have fallen asleep in Christ have perished.*

19 *If we have hoped in Christ in this life only, we are of all men most to be pitied.*

20 *But now Christ has been raised from the dead, the first fruits of those who are asleep.*

21 *For since by a man came death, **by a man also came the resurrection of the dead**.*

22 ***For as in Adam all die, so also in Christ all will be made alive.***

23 *But each in his own order: Christ the first fruits, after that those who are Christ's at His coming.*

The Intermediate State

What happens in the time between our physical death and the resurrection?

If the Kingdom is our hope and the resurrection happens when Christ returns, then what happens to us from the time we die until the resurrection? This period of time is referred to as the intermediate or interim state. What conditions will exist for us? Will we be conscious, semi-conscious, or in a state similar to sleep? Of course, no one can answer this question, though many have tried. Since no one can know for certain what exactly will happen, I feel that the best way to address this question is to let you come to your own conclusion. I am not certain that you need to decide what happens during this time, but I do want to convey that whatever it is, it is *not our Hope*, or a permanent state.

> Every writer on the subject of the intermediate state confesses that no attempt is made in any place whatever to describe it. The various theories and descriptions respecting it are drawn from inferences, and the admission is fully made by writers of all classes (who hold to a future personal Sec. Advent), that the eye of faith and the heart of hope is fixed, *not so much* on the condition after death *as to the condition after the Advent.* Now why such a procedure? The key lies in this simple fact, viz., that **the intermediate state (whatever it may be)** *__has no relationship whatever to the fulfilment of covenant and prophecy pertaining to Redemption,__* **and consequently is not portrayed.**[14]
>
> The doctrine of the immortality of the disembodied soul is sometimes substituted for the idea of an intermediate

---

[14] (Peters G. N., 1884)

state prior to resurrection, but without any warrant from Scripture. In modern theology a tendency to discount the historical has tended to displace the earlier discounting of the physical, but with much the same effect, at best a spiritualizing of postmortem existence, at worst a denial of any such existence. But it is clear from Scripture that the intermediate state is a state between two phases of embodiment, the present state of physical embodiment and that of "spiritual embodiment" (1st Cor. 15:44) which is to occur at Christ's second coming (1st Cor. 15:23).[15]

---

[15] (Elwell, 1988)

2

THE METHOD OF INTERPRETATION USED FOR THIS STUDY

Before discussing the method of Bible interpretation, it's important to address the oft-asked question regarding the accuracy of today's Bible translations. We trust in a book written over 2,000 years ago, so much that we stake our eternal destiny on it. How do we know it is actually what was originally written?

There are numerous works to answer that question, but the following quotes sum it up quite well. *The Baker Encyclopedia of Christian Apologetics* goes into great detail on this subject:

> There is overwhelming evidence in support of the reliability of the New Testament text. Testimony to the fidelity of the New Testament text comes primarily from three sources: Greek manuscripts, ancient translations, and quotations of Scripture by Christian writers.
>
> Through intensive comparative study of the readings in 5,686 Greek manuscripts, scholars have carefully weeded out errors and additions from "helpful" copyists and discerned which early manuscripts are most accurate.

Textual issues remain, but today's Bible reader, and especially those who read a recently edited Greek New Testament from the United Bible Society, can be confident that the text is extremely close to the autographs.[16]

The thousands of Hebrew manuscripts, with their confirmation by the LXX and the Samaritan Pentateuch, and the numerous other crosschecks from outside and inside the text provide overwhelming support for the reliability of the Old Testament text. Hence, it is appropriate to conclude with Sir Frederic Kenyon's statement, "The Christian can take the whole Bible in his hand and say without fear or hesitation that he holds in it the true word of God, handed down without essential loss from generation to generation throughout the centuries."[17]

The LXX referenced in the previous paragraph stands for the Septuagint, from the Latin word **septuaginta**, meaning seventy. The roman numerals for 70 are LXX (50+10+10). The Septuagint was the Greek translation of the Old Testament. According to tradition, Ptolemy II commissioned 70 scholars to translate the Hebrew Old Testament into Greek, because many of the Greeks in Alexandria did not speak or read Hebrew.

The LXX was the biblical text from which the NT writers, who wrote in Greek, quoted most often. Moreover, the translation of Hebrew words into Greek resulted in Greek words taking on Hebraic meanings, a fact of great significance for the interpretation of the NT. For example, the Greek word for "grace" (*charis*) came to mean God's benevolence (because it was used to translate Hebrew *khesed*), whereas in Greek literature prior to the LXX it had no particular religious significance, connoting only the human quality of kindness, charm, or pleasantness.[18]

---

[16] (Geisler N. L., 1999)
[17] (Geisler N. L., 1999)
[18] (Saldarini, 2011)

How inspired is the word of God? After all, it was written by humans, and the books and letters that make up the Bible were chosen by humans. Were those who chose this content as inspired as those who actually wrote it? Why did God decide that He would enlighten only a small group of geographically isolated men and only in a very narrow window of time? These are good questions you should consider in building your faith.

No one can answer these questions because it is a matter of faith. If you believe the Bible is the inspired word of God, then the following verses substantiate that faith.

2nd Peter 1:16–21

16 *For we did not follow cleverly devised tales when we made known to you the power and coming of our Lord Jesus Christ, but we were eyewitnesses of His majesty.*

17 *For when He received honor and glory from God the Father, such an utterance as this was made to Him by the Majestic Glory, "This is My beloved Son with whom I am well-pleased"—*

18 *and we ourselves heard this utterance made from heaven when we were with Him on the holy mountain.*

19 *So we have the prophetic word made more sure, to which you do well to pay attention as to a lamp shining in a dark place, until the day dawns and the morning star arises in your hearts.*

20 *But know this first of all, that no prophecy of Scripture is a matter of one's own interpretation,*

21 *for no prophecy was ever made by an act of human will, but men moved by the Holy Spirit spoke from God.*

2nd Timothy 3:16–17

16 *All Scripture is inspired by God and profitable for teaching, for reproof, for correction, for training in righteousness;*
17 *so that the man of God may be adequate, equipped for every good work.*

Inspiration does guarantee the truth of all the Bible teaches, implies, or entails (spiritually or factually). Paul said "all," not some, Scripture is God-breathed (2 Tim. 3:16), and Peter declared that "no prophecy of Scripture" came from man but that all came from God (2 Peter 1:20–21).

Jesus told His disciples that "the Counselor, [which is] the Holy Spirit, whom the Father will send in my name, will teach you *all things* and will remind you of *everything* I have said to you" (John 14:26). He added, "But when he, the Spirit of truth, comes, He will guide you into *all truth*" (John 16:13). As a matter of fact, the church is "built on the foundation of the apostles and prophets, with Christ Jesus himself as the chief cornerstone" (Eph. 2:20). And the early church "devoted themselves to the *apostles' teaching*" (Acts 2:42), which was recorded for us in the pages of the New Testament and was considered "Scripture" along with the Old Testament (cf. 2 Peter 3:15–16; 1 Tim. 5:18).

The inspiration of God, then, extends to every part of Scripture, including everything God affirmed (or denied) about any topic. It is inclusive of not only what the Bible *teaches* but what it *touches;* that is to say, it includes not only what the Bible teaches explicitly but also what it teaches implicitly, covering not only spiritual matters but factual ones as well. The omniscient God cannot be wrong about anything He teaches or implies.[19]

---

[19] (Geisler N. L., Systematic Theology, Volume One: Introduction, Bible, 2002)

Norman Geisler wrote in Volume One of his Systematic Theology that there are several things inspiration does not guarantee.

1. It does not guarantee that *every part* of a parable is conveying a truth (as opposed to the truthfulness of *the point* the parable is illustrating—Luke 18:2);

2. nor that everything *recorded* in the Bible is true (as opposed to only what is *taught* or implied—Gen. 3:4);

3. nor that no exaggerations (hyperboles) can be used (Col. 1:23);

4. nor that all statements about God and creation are purely literal (Heb. 4:13; Job 38:7);

5. nor that all factual assertions are technically precise by modern standards (as opposed to accurate by ancient standards—2 Chron. 4:2);

6. nor that all statements about the universe must be from a modern astronomical perspective (as opposed to a common observational standpoint—Josh. 10:12);

7. nor that all citations of Scripture must be verbatim (as opposed to faithful);

8. nor that all citations of Scripture must have the same *application* as the original (cf. Hos. 11:1; Matt. 2:15), rather than having the same *interpretation* (meaning);

9. nor that the same truth can be said in only one way (as opposed to many ways, such as in the Gospels);

10. nor that whatever a writer personally believed (as opposed to merely what he actually affirmed in Scripture) is true (Matt. 15:26);

11. nor that truth is exhaustively revealed or treated (as opposed to adequately presented) in the Bible (1 Cor. 13:12);

12. nor that quotations imply the truth of everything in the source it is citing, rather than only the part cited (Titus 1:12);

13. nor that the grammatical construction will always be the customary one (rather than an adequate one to convey the truth).[20]

How do we know that these are not included in what inspiration covers? The answer is called "the phenomena of Scripture"; that is, what the Bible *says* must be understood in view of what the Bible *shows.* What it *preaches* must be read in view of what it *practices.* The *doctrine* of Scripture is to be understood in the light of the *data* of Scripture.

All thirteen things listed above are part of the data of Scripture. For instance, the Bible uses round numbers; thus, when the Bible claims to be true it does not mean to exclude the use of round numbers. The same is true of hyperboles, figures of speech, observational language, and literary genre (poetry, parable, etc.). In short, everything the Bible affirms is true, but what is meant by truth must be understood in the light of the phenomena or data of Scripture.[21]

My goal in this book is to be as true as I can be to interpreting the Bible as the infallible, inspired, inerrant, authoritative word of God. It is not mechanical, robotic, or even spirit writing, but God-breathed. He chose to make this His method of communicating the truth to us. If we use common sense, contextual awareness, and the Holy Spirit to guide us, we will learn what He wants us to learn. The scriptures are our earthly/human handbook and, without adding or taking away from them, it is sufficient for each of us to spend our lifetime discovering our role of serving Him.

When referring to the Old Testament as the authoritative Word of God, the New Testament most often (over ninety times) uses the phrase "it is *written*" (cf. Matt. 4:4, 7, 10).

---

[20] (Geisler N. L., Systematic Theology, Volume One: Introduction, Bible, 2002)
[21] (Geisler N. L., Systematic Theology, Volume One: Introduction, Bible, 2002)

Jesus described this written word as that which "comes out of the mouth of God" (Matt. 4:4). So important were the exact words of God that Jeremiah was told:

This is what the LORD says: "Stand in the courtyard of the Lord's house and speak to all the people of the towns of Judah who come to worship in the house of the LORD. Tell them everything I command you; *do not omit a word*" (26:2).

So it wasn't simply God's message that men were free to state in their words; the very choice of words was from God. Exodus 24:4 records that "Moses then wrote down *everything the LORD had said.* ..." Again, Deuteronomy adds, "I [God] will raise up for them a prophet like you from among their brothers; I will put *my words* in his mouth, and *he will tell them everything I command him*" (Deut. 18:18)."[22]

Evangelicals believe the Bible is essential both to systematic thinking and to apologetics. It is the only infallible writing we have. It speaks with unerring authority on every topic it covers, whether spiritual or scientific, whether heavenly or earthly. However, the Bible is not God's only revelation to humanity. God has spoken in His world as well as in His Word. It is the task of the Christian theologian to appropriate the information from both and to form a worldview that includes a theocentric interpretation of science, history, human beings, and the arts. However, without God's revelation (both general and special) as the basis, this task is as impossible as moving the world with no place to put one's fulcrum. Without question, in building a solid systematic theology both special revelation and general revelation are necessary.[23]

---

[22] (Geisler N. L., Systematic Theology, Volume One: Introduction, Bible, 2002)

[23] (Geisler N. L., Systematic Theology, Volume One: Introduction, Bible, 2002)

It is noteworthy that in no other religious writings in the world do we find any specific predictive prophecies like we find in the Scripture. You will find no predictive prophecies whatsoever in the writings of Buddha, Confucius, Mohammed, Lao-Tse, or Hinduism. Yet in the Scripture there are well over two thousand prophecies, most of which have already been fulfilled.

They are so specific in nature that they burn all the bridges behind them. If they are not fulfilled, it leaves no room for excuse. How can these be explained? Of all the attacks that have ever been made upon the Scripture, there has never been one book written by a skeptic to disprove the prophecies of the Scripture. Though the Bible has been attacked at every other place, the one place where God rests His inspiration is that the things He foretells come infallibly to pass.

The Bible prophecies are altogether unexpected! I know of no one ever prophesying that any other human being would rise from the dead and ascend into heaven. That is exceedingly improbable. The chance of it happening by coincidence is incalculable. No, the Bible is not merely a book written by men; it is a book written by God through men, and the heart of its prophetic message is Jesus Christ.[24]

So then this question arises: if the Bible is a reliable source for God to communicate to us, then why are there so many different denominations? How do you know what the truth really is? If the Lord wants us to understand His Word and trust properly, why do we come up with so many differing doctrines?

One reason might be for us to learn tolerance. Perhaps God lets us interpret His word differently because He wants us to learn to love each other in spite of our differences. A good test of one's commitment

---

[24] (D. James Kennedy Ted Cabal et al., 2007)

to obeying Christ's commandment to love your neighbor is to see how you respond when someone disagrees with you about a doctrine. I have observed so much anger expressed over differing opinions of scriptural interpretation that I have to wonder what spirit is behind it. Is this the fruit of the Holy Spirit?

Many who read this book will have different opinions or doctrines than those expressed here. However, no matter which denomination or doctrine you follow, if you know Jesus Christ as Lord and that He has cleansed you from sin, then there is no doubt that you will enter into the Kingdom.

The main reason different doctrines arise from the same scriptures is that methods of interpreting them differ. Whenever interpreting scripture, certain rules must be applied consistently; otherwise, you can make the Bible say anything you want it to say. Different denominations and sects use different rules to interpret scripture, and in some cases they simply inconsistent. They usually do this to protect an already established doctrine to which they are committed, even if the Bible clearly does not teach it. In that case, they must try to interpret that particular scripture with different rules. Some have gone so far as to change the meanings of words in the original language or interpret a verse based on incorrect grammar. Others will deny the obvious meaning of a text and apply an allegorical interpretation to force it to fit their previously determined doctrine. This started to happen in the post-apostolic period.

> Martin Luther said if God wanted to reveal himself, it would follow that He must convey His truth to us accordingly to the well-known rules of language. He must use our mode of communicating thought and ideas. If He used words that obviously meant one thing literally, why should we try to find a hidden spiritual meaning?

I prefer the literal or grammatical interpretation of the Bible, which is how Jesus and those before him interpreted the Old Testament. The early Church also used the literal interpretation until the second or third century. When they started to think that Christ was not returning, they turned to an allegorical method of interpretation. Today, many orthodox denominations interpret the Scriptures allegorically. Most of this was started in the third century by two theologians: Origen and Augustine. Origen Adamantius (184–254) was a Christian theologian and Church Father credited with being one of the first theologians to use the allegorical method of interpreting the Bible. Origen had an influence on Augustine's use of allegorical interpretation. Augustine (354 -430) was another Christian theologian.

As popular as Augustine is in Church history, many point to him as the one who led the church astray and away from the truth of God by using allegory to interpret the Word. Augustine defined the Catholic Church as the Kingdom of God and the millennium starting with the first coming of Christ. Using allegorical interpretation, he came to the conclusion that Satan has been bound and cast into the pit even now during the present church age.

> By allegorization, it was believed, the mind of the inspiring Spirit could be ascertained; by allegorization, much in the Bible that was intellectually or ethically unacceptable in its literal sense could be made acceptable. This method, developed by the Alexandrian Fathers and taken over from them by many of the Western Fathers, in fact obscured the mind of the Spirit and obliterated the historical character of biblical revelation.[25]

> The early church fathers in Alexandria (Egypt), influenced by Greek philosophical thought, began a whole school of biblical interpretation in which the text was largely allegorized. That is, the meaning of the text was sought not in the plain or literal meaning of the words; the words were thought to stand for spiritual ideas in the mind of God. The

---

[25] (Wood D. a., 1996)

Alexandrians sought to understand Scripture by imagining what God would want to communicate. Imaginative interpretations piled on top of each other until they became bizarre or even fantastic, as the Alexandrian influence spread through the Western church in the Middle Ages. Another school of interpretation, not rejecting allegorizing entirely, but generally paying more attention to actual words of the Bible, grew up among the church fathers in Antioch (Syria). It had less influence than the Alexandrians on the medieval scholastic theologians, who for almost a thousand years obscured much of the literal, historical meaning of Bible passages with mystical interpretations.[26]

John Bunyan's *Pilgrim's Progress* is an allegory. However, with Bunyan the surface is to be entertaining, while the subsurface meaning is to be related to life; with the Bible the surface is actually tied to history, etc., and cannot be ignored. We are not to look beneath the surface unless there is warrant for doing so.

Allegorical interpretation was practiced extensively by the Greek philosophers and historians in their treatment of secular and sacred Greek texts. Schools at Alexandria, Egypt, given to the preservation of the Greek classics, exercised profound influence on Jewish interpreters who labored there in the interpretation of Old Testament texts.[27]

The challenge is to maintain a consistent method of interpretation, so I wrote this book trying my best to observe the following rules:

1. The obvious meaning is true.

    The correct understanding of any written document is a science. Indeterminate or capricious exegesis is excluded. A first and obvious principle of true interpretation is that of

---

[26] (Elwell, 1988)
[27] (Karleen, 1987)

objective listening to the writer or speaker in terms of what he has to say and not of alien or imported considerations or concerns. The plain, literal, and original meaning always has the right-of-way. All wresting of the passage, reinterpretation in terms of a different outlook, application to a clearly divergent matter, or reading-in of meanings that are not merely new but intrinsically improbable in the light of the context is unscientific and misleading.[28]

2. Allowances are made for obvious or documented figures of speech and idioms.
3. The language must be interpreted according to grammatical rules. Close attention should be paid to differences in original grammar and English interpretation, specifically the use of articles and prepositions.
4. All parts must be taken in context, including historical and geographical context.
5. If it is literally presented as an allegory, or as poetry, it should be interpreted as such.
6. Isolated passages must not be interpreted in a way that would contradict other biblical passages.
7. Allowances must also be made for the culture of the people and times in which the text was written.

The Bible should be interpreted grammatically, as one would any other book. To interpret any other way opens the door to any doctrine that man can conceive. Why even read the Bible if the most obvious reading is not the intended meaning? If there is no standard for interpretation, the Bible can be interpreted to support any idea. The Bible must be our standard in understanding God and His precepts.

There are two basic steps in interpretation. One must ask: (1) What did the passage mean for the person who first spoke these words or wrote them and for the people who

---

[28] (Geoffrey W. Bromiley, 1979-1988)

first heard or read them? (2) What should the passage mean to a reader today? The first task is to enter into the circumstances of the person who first wrote or heard or read the passage and then try to understand the meaning in the light of the whole Bible. The second is to try to make the meaning of the passage clear in the circumstances of the present century. Interpreters in every age have struggled to be faithful in these two steps.[29]

The more willingly an interpreter submits his proposed construction of a text to the scrutiny of others who have also worked hard to understand it, the higher will be the probability of achieving a consensus regarding the meaning its author wanted to transmit. The greatest difficulty to be overcome in the interpretation of texts is the famous "hermeneutical circle." (One's mind is so delighted with all the "evidence" and "coherency" its construction draws from the text that anger is easily generated against different constructions of that text, which also claim coherency and cite much "evidence" in their support.) But the interpreter who is aware of the alluring power of the hermeneutical circle and who desires truth more than the ego satisfaction of hanging onto his pet ways of construing a text will want to consider seriously the objections another interpreter brings against his way of gaining a supposedly coherent view of a text.[30]

As if all of this is not difficult enough, when we start looking at the prophetical writings in the Bible (and there are a lot of them), it becomes even more difficult. Remaining true to these rules of interpretation can be very difficult when trying to interpret prophecy and specific events relating to the end times. Many years have been spent trying to decipher scriptures regarding these things, and I have finally come to the conclusion that I am not able to honestly

---

[29] (Elwell, 1988)
[30] (Geoffrey W. Bromiley, 1979-1988)

determine all of the details of events relating to eschatology, the study of the end times. A lot of prophetic scriptures still remain a mystery to me.

Interpretations of prophetical scriptures cause more arguments over doctrines and core beliefs than anything else. So many people believe that the way they interpret the scriptures is the only way they can be interpreted. If you don't agree, then you are a heretic. Emotions get involved, and suddenly loving Christians can't agree on anything, from the color of the choir robes to the method of baptism and communion and on and on.

This is why we see a different church on each corner, or several on one street. Some of them may even be of the same denomination. Are we really supposed to divide the body of Christ because we cannot agree on interpretation?

Colossians 3:12–14

12 *So, as those who have been chosen of God, holy and beloved, put on a heart of compassion, kindness, humility, gentleness and patience;*
13 ***bearing with one another, and forgiving each other****, whoever has a complaint against anyone; just as the Lord forgave you, so also should you.*
14 *Beyond all these things **put on love, which is the perfect bond of unity**."*

1st Corinthians 1:10–13

10 *I beg you, brothers and sisters, by the name of our Lord Jesus Christ that all of you agree with each other and **not be split into groups**. I beg that you be **completely joined together** by having the same kind of thinking and the same purpose.*

> **11** *My brothers and sisters, some people from Chloe's family have told me quite plainly that there are quarrels among you.*
> **12** *This is what I mean: One of you says, "I follow Paul"; another says, "I follow Apollos"; another says, "I follow Peter"; and another says, "I follow Christ."*
> **13** ***Christ has been divided up into different groups****!*

What does the church divided say to the world? Does this show the power of God's love? In the beginning of Christianity, churches were only divided by location, not differences of opinion. No two people will agree on everything, but we need to learn to tolerate other opinions and be open minded enough to allow the Holy Spirit to lead us to the truth. If we only associate with those who agree with us, then how can we honestly say we are seeking the truth? This is not advocating fellowship with heretics, but we often are too quick to condemn those who believe minor doctrines differently. We need to be careful of what we define as heresy.

3

VARIOUS DOCTRINES REGARDING THE KINGDOM OF GOD

The study of Christian doctrines regarding the end times is called eschatology, from the term "Last Days" (ἔσχατον, or *eschaton*), translated from the original Koine Greek as "last, or pertaining to the last in a series of events." Koine (common, or *koinē*) Greek is the language of the New Testament and the common people, as opposed to classical Greek

There are three prevailing millennial views of the Kingdom within orthodox Christianity.

- Premillennial—Christ will return before the one thousand year Kingdom
- Amillennial—there is no one thousand year Kingdom
- Postmillennial—the Lord will come after the one thousand year Kingdom

PREMILLENNIALISM

Premillennialism posits that the coming of the Lord is before (pre) the millennium or Kingdom. The rest of this book is an attempt to show that the Bible adheres to the premillennial doctrine. Understanding that we as Christians will be resurrected to live with Christ in His Kingdom is a hope that purifies, strengthens, and enables us to undergo tribulations and trials that would otherwise not be endurable. The early church believed in the premillennial Kingdom, and it was not until the third century that the church started to declare itself the manifestation of the Kingdom due to the Gnostic and Alexandrian influence.

The premillennial view believes that the Kingdom is the 1,000-year reign of Jesus Christ here on earth. Christ will return (in a glorified body) and establish His Kingdom. Geographically, it will be based in the Promised Land, situated near Jerusalem. This is referred to as the millennial reign of Christ or the millennium as it is prophesized to be 1,000 years in length.

Premillennialism was the primary viewpoint of the Church from the first to the third centuries and embodied the hope that enabled them to shout praises to God while being devoured alive by wild animals, or burning on stakes, or hung on crosses. They "saw" clearly the life promised them with Christ and recognized that it was better than anything life afforded them here.

> Papias, Justin Martyr, Irenaeus, and Cyprian, among the earliest Fathers, all held the doctrine of a millennial Kingdom on earth; not till millennial views degenerated into gross carnalism was this doctrine abandoned.

> Chiliasm (from a Greek word meaning "a thousand") arose very early in the history of theology. Some of the early Church Fathers distinguished between a first and a second resurrection, and held that there would be an intervening millennial Kingdom in which Christ would reign with His saints upon the earth. This view may be found in Papias, Irenaeus, Barnabas, Hermas, Justin Martyr, and Tertullian (all from the second century). But by the time of Luther

and Calvin, the leading theologians (both Roman Catholic and Protestant) had rejected the doctrine of an earthly millennium. Calvin calls it a "fiction," and says that it is "too puerile to need or to deserve refutation."[31]

Premillennialism is not a radical concept. Grace, Talbot, and Dallas Theological Seminaries were all founded by premillennialists. Many leaders of the faith such as Scofield, Ryrie, D.L. Moody, John Walvoord, and even Billy Sunday believed in a premillennial Kingdom.

> The fact that Premillennialism was the initial view of the Church is quite significant because it favors the conclusion that Premillennialism is the correct millennial view. It should be noted, however, that correctness of a view is not proven conclusively by the fact that it was the original view. Initial impressions and conclusions of human beings in any realm of knowledge can be incorrect. Because this is true, the ultimate test of correctness for any view in the realm of theology is not the question of it being the original view, but the question of its agreement with the Scriptures. In order for a view concerning the Millennium to be correct, it must agree with the teaching of the Bible.[32]

> ...the Davidic Covenant and its fulfillment presented evidence that the premillennial view of the Millennium agrees with the teaching of the Bible. Further evidence to the same effect is found in an examination of the Kingdom of God concept in the Scriptures.[33]

> Joseph Mede (1586-1638), a prominent Anglican Church Bible scholar, pioneered the return to the literal interpretation of the Kingdom of God passages in the Bible. As a result, he "concluded that the Scriptures held

---

[31] (Jamieson, 1997)
[32] (Showers, 1990)
[33] (Showers, 1990)

the promise of a literal Kingdom of God," and that this Kingdom would come in the future. This conclusion prompted him to adopt the premillennial view of the early Church. Other scholars began to follow his example.[34]

Most of the Evangelicals I have talked to may claim to be premillennialists; however, they also strongly stress that the Kingdom is now, in your heart, and thus we should not cling to it as a hope. I address the issue of the Kingdom being in your heart in a later chapter, but I think it is very important we understand that is not the Kingdom. They are more certain of their stance on the rapture (Pre-, Mid-, or Post-) than understanding the Hope of the Kingdom.

It may be an eternal quality of life we receive when we are in a relationship with God through believing in Christ, but that is not the Kingdom. To consider our current walk with God as the Kingdom dilutes the hope and the promises. If the hope of the Kingdom is a hope that purifies and strengthens our walk with God in the present, then we must have a clear and concise understanding of that hope and its culmination of the return of Christ.

Why the Millennium? There are at least four answers to this question:

1. During the Millennium, Christ will openly manifest his kingdom in world history; the Millennium will provide an actual demonstration of the truthfulness of the divine witness borne by Christ and his followers during their lives on earth. It will be a time of the fulfillment of all God's covenant promises to His people.

2. The Millennium will reveal that man's rebellion against God lies deep in man's own heart, not in the devil's deception. Even when Satan is bound and

---

[34] (Showers, 1990)

righteousness prevails in the world, some people will still rebel against God. The final release of Satan will openly draw out this hidden evil.

3. The release of Satan after the Millennium shows the invulnerability of the city of God and the extent of the authority of Christ, since the devil is immediately defeated and cast into the lake of fire forever.

4. The Millennium will serve as a long period required to do the general "housecleaning" needed after the preceding ages of sin, during which sin was prevalent.[35]

The essence of Premillennialism is in its insistence that the reign will be on earth, not in heaven, for a period of time before the final judgment and the new heavens and earth...it is not of primary importance whether the years are actual **365**-day years or symbolic of a shorter or longer period of bliss enjoyed by believers as they reign with Christ on earth.[36]

AMILLENNIALISM

Amillennialists reject the literal interpretation of all the prophecies and references to the Kingdom. The Amillennial viewpoint doesn't deny the Kingdom, as there are too many scriptures promising the Kingdom to ignore them. They deny that it is a literal return of Christ physically, and they identify the Church as the Kingdom. "A-" is a Greek prefix for "no." So, they imagine no millennial reign on earth. They completely reject the promise of a political, physical reign of Christ upon the earth. St. Augustine was the first theologian to claim

---

[35] Gaebelein, Frank E., Leon Morris, Donald W. Burdick, Edwin A. Blum, Glenn W. Barker, and Alan F. Johnson. *The Expositor's Bible Commentary: Hebrews through Revelation.* Vol. 12. Grand Rapids, MI: Zondervan Publishing House, 1981.

[36] (Showers, 1990)

that the visible Catholic Church was the fulfillment of the Kingdom of God.

> After the fourth century the western church started to join the revolt against premillennial belief. Two major factors contributed to this change. First, Alexandrian theology was brought to the west by such influential church leaders as Jerome and Ambrose. As a result of being taught by Greek theologians in the east for several years, Jerome (345–420 AD) declared that he had been delivered from "Jewish opinions," and he ridiculed the early premillennial beliefs.[37]

> The second major factor which prompted the rejection of Premillennialism in the west was the teaching of Augustine (354–430 A.D.), the Bishop of Hippo, concerning the Church. Augustine himself had been a premillennialist in the early days of his Christian faith; however, through time he rejected that view in favor of a new one which he developed. That new view became known as Amillennialism.[38]

> Several things prompted this change in Augustine. First, the political situation of the Church had changed radically around the period of his life. By Augustine's time the persecution of the Church by Rome had stopped, and the state had made itself the servant of the Church. As the Roman Empire crumbled, the Church stood fast, ready to rule in place of the empire. It looked as if Gentile world dominion was being crushed and that the Church was becoming victorious over it.[39]

> Under these circumstances, Augustine concluded that Premillennialism was obsolete, that it did not fit the

---

[37] (Showers, 1990)

[38] (Showers, 1990)

[39] (Showers, 1990)

changed situation. In place of it he developed the idea that the Church is the Kingdom of Messiah foretold in such Scriptures as organized Catholic (universal) Church is the Messianic Kingdom and that the millennium began with the first coming of Christ. Augustine wrote, "The saints reign with Christ during the same thousand years, understood in the same way, that is, of the time of His first coming," and, "Therefore the Church even now is the Kingdom of Christ, and the Kingdom of heaven. Accordingly, even now His saints reign with Him."

The second factor which prompted Augustine to reject Premillennialism was his negative reaction to his own pleasure-seeking, self-indulgent, immoral lifestyle in his preconversion days. "After his conversion to Christianity, Augustine, a former bon vivant, consistently favored a world-denying and ascetic style of life." This led him to reject "as carnal any expectations of a renewed and purified world that the believers could expect to enjoy." [40]

The third factor in his change of view was the influence of Greek philosophy upon his thinking. Before his conversion Augustine was deeply immersed in the study of this philosophy, much of which asserted the inherent evil of the physical or material and the inherent goodness of the totally spiritual. This philosophy continued to leave its mark upon him even after his conversion. It also prompted him to reject as carnal the premillennial idea of an earthly, political Kingdom of God with great material blessings. To his way of thinking, in order for the Kingdom of God to be good, it must be spiritual in nature. Thus, "for him the millennium had become a spiritual state into which the Church collectively had entered at Pentecost ... and which the individual Christian might already enjoy through mystical communion with God. [41]

---

[40] (Showers, 1990)
[41] (Showers, 1990)

Concerning the premillennial opinion Augustine wrote,

And this opinion would not be objectionable, if it were believed that the joys of the saints in that Sabbath shall be spiritual, and consequent on the presence of God; for I myself, too, once held this opinion. But, as they assert that those who then rise again shall enjoy the leisure of immoderate carnal banquets, furnished with an amount of meat and drink such as not only to shock the feeling of the temperate, but even to surpass the measure of credulity itself, such assertions can be believed only by the carnal. They who do believe them are called by the spiritual Chiliasts, which we may literally reproduce by the name Millenarians. [42]

In order to avoid the implications of some of the millennial passages in the Bible, Augustine applied Origen's allegorical method of interpretation to the prophets and the Book of Revelation. For example, according to Augustine the abyss in which Satan is confined during the millennial reign of Christ (Rev. 20:1-3) is not a literal location or place. Instead, he said, "By the abyss is meant the countless multitude of the wicked whose hearts are unfathomably deep in malignity against the Church of God." His interpretation of Satan's being cast into the abyss was as follows: "He is said to be cast in thither, because, when prevented from harming believers, he takes more complete possession of the ungodly." He said that the binding and shutting up of Satan in the abyss "means his being more unable to seduce the Church." Augustine was convinced that this binding of Satan in the abyss is a reality during this present Church age.

In addition, Augustine interpreted the first resurrection (referred to by John in conjunction with the establishment of the millennial reign of Christ, Rev. 20:4–6) as being not

---

[42] (Showers, 1990)

the future bodily resurrection of believers but the present spiritual resurrection of the soul which takes place at the new birth.

"Augustine's allegorical millennialism became the official doctrine of the church," and Premillennialism went underground. Some aspects of Premillennialism were even branded as heretical. The Roman Catholic Church strongly advocated and maintained Augustine's amillennial view throughout the Middle Ages. During that span of time occasional premillennial groups formed to challenge the doctrine and political power of the major part of organized Christendom, but they were not able to restore Premillennialism to its original position as the accepted, orthodox view of the Church. Many Anabaptists were premillennial by conviction during the Reformation era. Some of these were quite radical in their Premillennialism, but many were not. The Lutheran, Reformed, and Anglican reformers rejected Premillennialism as being "Jewish opinions." They maintained the amillennial view which the Roman Catholic Church had adopted from Augustine.[43]

They spiritualized the promises because they grew impatient waiting for Christ's return. They wrongly interpreted the scriptures referring to the Kingdom and applied them to the church. This is why the rules of interpretation must be understood. They did not trust that the obvious meaning of these scriptures was true, so they applied a second meaning.

The church as a visible organization never had greater power over the minds of men. She controlled all departments of life from the cradle to the grave. She monopolized all the learning and made sciences and arts tributary to her. She took the lead in every progressive movement. She

---

[43] (Showers, 1990)

founded universities, built lofty cathedrals, stirred up the crusades, made and unmade kings, dispensed blessings and curses to whole nations. The mediaeval hierarchy centering in Rome re-enacted the Jewish theocracy on a more comprehensive scale. It was a **carnal** anticipation of the millennial reign of Christ.[44]

We must not confound this lofty conception of the church as the body of Christ with any particular ecclesiastical organization, which at best is only a part of the whole, and an imperfect approach to the ideal. Nor must we identify it with the still higher idea of the Kingdom of God or the Kingdom of heaven. A vast amount of presumption, bigotry, and intolerance has grown out of such confusion. It is remarkable that Christ speaks only once of the church in the organic or universal sense. But he very often speaks of the Kingdom, and nearly all his parables illustrate this grand idea. The two conceptions are closely related, yet distinct. In many passages we could not possibly substitute the one for the other without manifest impropriety.

We could not say "Thy church come" (Matt. 6:9); "to such (children) belongeth the church" (Mark 10:14); "the church cometh not with observation" (Luke 17:21); "neither fornicators, etc…shall inherit the church" (1 Cor. 6:10); "the church is not eating and drinking, but righteousness and peace and joy in the Holy Spirit" (Rom. 15:17). On the other hand, it would be improper to call the Kingdom of God "the body of Christ" or "the bride of the Lamb."[45]

The reformers denied that the Roman Church could be the fulfillment of the Kingdom, so they spiritualized it. They determined that the Kingdom was invisible and spiritual in nature. If one was saved, then Christ was their king and they were in the Kingdom.

---

[44] (Schaff, 1997)

[45] (Schaff, 1997)

This interpretation does not induce much hope, especially when one is at death's door. Proponents of this theology base a lot of this interpretation on Luke 17:20-21. This is Jesus saying, "The Kingdom is within you." I will address this verse in a later chapter. Suffice it to say, this does not follow the rules of interpretation because they do not take the verse in context.

I cannot fathom scholars would actually imagine this present age is the Kingdom and that paradise has been restored. There is, however, an association called the International Preterist Association. The term *preterist* means one who believes the Kingdom has been fulfilled in the past, as compared to a *futurist* who would suppose the Kingdom is in the future. This quickly growing organization refers to the hope of a physical return of Christ and His Kingdom as a false hope and calls the premillennial viewpoint "pie in the sky, bye and bye." They believe Christ's plan of redemption was consummated with the destruction of Jerusalem in 70 AD and we now live in the Garden of Eden if we are in Christ.

Here are a few excerpts from the website of the International Preterist Association (www.preterist.org):

> Bible prophecy absolutely makes sense when approached from this past-fulfillment (preterist) perspective! It puts emphasis on the spiritual nature of God's Kingdom, not on the physical, materialistic, sensual, and sensational. It teaches a realized spiritual salvation in Christ and the Church now, instead of a frustrated hope for a postponed sensually-gratifying paradise way off in the future. It has an optimistic worldview that gets involved, makes a positive difference, and lights a candle, rather than cursing the darkness, longing for a rapture-escape, or retreating from society. It doesn't engage in wild-eyed speculation like futurist views. It's just simple, straight-forward Bible interpretation.[46]

---

[46] (The International Preterist Association Website)

> Many knew the destruction of Jerusalem in 70 AD was important in God's scheme of redemption, but never understood its full significance. It has to do with the consummation of the plan of redemption. The final events of the redemptive drama came to pass in the first century within the apostles' generation (before A.D. 70). Christ's Kingdom is here now. Paradise has been restored in Christ (spiritually-speaking). We live in the Garden of Eden now (if we are in Christ), just as sure as we can know we have "eternal life." These are present and abiding benefits, not pie-in-the-sky bye-and-bye. Christ has conquered all His enemies and has given us the Kingdom.[47]

Life in Christ is truly marvelous, but it will be much more wonderful to be in His physical presence, to sit down at a table and have communion with Him, Abraham, Isaac, and Jacob. As believers, Christ comforts us in times of tragedy and death, but we have a hope of the resurrection. Death has been defeated! The preterist view does not seem to express that hope. If this is it, then why do I not see the lame leaping like deer, nor the child playing at the adder's den? I still see creation groaning in corruption waiting for the revealing of the sons of God.

It is the popularity of viewpoints like this that inspired me to write this book.

POSTMILLENNIALISM

"Post-" is a prefix for *after*, so postmillennialists believe **Christ will return after the Millennium**. This doctrine is based on the teachings of Daniel Whitby, an English Unitarian. He taught that as Christianity spread throughout the world, the entire population would eventually become followers of Christ and subjects of the

---

[47] (The International Preterist Association Website)

righteous King ruling from Heaven. After this thousand-year period of Christians ruling the earth, Jesus would then return and eternity would begin. Based on man progressing towards goodness, this is demonstrated by things like the abolishment of slavery and the education of the masses. Science and righteous leaders would solve all of mankind's problems in due time.

> From the time of its early development in the 17th century until the 20th century, Postmillennialism increased in popularity until it became "one of the most important and influential millennial theories. It was probably the dominant Protestant eschatology of the nineteenth century and was embraced by Unitarian, Arminian, and Calvinist alike." It seemed to fit the optimistic spirit of the times. The rise of new democracies, the greater abundance of material goods and rising standard of living made possible by the industrial revolution in the west, the major discoveries in the fields of medicine, transportation, and communication, the rise of many new colleges and universities, and the relative peace maintained by Great Britain around the world for almost 100 years during the 19th century all made it appear that man was, indeed, on the verge of entering an unprecedented golden age of history. On the surface it appeared that Postmillennialism was the correct view of eschatology.[48]

> The optimism of Postmillennialism was dealt a severe blow, however, with the outbreak of World War I in 1914. Never before had the world seen a war of such magnitude involving so many nations. Science, which was supposed to help man usher in the age of peace and righteousness, now provided him with new tools with which to destroy great masses of humanity and thereby demonstrate his depraved nature more vividly than in the past. As a result, some theologians, such as Karl Barth, began to reject the

---

[48] (Showers, 1990)

concept of the inherent goodness of man which they had
been taught by liberal theologians. Barth began to declare
that man is sinful by nature and that the liberal view does
not fit reality.[49]

A revival of this old theology is becoming very popular among some
Christian groups. This is being taught as "dominion theology," which
is a teaching of postmillennial theology. The basic teachings predict
that Christians living on earth will set up the Kingdom here through
the power of positive confession and "faith in faith." Jesus will return
only after they have accomplished this—not through the power of the
Holy Spirit, but through positive confession.

Some people view the condition of mankind as steadily improving;
others view it as heading into the toilet. The increase of divorce,
abortion, drug use, illicit sex, homosexuality, and the recent uprising
of terrorism convince me that mankind will never bring about peace
or righteousness. If the organized church is supposed to put an end
to these manifestations of man's sinful nature, then we would not
have the rash of scandalous affairs recently uncovered within the
organized church. We have seen many examples of TV evangelists,
catholic priests, and respected teachers of God's word caught in sin.
I am not condemning them, just their actions; to me, though, this
shows that man is unable to defeat sin. It requires a truly divine
intervention, which the premillennial viewpoint anticipates.

To fully understand the Kingdom, we must be able to correctly
interpret prophecies. We cannot change our method of interpretation
to accommodate our prejudices or lack of patience.

> The premillennialist strongly affirms that this sequence
> demands that the millennium, the reign of Christ, be
> understood as a real, future event following Christ's
> return. None of the variations of amillennialism or

---

[49] (Showers, 1990)

postmillennialism that see the millennium in the present church age before Christ returns or even in the Future before Christ comes again adequately accounts for the sequence of events in Revelation.[50]

In addition to the literary argument, there is the theological point that the premillennial position places the real triumph of Christ within history. That is, the victory that the church believes was accomplished through Christ's death on the cross will be made visible to the world and the forces of evil at Christ's return and reign on earth. This is not faith in a merely spiritual or heavenly triumph, but faith that God will genuinely intervene in the course of the world to bring justice and peace.[51]

We must know the background of these other viewpoints on Millennialism. These viewpoints are not due to different opinions on a translation of a few verses, but to a totally corrupt abandonment of the biblical interpretation the early church believed during the first two or three centuries.

---

[50] (Elwell, 1988)

[51] (Elwell, 1988)

4

ERRONEOUS CONCEPTS REGARDING THE KINGDOM

It amazes me how many people read the Bible and try to interpret the "Kingdom," "Kingdom of God," and "Kingdom of Heaven" as different events. These terms all refer to the same thing. In the original Greek language, both of the terms "Kingdom of God" and "Kingdom of Heaven" use the Genitive case, which is the attributive case. This means the power of the Kingdom is ***attributed*** to God or heaven. They both have the same meaning.

> **John 18:36–37**
> **36** *Jesus answered, "My Kingdom is not of this world. If My Kingdom were of this world, then My servants would be fighting, that I might not be delivered up to the Jews; but as it is, My Kingdom is not of this realm."*
> **37** *Pilate therefore said to Him, "So You are a king?" Jesus answered, "You say correctly that I am a king. For this I have been born, and for this I have come into the world, to bear witness to the truth. Everyone who is of the truth hears My voice."*

When He said that His Kingdom is not of this world, it uses the same Genitive case and the same preposition. He is literally saying, "My Kingdom does not derive its power from this world." It is not attributed to this world. This is reemphasized when He states the His Kingdom is not of this realm.

> If there had been no actual Kingdom to come would not Christ have said, "Ye have misunderstood the word—My Kingdom is not a literal one; it is only spiritual"?

> If it be answered that Jesus did say, "My Kingdom is not of this world," we reply, "That is no proof that it was not to be in the world." The phrase "of the world," as employed in the New Testament, commonly means partaking of its evil spirit, and **has no reference whatever to location**. On His own authority His disciples were "not of the world," and yet they were in it. He was "not of the world," and yet "He was in the world!"[52]

> "The kingdom of the heavens": i.e., the kingdom which has its origin and source from the heavens. It might be taken as the genitive of character, "heavenly kingdom"; but still only in the above sense, as the words of the Lord teach in John 18:36: "My kingdom is not of this world." The word "of" there is not the sign of the genitive case, but is the preposition ἐκ (ek), out of, from, as to its origin. The kingdom depends on the Person of the King. It is the king that makes a kingdom, and not the kingdom the king. It is king-dom, the termination *dom* denoting jurisdiction. *Dom* is an abbreviation of doom or judgment. Hence it denotes the sphere in which anything is exercised, as earl-dom, wis-dom, Christen-dom. Hence a king-dom is the sphere where a king exercises his rule and jurisdiction. In his absence, therefore, there can be no kingdom. When the Lord said to His enemies, "The kingdom of God is among

---

[52] (Riley, 1913)

you" (Luke 17:21, margin), He meant in the person of the king. He could not mean that it was "within" the hearts of His enemies, who rejected the King and sought His life.

The kingdom, for which we pray, therefore, is not "from hence," but from heaven.[53]

Whenever the terms Kingdom, Kingdom of God, or Kingdom of Heaven are used in the Greek New Testament, it is always with the definite article. In Greek grammar, that is called articular construction. Articular construction in Greek shows that it is one specific identity, not a general term. The best way to translate it in English is *the* Kingdom. The definite article means that there is one specific Kingdom, not a generic term to describe several nebulous concepts.

The function of the article is to point out an object or to draw attention to it. Its use with a work makes the word stand out distinctly.

Probably the most convincing argument that these terms mean the same thing is the fact that Matthew uses the expression "Kingdom of Heaven," while Mark and Luke call it "the Kingdom of God." They use it when describing the exact same events.

In **Matthew 13:11-12**, the term used is Kingdom of Heaven.

> **11** *And He answered and said to them, "To you it has been granted to know the mysteries of the **Kingdom of heaven**, but to them it has not been granted.*
> **12** *For whoever has, to him shall more be given, and he shall have an abundance; but whoever does not have, even what he has shall be taken away from him."*

---

[53] (Bullinter, 1898)

As compared to **Mark 4:10–11**, in which the term used is Kingdom of God:

> **10** *And as soon as He was alone, His followers, along with the twelve, began asking Him about the parables.*
> **11** *And He was saying to them, "To you has been given the mystery of the **Kingdom of God**; but those who are outside get everything in parables."*

As compared to **Luke 13:29**:

> *And they will come from east and west and from north and south, and will recline at the table in the **kingdom of God**.*

And **Matthew 18:3–4**:

> **3** *...and said, "Truly I say to you, unless you are converted and become like children, you will not enter the **kingdom of heaven**.*
> **4** *Whoever then humbles himself as this child, he is the greatest in the **kingdom of heaven**."*

As compared to **Luke 18:16–17**:

> **16** *But Jesus called for them, saying, "Permit the children to come to Me, and do not hinder them, for the **kingdom of God** belongs to such as these.*
> **17** *Truly I say to you, whoever does not receive the **kingdom of God** like a child will not enter it at all."*

The Greek phrases translated as "of Heaven" (τῶν οὐρανῶν or *tōn ouranōn*) and "of God" (τοῦ θεοῦ or *ton theon*) mean the same thing. Even the term "Kingdom" as used in the New Testament refers to the same Kingdom of our Lord Jesus Christ.

The very fact that the expressions are interchangeable both in the MSS and in the Synoptic parallels forces us to the conclusion that they are used **promiscue** (not separate or distinct, mixed; mutual, shared) and have exactly the same meaning. It is open to dispute whether Jesus used the one or the other in the original Aramaic. The possibility must also be taken into account that there is at least a nuance in the kingdom of heaven in so far as this refers to the lordship which comes down from heaven into this world. If so, this gives us two important insights. The first is a plain reassurance that the essential meaning is reign rather than realm. The second is the related indication that this reign cannot be a realm which arises by a natural development of earthly relationships or by human efforts, but is one which comes down by divine intervention. Since heaven can be substituted for God by later Jewish usage, what is true of βασιλεία τῶν οὐρανῶν is also true of βασιλεία τοῦ θεοῦ. The same holds good also of βασιλεία τοῦ πατρός ("kingdom of the Father") in Mt. 13:43; 26:29 (cf. Mt. 6:10:"Thy kingdom come," i.e., the kingdom of "our Father"); 25:34 and Lk. 12:32 ("It hath pleased your Father to give you the kingdom").[54]

IS THE KINGDOM IN YOUR HEART?

Most of the people I talk to about the Kingdom tell me that the Kingdom is in the heart of the Christian. I strongly disagree. While Christ may be figuratively on the throne of my life, this is by no means the promised Kingdom that Jesus talked about so often. They usually will then misquote Luke 17:20 as proof that the Kingdom is in your heart and not a physical Kingdom. One such proponent of that doctrine is the popular radio preacher, John MacArthur.

If you be heirs of glory, "the Kingdom of God is within you" (Lk. 17:21) by virtue of your regeneration and union with

---

[54] (Kittel G. B., 1964)

Christ. The Kingdom of heaven has the throne in your heart, if you have a right to that Kingdom. Christ is in you, and God is in you; and having chosen Him for your portion, your soul has taken up its everlasting rest in Him, and gets no true rest but in Him; as the dove, until she came into the ark.[55]

Let's take a closer look at that verse.

Luke 17:20–21

20 *Now having been questioned by the Pharisees as to when the Kingdom of God was coming, He answered them and said, "The Kingdom of God is not coming with signs to be observed;*
21 *nor will they say, 'Look, here it is!' or, 'There it is!' For behold, the Kingdom of God is in your midst."*

Jesus was talking to the Pharisees. We normally do not think of this group as good Christians.

Matthew 23:27

"Woe to you, scribes and Pharisees, hypocrites! For you are like whitewashed tombs which on the outside appear beautiful, but inside they are full of dead men's bones and all uncleanness."

If the Kingdom of God were in their hearts, what would this imply? I seriously doubt that He was telling them that the Kingdom was in their hearts. Besides, He doesn't say heart; He says "in your midst." The English Standard Version of the Bible translates it as *"the kingdom of God is in the midst of you."* The New Revised Standard Version translates it as *"the kingdom of God is among you."*

"In their midst" or "among them" means that He was standing there in their midst, among them. So what does that have to do with the

---

[55] (MacArthur J., 1996)

Kingdom of God? It means where Christ is, so is the Kingdom. He is the King, so where He is, that is where the Kingdom is.

It is always important to look at the context of verses that create a doctrine. Luke 17:21 is where the concept of the Kingdom being within us originates, but the next group of verses (23–24) talks about the coming of Christ, His day.

> **Luke 17:23–24**
> **23** *"They will say to you, 'Look there! Look here!' Do not go away, and do not run after them.*
> **24** *For just like the lightning, when it flashes out of one part of the sky, shines to the other part of the sky, so will the Son of Man be in His day."*

Is the Kingdom now? Are we in it as Christians walking with the Christ?

> **1st Corinthians 15:50**
> *Now I say this, brethren, that flesh and blood cannot inherit the Kingdom of God; nor does the perishable inherit the imperishable.*

Notice that is says specifically "Flesh and **blood**." This appears to indicate that it is not a physical Kingdom here on earth where saints will dwell. Jesus experienced the same kind of resurrection that we will and His resurrected body did not have blood. The only way we can enter the Kingdom is with a resurrected glorified body. The bodies that we will have when we enter the Kingdom will not be flesh and blood, but flesh and bone: no blood, an imperishable body.

> **1st Corinthians 15:51–58**
> **51** *Behold, I tell you a mystery; we shall not all sleep, but we shall all be changed,*

52 in a moment, in the twinkling of an eye, at the last trumpet; for the trumpet will sound, and the dead will be raised imperishable, and we shall be changed.

53 For this perishable must put on the imperishable, and this mortal must put on immortality.

54 But when this perishable will have put on the imperishable, and this mortal will have put on immortality, then will come about the saying that is written, "Death is swallowed up in victory.

55 O death, where is your victory? O death, where is your sting?"

56 The sting of death is sin, and the power of sin is the law;

57 but thanks be to God, who gives us the victory through our Lord Jesus Christ.

58 Therefore, my beloved brethren, be steadfast, immovable, always abounding in the work of the Lord, knowing that your toil is not in vain in the Lord.

What kind of body did Jesus have after the resurrection? The disciples could touch Him, feel His wounds. He could pass through walls, appear and disappear at will, and eat food. Jesus appeared to two of His followers and walked with them to Emmaus, a small village about seven and a half miles from Jerusalem. They did not recognize Him until He broke bread. As soon as they realized that it was Jesus, He vanished. They hurried back to Jerusalem to tell the others, and, according to John, they were in a room with the doors shut because they were afraid of persecution from the Jews. Look what happened then:

Luke 24:36–43

36 And while they were telling these things, He Himself stood in their midst.

37 But they were startled and frightened and thought that they were seeing a spirit.

38 *And He said to them, "Why are you troubled, and why do doubts arise in your hearts?*
39 *See My hands and My feet, that it is I Myself; touch Me and see, for a spirit does not have **flesh and bones** as you see that I have."*
40 *[And when He had said this, He showed them His hands and His feet.]*
41 *And while they still could not believe it for joy and were marveling, He said to them, "Have you anything here to eat?"*
42 *And they gave Him a piece of a broiled fish;*
43 *and He took it and ate it before them.*

Jesus had a different body—not flesh and blood, but an imperishable and immortal body. Jesus gave a glimpse to Peter, James, and John of how He will appear in His glory:

Matthew 17:1–2
1 *And six days later Jesus took with Him Peter and James and John his brother, and brought them up to a high mountain by themselves.*
2 *And He was transfigured before them; and His face shone like the sun, and His garments became as white as light.*

This is the body that Jesus still has and will have when He returns. Many think of Jesus as being in heaven in a pure spirit form, but that is not the case. He will return with the same glorified body.

Acts 1:9
And after He had said these things, He was lifted up while they were looking on, and a cloud received Him out of their sight.

We have here Christ's ascending on high; not fetched away, as Elijah was, with a chariot of fire and horses of fire, but rising to heaven, as he rose from the grave, purely by his own power, his body being now, as the bodies of the saints will be at the resurrection, a spiritual body, and raised in power and incorruption.[56]

Acts 1:10–11

10 *And as they were gazing intently into the sky while He was departing, behold, two men in white clothing stood beside them;*

11 *and they also said, "Men of Galilee, why do you stand looking into the sky? This Jesus, who has been taken up from you into heaven, will come in just the same way as you have watched Him go into heaven."*

Jesus will return in just the same way as He left. This has several implications:

- He is coming back! Visibly, personally, and in His Glory.
- He will return in a Cloud: "And behold, with the clouds of heaven, One like a Son of Man was coming" (Daniel 7:13).
- He will come back with the same glorified body with which He left.

Today, Jesus is currently seated at the right hand of God.

Mark 16:19

So then, when the Lord Jesus had spoken to them, He was received up into heaven and <u>sat down at the right hand of God</u>.

As he was about to be stoned to death, Stephen actually saw Christ there:

---

[56] (Henry, 1996, c 1991)

Acts 7:55–56

55 *But being full of the Holy Spirit, he gazed intently into heaven and saw the glory of God, and Jesus <u>standing at the right hand</u> of God;*

56 *and he said, "Behold, I see the heavens opened up and the Son of Man <u>standing at the right hand of God</u>."*

Colossians 3:1

Therefore if you have been raised up with Christ, keep seeking the things above, <u>where Christ is, seated at the right hand of God</u>.

1st Peter 3:21–22

21 *Corresponding to that, baptism now saves you— not the removal of dirt from the flesh, but an appeal to God for a good conscience—through the resurrection of Jesus Christ,*

22 *<u>who is at the right hand of God</u>, having gone into heaven, after angels and authorities and powers had been subjected to Him.*

"Christ is seated at the right hand of God;" not on the throne— not yet—but He will be revealed in glory! Jesus told us to take communion in remembrance of Him. He told us that someday He would join us to drink the cup in the Kingdom. How could the Kingdom be now, since Jesus is not here?

Having just quoted 1st Peter 3:21 ("*Corresponding to that, baptism now saves you—not the removal of dirt from the flesh, but an appeal to God for a good conscience—through the resurrection of Jesus*

Christ"), I must explain what this means. Baptism does not save you from sin and does not save you as far as entering into the Kingdom. It saves you from a guilty conscience. It is an appeal to God for a clear conscience. It changes us, not God.

The Kingdom is not now, it is not in your heart, and we will not usher the Kingdom in with our works. The only way we can influence the coming of Christ is to preach the Kingdom.

Matthew 24:14
*"This gospel of the kingdom shall be preached in the whole world as a testimony to all the nations, **and then the end will come**."*

5

DEFINITION OF THE KINGDOM

The term "Kingdom" is used to describe a political government in which a king rules over all of the subjects in that land or country. It is a shortened form of the words "king's domain." The king is considered royalty, and everyone who lives in that kingdom bows down before him and pays homage to him. A theocracy is a government ruled by God or a representative of God. The Greek word for "theocratic" literally means the "power of God." The theocratic Kingdom of God is a political government with Christ as the King.

Israel became a theocracy during the time of Moses. The tabernacle Moses built was the palace of the King. Saul was the first human king of Israel, but he was supposed to be God's delegated representative. He willfully and constantly disobeyed God and had to be removed from office. Saul had been the choice of the people; David was chosen by God. During the reign of David, God promised David that his descendant would inherit the kingdom and David's Throne.

While a king has supreme rule, he is not a dictator. The difference between a dictator and a king is the dictator usually takes power by force, while a king inherits the throne.

The theocratic kingdom is yet in the future. Jesus Christ will inherit the land that was promised to Abraham, and He will inherit the

Throne of David. The promised King had to be a descendant of both Abraham and King David. This is why Matthew starts off with the genealogy of Jesus.

Matthew 1:1

The record of the genealogy of Jesus the Messiah, the son of David, the son of Abraham:

This is the very first verse in the entire New Testament, making evident the importance of Jesus being a descendant of Abraham and David. The entire ministry of Christ is based upon Him being the Messiah, the One who will set up the Kingdom of God. Matthew obviously thought it was important to establish that Jesus was a physical descendant of David and Abraham.

He speaks of Abraham because that is to whom the first promises regarding the Messiah were made.

This Kingdom has been prophesized and promised throughout the entire Bible. These prophecies describe a physical return of Jesus Christ to the earth to establish the Kingdom in which He will rule from His Throne in Jerusalem for one thousand years. The Kingdom will last one thousand years.

Revelation 20:4–6

4 *Then I saw thrones, and they sat on them, and judgment was given to them. And I saw the souls of those who had been beheaded because of their testimony of Jesus and because of the word of God, and those who had not worshiped the beast or his image, and had not received the mark on their forehead and on their hand; and they <u>came to life and reigned with Christ for a thousand years.</u>*

5 *The rest of the dead did not come to life until the thousand years were completed. This is the first resurrection.*

6 <u>*Blessed and holy*</u> *is the one who has a part in the first resurrection; over these the second death has no power, but they will be priests of God and of Christ and will reign with Him for a thousand years.*

It can be seen from this passage that Christian martyrs and those who make it through the tribulation without worshipping Satan or the Anti-Christ will be in the Kingdom. The tribulation and the Anti-Christ will be discussed in more detail in a later chapter. The Kingdom will last for one thousand years, and at the end of that time Jesus will turn the Kingdom over to His Father.

1st Corinthians 15:24–26

24 *...then comes the end, when He hands over the kingdom to the God and Father, when He has abolished all rule and all authority and power.*

25 *For He must reign until He has put all His enemies under His feet.*

26 *The last enemy that will be abolished is death.*

Today, many Christians suppose that the reward for being a "good Christian" is eternal life in the presence of God in heaven. The term "eternal life" as used in the Bible relates strongly to the *quality* of life and more lightly to the length of time. The Greek interlinear shows the Greek words for "have eternal life" as it appears in John 3:15 and 3:16.

have		eternal		life	.
ἔχη		αἰώνιον		ζωὴν	
echē		aiōnion		zōēn	

...αἰώνιον (aiōnion or eternal) in combination with ζωή (zōēn or life) there is evidently not only a temporal element, but also a **qualitative** distinction. In such contexts, αἰώνιος evidently carries certain implications associated with αἰώνιος in relationship to divine and supernatural attributes. [57]

This is not to say that Christians will not spend eternity with God, but that a lot of the reward for receiving Christ is the quality that can be enjoyed knowing personally the love and forgiveness God pours out on us and the ability to approach Him as our Dad. That quality of life will be even better and fuller in the Kingdom.

Life after death has been promised to Christians, and it is part of our hope. Many Christians interpret this as heaven and nothing more. They imagine they will exist in a purely spiritual form and have no idea of what will take place there or what they will be doing. They have no concept of an earthly reign of Jesus Christ, or, if they do, they place little or no emphasis on it.

The study of what happens in the end times is referred to as "eschatology." No one can really know exactly how all the details of the end time events will take place, but a basic understanding of the promises is important to an understanding of God and man's relationship with Jesus Christ. Prophecy concerning the end times can be difficult to interpret, and this leads to many differing theories. Sometimes, so much emphasis is placed on the different theories or speculations that it distracts from the main hope of the Kingdom.

The Kingdom is not the same as heaven and it should not be interpreted that way. This will be discussed later in more detail, but the term "heaven" is by no means synonymous with the Kingdom. The Kingdom will be physically located on the earth in the Valley of Jehoshaphat near Jerusalem.

---

[57] (Louw, 1996)

Like Rome, Jerusalem is a city set on hills. A cluster of five hills comprise the denuded quadrilateral land mass roughly one mile long and one-half mile wide, bordered on all sides, except the north, by deep ravines. Skirting the city on the west and south is the Valley of Hinnom (Greek Gehenna); hedging Jerusalem on the east is the Kidron Valley (compare the Valley of Jehoshaphat, Jl. 3:2, 12).[58]

Joel 3:2

"I will gather all the nations
And bring them down to the valley of Jehoshaphat.
Then I will enter into judgment with them there
On behalf of My people and My inheritance, Israel,
Whom they have scattered among the nations;
And they have divided up My land."

Joel 3:11–17

11 *Hasten and come, all you surrounding nations,*
And gather yourselves there.
Bring down, O LORD, Your mighty ones.
12 *Let the nations be aroused*
And come up to the valley of Jehoshaphat,
For there I will sit to judge
All the surrounding nations.
13 *Put in the sickle, for the harvest is ripe.*
Come, tread, for the wine press is full;
The vats overflow, for their wickedness is great.
14 *Multitudes, multitudes in the valley of decision!*
For the day of the LORD is near in the valley of decision.
15 *The sun and moon grow dark*
And the stars lose their brightness.
16 *The LORD roars from Zion*
And utters His voice from Jerusalem,
And the heavens and the earth tremble.

---

[58] (Elwell, 1988)

But the LORD is a refuge for His people
And a stronghold to the sons of Israel.
17 *Then you will know that I am the LORD your God,*
Dwelling in Zion, My holy mountain.
So Jerusalem will be holy,
And strangers will pass through it no more.

Its exact location is disputed. Some identify it with the Kidron Valley, east of Jerusalem, pointing to early Christian tradition, notably, Jerome; others prefer the valley of Hinnom, south of Jerusalem. This tradition may be traced back through Eusebius to the book of 1 Enoch (53:1). Still others say the name is symbolic and refers only to coming judgment, not to a specific place.[59]

The Kingdom is our reward for believing in the atoning blood of Christ. The Kingdom as our hope is not a new idea. The Jews had held to a traditional hope of the Kingdom ruled by a righteous King from the time of Moses.

The Jews expected that when the Messiah came He would establish a glorious earthly kingdom at Jerusalem; that those who had died in the faith should be raised from the dead to share in the blessings of the Messiah's reign; that all nations and peoples on the face of the whole earth should be subject to them; and that any nation that did not serve them should be destroyed. All the riches and honours of the world were to be at their disposal. The event disappointed these expectations; and the principles of prophetic interpretation on which those expectations were founded were proved to be incorrect.[60]

---

[59] (Elwell, 1988)
[60] (Hodge, 1997, Originally published in 1872)

At the time of Christ, The Kingdom was a concept that every Jew understood. There was no need to explain the Kingdom. The hope of the Kingdom was also clung to and taught by the early church fathers.

Will Durant, the 20th-century historian who produced the multi-volume set entitled *The Story of Civilization*, wrote the following concerning Jesus Christ's view of the Kingdom of God:

> What did he mean by the Kingdom? A supernatural heaven? Apparently not, for the apostles and the early Christians unanimously expected an earthly Kingdom. This was the Jewish tradition that Christ inherited; and he taught his followers to pray to the Father, "Thy Kingdom come, thy will be done on earth as it is in heaven…"

> Durant further declared that "The apostles were apparently unanimous in believing that Christ would soon return to establish the Kingdom of Heaven on earth."[61]

> In reading the NT it is important to remember the basic meaning of "kingdom." It refers to the realm in which a ruler acts to carry out his will. If we operate from this basic definition, Scripture will break down our stereotypes as well and reveal an exciting aspect of the kingdom of heaven that Christians too often miss.[62]

The Kingdom of God requires that three conditions be fulfilled:

1. It will include God's people.
2. It will be in God's place.
3. It will be directly under God's rule.

---

[61] (Showers, 1990)
[62] (Richards L. O., 1999)

GOD'S PEOPLE

Many non-Christians ask, "If God is a loving God, why won't everyone enter into the Kingdom or go to heaven?" The answer is that God is a loving God, and He has made it very easy for everyone to be there. In fact, He sent His only begotten Son to die for the world so they could all come to the party.

It would not make sense for anyone that does not want to submit to God today to enter into the future Kingdom. If you were walking down a dark alley in the inner city, you would probably be very nervous and afraid. Not from the people that say "Lord your will, not mine" but from those that say to God today "Lord my will, not yours". This attitude is why this world has so much pain and suffering inflicted by others. It would not be much of a hope if those people were there with that attitude, but they are given the choice. It is their decision.

We can trace throughout history who God's people were, but the promise of the Kingdom, and all that is associated with it, started with Abraham. This promise was extended to his heirs. Those who believe as Abraham did are heirs of those promises or, put another way, heirs of the land and heirs of the Kingdom.

Who are the heirs to the Kingdom? Anyone who exhibits the same faith in God that Abraham demonstrated, a faith that leads to action, is what really makes one an inheritor of the same things that God promised to Abraham.

Abraham, Isaac, and Jacob:

Hebrews 11:8–9
8 *By faith Abraham, when he was called, obeyed by going out to a place which he was to receive for an*

inheritance; and he went out, not knowing where he was going.

*9 By faith he lived as an alien in the land of promise, as in a foreign land, dwelling in tents with Isaac and Jacob, **fellow heirs** of the same promise...*

Moses and the Israelites:

Exodus 19:3–6

3 Moses went up to God, and the LORD called to him from the mountain, saying, "Thus you shall say to the house of Jacob and tell the sons of Israel:

4 'You yourselves have seen what I did to the Egyptians, and how I bore you on eagles' wings, and brought you to Myself.

5 Now then, if you will indeed obey My voice and keep My covenant, then you shall be My own possession among all the peoples, for all the earth is Mine;

6 and you shall be to <u>Me a kingdom of priests and a holy nation.</u>' These are the words that you shall speak to the sons of Israel."

Jesus:

One specific descendant of Abraham who will be there is Jesus.

Hebrews 1:1–2

1 God, after He spoke long ago to the fathers in the prophets in many portions and in many ways,

*2 in these last days has spoken to us in His Son, whom **He appointed heir of all things**, through whom also He made the world.*

As described in verse 2 above, God has appointed Jesus as the heir of all things. He has also allowed those who trust in Him to be adopted and also become heirs.

The Saints:

Saints are those who have set their lives apart from this world for God Almighty, made themselves subject to Him, and are devoted to Him. It doesn't mean they are without sin; it means that they believe their sin has been paid for at Christ's death. Paul addressed the Corinthians as "saints," but they were far from sinless.

> Both Catholics and Protestants consider all the saved in heaven as saints, but the term *saint* is customarily used specifically for those persons of conspicuous holiness whom the church officially recognizes.[63]

The Hebrew word used in Daniel below is שַׂיּ.דָק (*qaddiysh*). According to the *Enhanced Strong's Lexicon* it is in this case plural, masculine, and an adjective meaning "saint" or "holy one." It also says that it corresponds to the root שַׁ.דָק (*qadash*), which means "to be set apart," "consecrated," or "hallowed."

> The Greek word (ἁγίοις) hagiois means (according to the Louw-Neda *Greek-English lexicon of the New Testament: based on semantic domains)* "persons who belong to God, and as such constitute a religious entity - 'God's people.'"[64]

Daniel's vision clearly explains that the saints will also have a part in this Kingdom.

---

[63] (Reid, 1990)
[64] (Louw, 1996)

Daniel 7:18, 21–22

18 _**But the saints of the Highest One will receive the Kingdom and possess the Kingdom forever**, for all ages to come.'_

21 _I kept looking, and that horn was waging war with the saints and overpowering them_

22 _until the Ancient of Days came, and judgment was passed in favor of the saints of the Highest One, and the time arrived when **the saints took possession of the Kingdom**._

The Kingdom is the literal, physical government (reign) of Jesus Christ upon the earth as King after His glorious return. He will reign over all the nations of the earth with His risen and glorified saints for a thousand years.

Matthew 25:31–34

31 _But when the Son of Man comes in His glory, and all the angels with Him, then He will sit on His glorious throne._

32 _All the nations will be gathered before Him; and He will separate them from one another, as the shepherd separates the sheep from the goats;_

33 _and He will put the sheep on His right, and the goats on the left._

34 _Then the King will say to those on His right, 'Come, you who are blessed of My Father, **inherit the kingdom** prepared for you from the foundation of the world._

Note the word "inherit." The Kingdom is promised to the heirs of Abraham. It is an inheritance not only to the Jews, but to all those who have the faith of Abraham.

Romans 4:16–17

16 *For this reason it is by faith, in order that it may be in accordance with grace, so that the promise will be guaranteed to all the descendants, not only to those who are of the Law, but also to those who are of the faith of Abraham, who is the father of us all,*

17 *(as it is written, "A FATHER OF MANY NATIONS HAVE I MADE YOU") in the presence of Him whom he believed, even God, who gives life to the dead and calls into being that which does not exist.*

Revelations 5:8–10

8 *When He had taken the book, the four living creatures and the twenty-four elders fell down before the Lamb, each one holding a harp and golden bowls full of incense, which are the prayers of the saints.*

9 *And they sang a new song, saying, "Worthy are You to take the book and to break its seals; for You were slain, and purchased for God with Your blood men from every tribe and tongue and people and nation.*

10 *<u>You have made them to be a kingdom and priests to our God; and they will reign upon the earth.</u>"*

Daniel 7:13–14, 18

I kept looking in the night visions, and behold, with the clouds of heaven One like a Son of Man was coming, and He came up to the Ancient of Days and was presented before Him. And to Him was given dominion, glory and a kingdom, that all the peoples, nations and men of every language might serve Him. His dominion is an everlasting dominion which will not pass away; and His kingdom is one which will not be destroyed...<u>But the saints of the Highest One will receive the kingdom and possess the kingdom forever,</u> for all ages to come.

The term "One like a Son of Man" is a reference to the Messiah. Although the term was used several times to refer to Ezekiel and even once to Daniel, this time it is referring to Christ. The term is used to refer to Jesus 84 times in the four Gospels. Jesus also refers to Himself as the Son of Man many times, such as in Matthew 8:20.

> **Matthew 8:20**
> *Jesus said to him, "The foxes have holes and the birds of the air have nests, but the Son of Man has nowhere to lay His head."*

Stephen also specifically calls Jesus the Son of Man. When he was about to be killed, he saw a vision and exclaimed what he saw.

> **Acts 7:55–56**
> **55** *But being full of the Holy Spirit, he gazed intently into heaven and saw the glory of God, and Jesus standing at the right hand of God;*
> **56** *and he said, "Behold, I see the heavens opened up and the Son of Man standing at the right hand of God."*

We know that Jesus was the Son of God, but we also must realize that He was the Son of Man.

> The fallen, guilty race of Adam could not have their sins atoned for except by a Sin-Bearer who represented them as a true human being as He laid down His life for their sake.[65]

And:

> For only as man could He serve as Messiah and redeem His people through His sacrificial death. And of course,

---

[65] (Showers, 1990)

it was only as man—the Man who had lived a completely sinless life—that He could be qualified to sit in judgment on the sins of men at His second coming. As the man who perfectly obeyed the law of God and never yielded to temptation, Christ is in a position to condemn those who have transgressed the moral law and who have in addition rejected His atonement and lordship for their lives.[66]

Daniel's vision is further explained, clearly showing that the saints will also have a part in this Kingdom.

Daniel 7:17–18

17 *These great beasts, which are four in number, are four kings who will arise from the earth.*
18 *But the saints of the Highest One will receive the Kingdom and possess the Kingdom forever, for all ages to come.*

Daniel 7:21–22

21 *I kept looking, and that horn was waging war with the saints and overpowering them*
22 *until the Ancient of Days came, and judgment was passed in favor of the saints of the Highest One, and the time arrived when the saints took possession of the Kingdom.*

John in his prophecy saw that the saints will become a Kingdom and priests and they will reign on the earth with Jesus. Through the blood of Christ, we were purchased to be a part of the Kingdom. Reigning upon the earth does not quite fit the concept most Christians have of life after death or Heaven. The difference between the hope of eternal life in heaven and the hope of the Kingdom is not a matter of semantics; there is a real and tangible difference. This is not some

---

[66] (Archer, 1982)

dreamy state of euphoria. It is a real event in a real place with real people, and Jesus will be King!

Most of the Christians I have met would tell you that eternal life and heaven are the same thing. They would also tell you that entry into heaven is assured to all who have said a prayer inviting Christ into their hearts. The Bible does not teach this prayer (Revelation 3:20 is talking to the church of Laodicea, not your heart), nor does it say that a one-time prayer will give you a ticket into the Kingdom. That prayer can be the start of a wonderful relationship with God, but by saying it, you cannot change God or cause Him to forgive you of your sins. If that prayer or any other event in your life is the start of a relationship that allows your conscience to be cleansed by believing in what Christ did at the cross for you, then it will change you. Your sins were forgiven at the cross. Now we are to live in that knowledge and allow His love to flow through us and produce loving works in us—not from us trying to earn anything, but from the Holy Spirit leading us in righteousness.

Notice what the Lord says about the decision about who enters into the Kingdom.

Matthew 25:31–40

31 *"But when the Son of Man comes in His glory, and all the angels with Him, then He will sit on His glorious throne.*
32 *And all the nations will be gathered before Him; and He will separate them from one another, as the shepherd separates the sheep from the goats;*
33 *and He will put the sheep on His right, and the goats on the left.*
34 *Then the King will say to those on His right, 'Come, you who are blessed of My Father, inherit the Kingdom prepared for you from the foundation of the world.*

> **35** *'For I was hungry, and you gave Me something to eat; I was thirsty, and you gave Me something to drink; I was a stranger, and you invited Me in;*
> **36** *naked, and you clothed Me; I was sick, and you visited Me; I was in prison, and you came to Me.'*
> **37** *Then the righteous will answer Him, 'Lord, when did we see You hungry, and feed You, or thirsty, and give You something to drink?"*

Notice that the righteous were not even conscious of doing good works; they did not remember doing them. These works were the natural result of being led by the Holy Spirit, the Truth of God.

> **38** *"And when did we see You a stranger, and invite You in, or naked, and clothe You?*
> **39** *When did we see You sick, or in prison, and come to You?*
> **40** *The King will answer and say to them, 'Truly I say to you, to the extent that you did it to one of these brothers of Mine, even the least of them, you did it to Me.'"*

From this passage, it is obvious that the Kingdom is set up after the return of Christ and His judgment. This judgment described is to determine if one is a sheep or a goat. It appears that the sheep are the ones who Christ knows, and the goats are the ones to whom Jesus says, "I do not know you."

Matthew 7:21–23

> **21** *"Not everyone who says to Me, 'Lord, Lord,' will enter the Kingdom of heaven; but he who does the will of My Father who is in heaven.*
> **22** *Many will say to Me on that day, 'Lord, Lord, did we not prophesy in Your name, and in Your name*

cast out demons, and in Your name perform many miracles?'

23 *And then I will declare to them, 'I never knew you;* DEPART FROM ME, YOU WHO PRACTICE LAWLESSNESS.'"

It plainly says here that it is the one who does the will of God who will enter the Kingdom. Not everyone who preaches, casts out demons, or performs miracles in the name of Christ will be allowed in. This is where the commandment to love our neighbor as ourselves comes into play.

Revelation 20:4–6

4 *I saw thrones, and they sat upon them, and judgment was given to them. And I saw the souls of those who had been beheaded because of the testimony of Jesus and because of the word of God, and those who had not worshipped the beast or his image, and had not received the mark upon their forehead and upon their hand; <u>and they came to life and reigned with Christ for a thousand years</u>.*

5 *The rest of the dead did not come to life until the thousand years were completed. This is the first resurrection.*

6 *Blessed and holy is the one who has a part in the first resurrection; over these the second death has no power, but they will be priests of God and of Christ and <u>will reign with Him for a thousand years</u>.*

The resurrection must take place for the Kingdom. The passages above do not sound to me like heaven. How could anyone reading the above passages say that the Kingdom is in your heart?

Revelations 12:5

And she gave birth to a son, a male child, who is to rule all the nations with a rod of iron; and her child was caught up to God and to His throne.

Not only will Christ rule with a rod of iron, but the disciples and the saints will rule along with Him.

Luke 22:28–30

28 *"You have stayed with me all through my trials;*
29 *and just as my Father has given me the right to rule, so I will give you the same right.*
30 *You will eat and drink at my table in my Kingdom, and you will sit on thrones to rule over the twelve tribes of Israel."*

2nd Timothy 2:11–12

11 *This is a true saying: "If we have died with him, we shall also live with him.*
12 *If we continue to endure, we shall also rule with him."*

The Kingdom is the literal, physical government (reign) of Jesus Christ upon the earth as King after His glorious return. He will reign over all the nations of the earth with His risen and glorified saints for a thousand years.

Daniel 2:44–45

44 *And in the days of those kings the God of heaven will set up a kingdom which will never be destroyed, and that kingdom will not be left for another people; it will crush and put an end to all these kingdoms, but it will itself endure forever.*
45 *In as much as you saw that a stone was cut out of the mountain without hands and that it crushed the*

iron, the bronze, the clay, the silver, and the gold, the great God has made known to the king what will take place in the future; so the dream is true, and its interpretation is trustworthy.

Revelation 5:9–10

9 *And they sang a new song, saying, "Worthy are You to take the book and to break its seals; for You were slain, and purchased for God with Your blood men from every tribe and tongue and people and nation.*
10 *You have made them to be a kingdom and priests to our God; and they will reign upon the earth."*

Romans 8:14–17

14 *For all who are being led by the Spirit of God, these are sons of God.*
15 *For you have not received a spirit of slavery leading to fear again, but you have received a spirit of adoption as sons by which we cry out, "Abba! Father!"*
16 *The Spirit Himself testifies with our spirit that we are children of God,*
17 *and if children, **heirs also, heirs of God and fellow heirs with Christ**, if indeed we suffer with Him so that we may also be glorified with Him.*

Some doctrines teach that the Kingdom promises only apply to the nation of Israel because they are the descendants of Abraham. Paul teaches that if you belong to Christ, then you are part of the nation of Israel.

> The term "Israelite" refers to him as a member of the theocracy, and a partaker of the theocratic privileges and glorious vocation of the nation Israel and an heir of the promises.[67]

---

[67] (Wuest, 1997, c1984)

Galatians 3:29
*And if you belong to Christ, then you are Abraham's descendants, **heirs according to promise**.*

Galatians 4:7
*Therefore you are no longer a slave, but a son; and if a son, **then an heir** through God.*

Ephesians 3:6
*...to be specific, that the Gentiles are **fellow heirs** and fellow members of the body, and fellow partakers of the promise in Christ Jesus through the gospel...*

Titus 3:7
...so that being justified by His grace we would be made heirs according to the hope of eternal life.

Christians are heirs, but heirs of what? Being an heir means that you will inherit an estate or something owned. The saints will inherit the Land promised to Abraham. That Land is the geographic location of the Kingdom.

James 2:5
*Listen, my beloved brethren: did not God choose the poor of this world to be rich in faith and **heirs of the Kingdom** which He promised to those who love Him?*

GOD'S PLACE

The place is on the earth. As mentioned in verse 10 above, "*and they will reign upon the earth*." The land that was promised to Abraham is the location of the kingdom. The Land was such an important promise that when Abraham asked God, "How will I know that I will possess it?" God made a covenant with him to guarantee that

He would own it. Another word for that guarantee or covenant is *testament*. The Old Testament is named after the promise made by God to Abraham. The Kingdom will start when Jesus inherits the land that was promised by God to Abraham. I will describe this in detail in a later chapter and deal with the Promise and Covenant regarding the Land where the Kingdom will reside.

This Kingdom has been prophesized and promised throughout the entire Bible. These prophecies describe a physical return of Jesus Christ to the earth to establish the Kingdom in which He will rule from His Throne in Jerusalem for one thousand years. The Kingdom will last one thousand years.

The promise made to Abraham was that he would possess the land of his sojourning. This land became known as the Promised Land. The covenants are all based on this promise that Abraham or his heirs will own the Promised Land. Many people might think that this promise was fulfilled after the children of Israel moved into the Promised Land after Moses led them to it. I will address this in much more detail later, but one should know that the Promised Land has never been completely possessed by Abraham or his descendants. We will see the importance of this later, but this land is critical to the fulfillment of the Kingdom.

GOD'S RULE

In the Kingdom, the Lord Jesus Christ will reign as king.

Romans 15:12
*Again Isaiah says, "There shall come the root of Jesse, And He who arises **to rule** over the Gentiles, In Him shall the Gentiles hope."*

Luke 1:33

...and He will reign over the house of Jacob forever, and His Kingdom will have no end.

Revelation 11:15

Then the seventh angel sounded; and there were loud voices in heaven, saying, "The Kingdom of the world has become the Kingdom of our Lord and of His Christ; and He will reign forever and ever."

Christ will rule the entire earth with a rod of iron, but the Kingdom itself is described as a place where there will not be any more war, the wolf will dwell with the lamb, little kids will play at the den of cobras and vipers and not be hurt, no one will be sick, the blind will see, the deaf will hear, the lame will leap like deer, and there will be no more death. If we keep these promises in mind, we can know for sure that the Kingdom is not now, nor has it ever been. Obviously, the church or the walk with Christ today does not fulfill these promises.

There are only two times that the three essential aspects (God's people, place and rule) can be met. One is the Garden of Eden:

> Prior to the fall of man, the Theocratic Kingdom of God existed on planet Earth. God made Adam the human administrator of His rule over the earthly province of His Universal Kingdom. Adam did not obtain his position or authority on his own; it was given to him by God (Gen. 1:26, 28; Ps. 8:3–9). Thus, it was God's rule that was administered over the world system by Adam from the time of his creation to the time of his fall. [68]

The only other time is in the future when Christ will set up a literal physical government in a defined place for a defined period of time. It will be the reign of Jesus Christ upon the earth (God's place) as

---

[68] (Showers, 1990)

King after His glorious return. He will reign (God's rule) over all the nations of the earth with His risen and glorified saints (God's people) for a thousand years.

Let's look at some scriptures to support this. In the book of Daniel, we read that the King of Babylon, Nebuchadnezzar, had a dream and Daniel is describing to him the meaning of that dream. He explains that God will establish His Kingdom, which will put an end to all manmade Kingdoms.

Daniel 2:44
And in the days of those kings the God of heaven will set up a Kingdom which will never be destroyed, and that Kingdom will not be left for another people; it will crush and put an end to all these Kingdoms, but it will itself endure forever.

As I mentioned earlier, the definition of the Kingdom requires three conditions to be fulfilled. It will consist of God's people, it will be in God's place, and it will be directly under God's rule.

1. God's people are those who are willing subjects of His rule.
2. God's place is where the King is unchallenged as The Lord.
3. God's Rule is when all of its inhabitants say "Lord your will, not mine."

Originally, God created man to have a specific relationship with Him, which was in effect in the Garden of Eden before the fall. The three essential aspects that define the Kingdom existed at that time. In the Garden of Eden we find God's people (Adam and Eve), In God's place (the Garden of Eden), all under God's rule.

Not only did we have a special close relationship with God, but we were also given dominion over the earth. We were to rule over all of the earth and the animals.

Genesis 1:25

Then God said, "Let Us make man in Our image, according to Our likeness; and let them rule over the fish of the sea and over the birds of the sky and over the cattle and over all the earth, and over every creeping thing that creeps on the earth."

When Adam and Eve ate of the tree of knowledge of good and evil, they were no longer willing subjects of His rule. They had challenged the rule of God by desiring to become like God, and they had the attitude of "my will, not yours."

Genesis 3:17–19

17 *Then to Adam He said, "Because you have listened to the voice of your wife, and have eaten from the tree about which I commanded you, saying, 'You shall not eat from it';*
Cursed is the ground because of you;
In toil you shall eat of it
All the days of your life.
18 *Both thorns and thistles it shall grow for you;*
And you shall eat the plants of the field;
19 *By the sweat of your face*
You shall eat bread,
Till you return to the ground,
Because from it you were taken;
For you are dust,
And to dust you shall return."

We no longer had dominion over the earth—we became slaves to the toil required to get the earth to meet our needs.

God removed mankind from the garden to prevent us from eating the Tree of Life and living forever in rebellion against Him. His plan was to get us back into that relationship as willing subjects, thus the plan of salvation. God's plan of salvation is to get mankind to become willing subjects, back in His Kingdom.

2nd Samuel 7:11–16

11 *"The Lord also declares to you that the Lord will make a house for you.*

12 *When your days are complete and you lie down with your fathers, I will raise up your descendant after you, who will come forth from you, and I will establish his Kingdom.*

13 *He shall build a house for My name, and I will establish the throne of his Kingdom forever.*

14 *I will be a father to him and he will be a son to Me; when he commits iniquity, I will correct him with the rod of men and the strokes of the sons of men,*

15 *but My loving kindness shall not depart from him, as I took it away from Saul, whom I removed from before you.*

16 *And your house and your Kingdom shall endure before Me forever; your throne shall be established forever."*

The Kingdom here refers to the coming eschatological Kingdom of our Lord, Jesus Christ, not the reign of God now. God is in charge and reigns over the entire universe, but we do not have the three essential conditions required.

6

THE IMPORTANCE OF
THE KINGDOM

The Kingdom of God is the main theme of the entire Bible. It is the thread that ties all of scripture together from Genesis to Revelation. From the time Adam and Eve left the Garden of Eden, God's plan has been to bring his children back into a Kingdom relationship with Him. Abraham, Isaac, Jacob, Moses, Samuel, David, Solomon, Isaiah, Jeremiah, Ezekiel, Daniel, Hosea, Joel, Amos, Obadiah, Micah, Habakkuk, Haggai, Zechariah, Malachi, all of the apostles, and Jesus mention it and talk of its glory. It was the hope of the Jews in the time of Christ. They were looking for it to be fulfilled, but they were looking for a conquering King, not this man of peace.

> The central current and ultimate aim of universal history is the Kingdom of God established by Jesus Christ. This is the grandest and most comprehensive institution in the world, as vast as humanity and as enduring as eternity. All other institutions are made subservient to it, and in its interest the whole world is governed. It is no after-thought of God, no subsequent emendation of the plan of creation, but it is the eternal forethought, the controlling idea, the beginning, the middle, and the end of all his ways and works.[69]

---

[69] (Schaff, 1997)

An understanding of the premillennial theocratic Kingdom is necessary to properly understand salvation, judgment, and prophecy.

> It is utterly impossible for us to determine the true significance, the Divine course, and the development of the plan of salvation without a deep insight into that of the Kingdom itself.[70]

> Indeed, the Kingdom of God concept is the heart of the biblical philosophy of history and, therefore, is the central theme of the Bible.[71]

There is a lot of confusion today about the end times, and few people will take the time to study it themselves. Many books have been written that teach many different concepts of the Kingdom and the return of Christ. A solid understanding of the Kingdom and Christ's return is critical for Christians to understand. It not only is important to help us understand the scriptures, but if or when we suffer persecution, we may know there is an end in sight and that Christ will triumph and be true to His promises. Without a strong hope in the fulfillment of the Kingdom promises, we can easily become discouraged and give up on our faith.

This is why I have such a strong conviction that the Kingdom of God, defined as a physical earthly reign of Christ, must be taught, especially as we draw closer towards the last days.

Why put so much emphasis on the Kingdom of God? First of all, the scriptures put an emphasis on this topic. Secondly, Jesus emphasized it. The word "Kingdom" appears 120 times in the four gospels alone.

---

[70] (Peters G. N., 1884)
[71] (Showers, 1990)

Jesus said in **Luke 4:43**, *"I must preach the Kingdom of God to the other cities also, for I was sent for this purpose."*

Here, Jesus states the very purpose He was sent to earth by the Father was to preach the Kingdom of God.

Jesus told us to make seeking the Kingdom our number one priority. It is more important than anything else to live a life truly dedicated to seeking the Kingdom and trusting the Lord to meet all of our needs.

Matthew 6:25–33

25 *"For this reason I say to you, do not be worried about your life, as to what you will eat or what you will drink; nor for your body, as to what you will put on. Is not life more than food, and the body more than clothing?*

26 *Look at the birds of the air, that they do not sow, nor reap nor gather into barns, and yet your heavenly Father feeds them. Are you not worth much more than they?*

27 *And who of you by being worried can add a single hour to his life?*

28 *And why are you worried about clothing? Observe how the lilies of the field grow; they do not toil nor do they spin,*

29 *yet I say to you that not even Solomon in all his glory clothed himself like one of these.*

30 *But if God so clothes the grass of the field, which is alive today and tomorrow is thrown into the furnace, will He not much more clothe you? You of little faith!*

31 *Do not worry then, saying, 'What will we eat?'*
or 'What will we drink?' or 'What will we wear for
clothing?'
32 *For the Gentiles eagerly seek all these things; for your*
heavenly Father knows that you need all these things.
33 *But seek first His kingdom and His righteousness,*
and all these things will be added to you."

In verse 33, the verb used in the original Greek, ζητεῖτε (*zeteite*), translated "seek," is in the present tense, active voice and imperative mood. That implies that Christ is exhorting us to actively, and continually, seek His Kingdom. Seek and continue to seek. We should treat it with the great significance it deserves.

The next word is πρῶτον (*proton*), translated as "first." While it does mean first in a series, the *Kittle Theological Dictionary of the New Testament* says:

> The meaning here cannot be that one must first seek after God's kingdom and then after other things. "Above all" is the only meaning which corresponds to the central position which orientation to the kingdom of God has in the proclamation of Jesus. Indeed, πρῶτον (proton) is so exclusive here that it carries the implication of "only."[72]

Another place where the Kingdom is mentioned is in the Lord's Prayer. Here, when Jesus is teaching us how to pray—or, maybe more appropriately, what the outline of our prayers should cover—it is mentioned twice.

Matthew 6:9–13
9 *"Pray, then, in this way:*
'Our Father who art in heaven,
Hallowed be Thy name.

---

[72] (Kittel G. B., 1964)

10 '***Thy Kingdom come***.
Thy will be done,
On earth as it is in heaven.
11 *'Give us this day our daily bread.*
12 *'And forgive us our debts, as we also have forgiven*
our debtors.
13 *'And do not lead us into temptation, but deliver us*
*from evil. [For **Thine is the Kingdom**, and the power,*
and the glory, forever. Amen.]'"

From the first days of the Christian Church to today, we have been looking for the return of Jesus Christ to this earth.

Luke 21:27–31
27 *"And then they will see the Son of Man coming in*
a cloud with power and great glory.
28 *But when these things begin to take place,*
straighten up and lift up your heads, because your
redemption is drawing near."
29 *And He told them a parable: "Behold the fig tree*
and all the trees;
30 *as soon as they put forth leaves, you see it and*
know for yourselves that summer is now near.
31 *Even so you, too, **when you see these things***
happening, recognize that the Kingdom of God is
near."*

After years of thinking He could come any time, we started to think we must have misunderstood because He had not shown up yet. It is discouraging at times. Even in my own lifetime there have been several times when it appeared that prophecy was being fulfilled and the time was at hand.

Those truly seeking but not studying correct doctrines are constantly being seduced by false teachings. From Jim Jones at Jonestown in

Guyana; to the Branch Davidians at Waco, Texas; the Heaven's Gate group of web page designers who committed suicide; to The Church of The Lamb of God led by Ervil LeBaron, who was responsible for over 24 murders—all of them were seeking God and all were led terribly astray.

We have seen fanatics predicting the time, contrary to the teaching that no one will know the time or place.

> **Mark 13:32–37**
> **32** *"But of that day or hour **no one knows, not even the angels in heaven, nor the Son**, but the Father alone.*
> **33** *Take heed, keep on the alert; for you do not know when the appointed time is.*
> **34** *It is like a man, away on a journey, who upon leaving his house and putting his slaves in charge, assigning to each one his task, also commanded the doorkeeper to stay on the alert.*
> **35** *Therefore, be on the alert—for you do not know when the master of the house is coming, whether in the evening, at midnight, at cockcrowing, or in the morning—*
> **36** *lest he come suddenly and find you asleep.*
> **37** *And what I say to you I say to all, 'Be on the alert!'"*

How do we stay on the alert for so long? I have heard the expression, "Live as if He could return any minute, but plan as if He won't return for a one thousand years." I think this expectation of His return at the next minute can have a drastic effect on our walk with Christ, but we must not grow weary and think like the evil servant who says in his heart, "My master delays in His coming."

Matthew 24:48–51

48 *"But if that evil slave says in his heart, 'My master is not coming for a long time,'*

49 *and shall begin to beat his fellow slaves and eat and drink with drunkards;*

50 *the master of that slave will come on a day when he does not expect him and at an hour which he does not know,*

51 *and shall cut him in pieces and assign him a place with the hypocrites; weeping shall be there and the gnashing of teeth."*

I think that Paul thought it would happen in his lifetime, but I also think we are to consider that it could happen in our lifetime. Most of the prophecies regarding what must happen before the return of Christ have been fulfilled. I truly think the time is near.

There are so many parables and references to the concept of *"my master delays in His coming;"* it must seem to us to be a long time before it occurs. But indeed, He is coming and the time is getting closer. It may be another 2,000 years, or it may be tomorrow.

2nd Peter 3:10–15

10 *But the day of the Lord will come like a thief, in which the heavens will pass away with a roar and the elements will be destroyed with intense heat, and the earth and its works will be burned up.*

11 *Since all these things are to be destroyed in this way, what sort of people ought you to be in holy conduct and godliness,*

12 *looking for and hastening the coming of the day of God, on account of which the heavens will be destroyed by burning, and the elements will melt with intense heat!*

13 *But according to His promise we are looking for new heavens and a new earth, in which righteousness dwells.*

14 *Therefore, beloved, since you look for these things, be diligent to be found by Him in peace, spotless and blameless,*

15 *and regard the patience of our Lord to be salvation...*

Unless we study and learn the truth, when someone comes performing what may seem like miracles and preaches a message that seems to offer a solution to the world's woes, how can we be immune to being led astray?

7

THE GOSPEL AND THE MESSIAH

THE GOSPEL

In modern vernacular, the term "gospel" is sometimes used to refer to the entire Bible, or a truth (as in, "that's the gospel truth") but, technically, it refers to any of the first four books of the New Testament. Sometimes it is used as "good news" (as in, "have you heard the gospel of Christ?").

The Merriam-Webster Dictionary defines the word gospel as follows:

> Etymology: Middle English, from Old English Godspel (translation of Late Latin evangelium), from God good + spell tale. Date: before 12th century
>
> **1 a** often capitalized: the message concerning Christ, the Kingdom of God, and salvation.

The Greek word that is translated as "gospel" in the New Testament is εὐαγγέλιον (*euangelion*). Our word "evangelist" comes from the Latin word closely related to it. Originally, the root meaning of the word meant a "reward for good tidings." By the time it was used in the Bible, it had come to mean "good news about that reward." *Vines Greek English Dictionary* defines the word gospel by saying

97

it "denotes the good tidings of The Kingdom of God and salvation through Christ."

Thayer's Greek English Dictionary defines the word gospel as "glad tidings of the Kingdom of God soon to be set up and of Jesus, the Messiah, the Founder of this Kingdom."

Today in modern English, the word means the absolute truth. In Christian context, we usually think of it as the message of salvation. While that is still true, I think we miss the rest of the message. We need to understand that it means preaching the good news that the Kingdom of God is coming.

You might ask if this is this really a fair definition. Does "gospel" really mean preaching the good news of the Kingdom? Let's look at how it is used in Luke 9. Jesus sent the disciples out to proclaim the Kingdom, but they preached the gospel.

> **Luke 9:2**
> *And He sent them out to proclaim the Kingdom of God, and to perform healing.*

Jesus sent them to preach the Kingdom, but later it tells that they did something different: they preached the Gospel.

> **Luke 9:6**
> *And departing, they began going about among the villages, preaching the gospel, and healing everywhere.*

Either it means the same thing, or they disobeyed Him. Matthew defines the gospel as the gospel of the Kingdom.

Matthew 24:14

And this gospel of the Kingdom shall be preached in the whole world for a witness to all the nations, and then the end shall come.

It appears from this verse that Jesus will not return until the Kingdom has been preached to the whole world. This is another reason I feel I must share this message. Maybe now you can see the reason I am so passionate about this topic and why I am writing this book.

I think it is clear that we are commissioned to preach the gospel, and that means that we should be preaching that the Kingdom of God will be the reign of Jesus Christ upon the earth as King after His glorious return. He will reign over all the nations of the earth with His risen and glorified saints for a thousand years. The only way we can enter into that Kingdom is to have a relationship with God through accepting the sacrifice that Jesus made in our place. He died for us so we might enter into this Kingdom.

> When it was time for Jesus to begin his public ministry, John the Baptist began to preach, "Repent, for the kingdom of heaven is near" (Mt 3:2). God was about to break into history, to act in a bold, fresh way. This message, which was also the theme of Jesus' early ministry (Mt 4:17; Mk 1:15), is "the good news of the kingdom" (Mt 4:23).

> Jesus' message was stronger than that of John. John said the kingdom was coming. Jesus announced that it had arrived! Confronting men who accused him of doing his miracles by Satan's power, Jesus said, "If I drive out demons by the Spirit of God, then the kingdom of God has come upon you" (Mt 12:28; cf. Lk 11:20). Most of Jesus' miracles belong to this time period, the time of his preaching the gospel of the kingdom. The king had come and had demonstrated his power to act, revealing his authority over every natural and supernatural power.

In the NT, the kingdom and Jesus are inseparable, even as the concept of kingdom is meaningless apart from the person of the king.

In a significant sense, then, any announcement of the gospel of the kingdom must focus on the person of Jesus, promising that he is or soon will be present, able to act in all his sovereign power.[73]

CHRIST THE MESSIAH

When I teach this topic in adult Sunday school classes, I ask the class to tell me what "Christ" means. I am amazed at the answers I get. Usually, the first response is, "It means Savior." Others think it means "Son of God." No one will admit they think it might be the last name of Jesus, but I sometimes wonder. The word Christ is a direct transliteration of the Greek word Χριστού, the root of which is Χριστος (*Christou* or *Christos*). The basic meaning of Christos is "Anointed One."

In the Greek translation of the Hebrew Old Testament, the Septuagint (or LXX), Christos is used everywhere the Hebrew word "Messiah" is used. "Messiah" also means "The Anointed One." It refers to a priest or a king after he has been anointed into that office.

See how the New American Standard Bible translates the word *Messiah*:

John 1:40–41
40 *One of the two who heard John speak, and followed Him, was Andrew, Simon Peter's brother.*

---

[73] (Richards L. O., 1999)

41 *He found first his own brother Simon, and said to him, "We have found the Messiah" (which translated means Christ)."*

In the Old Testament, the first person referred to as an anointed one as king was Saul, the first king of the nation of Israel.

1st Samuel 24:5–6
5 *And it came about afterward that David's conscience bothered him because he had cut off the edge of Saul's robe.*
6 *So he said to his men, "Far be it from me because of the Lord that I should do this thing to my lord, the Lord's anointed, to stretch out my hand against him, since he is the Lord's anointed."*

Here, David is referring to Saul as the Lord's anointed one. Where we see lord in small letters, it is referring to Saul. The capital letters refer to the LORD, Jesus Christ. The Septuagint uses the words *Christos kurios* (lord) here. The difference is the use of the definite article with the word. It is "christ lord" for Saul, and "the Christ Lord" when referring to Jesus. David is calling Saul the Lord's "christ" or anointed one, The Lord's anointed king of Israel.

All of the kings of Israel were anointed. David refers to himself as anointed, but then in Psalms 2:2, he refers to the Messiah as anointed. When the word *kristos* (in the Septuagint text) is used to describe Saul or David, it does not have a definite article with it. In English, this would translate **a** christ (not capitalized). They were kings, but not **_The_** King. When the definite article is used with the word Christos, it means **_The_** King, The Messiah, The Christ, who we know is Jesus.

The idea that "anointed" relates to priests comes from Exodus.

Exodus 28:40–41

40 *"And for Aaron's sons you shall make tunics; you shall also make sashes for them, and you shall make caps for them, for glory and for beauty.*
41 *And you shall put them on Aaron your brother and on his sons with him; and you shall anoint them and ordain them and consecrate them, that they may serve Me as priests."*

The Messiah, or the Christ, was an office, a promise, and a hope. This hope was very real with the children of Israel, and they strongly believed in His coming. When Jesus came as the Savior of all Mankind, most of them began to lose the hope of the coming of "The Anointed One" or "The Messiah."

Many professing Christians do not understand the full meaning of the title of Christ. That is one of the inspirations I have for writing this book. We need to understand all of the implications of that title of Messiah. It is critical that we know Jesus as "The Christ."

Jeremiah 23:5

"Behold, the days are coming," declares the Lord,
"When I shall raise up for David a righteous Branch;
And He will reign as king and act wisely And do justice and righteousness in the land."

The movie *The Greatest Story Ever Told* did a great job of showing the tremendous excitement that Andrew felt when he announced to Peter, "We have found the Messiah!" You could tell he was really excited. I suppose we will be just as excited, if not more. We need to make it our hope to see Jesus return as King. Later on, we read that Nathanael recognized Jesus as the Son of God and the King of Israel.

John 1:49

Nathanael answered Him, "Rabbi, You are the Son of God; You are the King of Israel."

Matthew 16:13–16

13 *Now when Jesus came into the district of Caesarea Philippi, He began asking His disciples, saying, "Who do people say that the Son of Man is?"*
14 *And they said, "Some say John the Baptist; and others, Elijah; but still others, Jeremiah, or one of the prophets."*
15 *He said to them, "But who do you say that I am?"*
16 *And Simon Peter answered and said, "Thou art the Christ, the Son of the living God."*

The Jewish background of Peter, knowing that all of Israel was looking for the Messiah, makes this statement very powerful. Peter finally understood that this man in front of him was the fulfillment of the scriptures and the hope of all mankind.

Matthew 16:17–19

17 *And Jesus answered and said to him, "Blessed are you, Simon Barjona, because flesh and blood did not reveal this to you, but My Father who is in heaven.*
18 *And I also say to you that you are Peter, and upon this rock I will build My church; and the gates of Hades shall not overpower it."*

It also appears that since Peter had this revealed to him from God, he gets the keys to the Kingdom.

19 *"I will give you the keys of the Kingdom of heaven..."*

When Peter recognized Jesus was the Christ, he was told that Christ would build His Church upon that rock. Is it possible that the principle that Peter had just expressed—the fact that Jesus was the Christ—is the rock or foundation that the Church is built upon?

Peter made a remarkable, history-changing proclamation. He declared that Jesus was "the Christ, the Son of the living God," to which Jesus responded, "Blessed are you, Simon, son of Jonah, because flesh and blood did not reveal this to you, but my Father in heaven. And I also say to you, that you are Peter, and upon this rock I will build my church" (Matt. 16:16–18). As "Peter" and "rock" are one word in the dialect spoken by Jesus (Aramaic), the wordplay in this verse can be seen only in languages that have one word for both. In the Greek, the word for "Peter" is petros meaning "stone" or "fragment of a rock"; the word for "rock" is petra which is more specifically "rock mass." Some commentators have indicated that though the two words are nearly synonymous, Jesus intended a distinction—Peter is but a fragment of the whole, while Christ Himself is the entire rock. Thus, it could be said that the church would be built on Christ, the Rock. Others have maintained that Jesus is saying in this passage that the church will be built on Peter's confession that Jesus is the Son of God.[74]

However we interpret this passage, it is clear that Peter himself never declared that he was the single rock upon which the church was built. Rather, he told the believers: "you also as living stones are being built up a spiritual house" (1 Pet. 2:5). The word "also" shows that he put all other believers in the same category as he: We all are living stones in the church God is building.[75]

---

[74] (Carpenter, 2000)
[75] (Carpenter, 2000)

He confessed that Jesus is "The Christ," not just the Son of God. The definite article to emphasize "the" can be seen in the original Greek: ὁ (The) χριστὸς (Christ) ὁ (The) υἱὸς (Son) τοῦ (of the) θεοῦ (God) τοῦ (The) ζῶντος (The Living).

Anyone who **denies** that Jesus is the Christ, the Messiah, the coming King, is a liar. Harsh words, but not mine:

1st John 2:22–23

22 *"Who is the liar but the one who denies that Jesus is the Christ? This is the antichrist, the one who denies the Father and the Son.*

23 *Whoever denies the Son does not have the Father; the one who confesses the Son has the Father also."*

The Jewish people who lived at the time of Jesus believed the Messiah was coming, and I think they fully understood the concept of the Kingdom. A good example of this is a man named Simeon.

Luke 2:25–32

25 *And behold, there was a man in Jerusalem whose name was Simeon; and this man was righteous and devout, looking for the consolation of Israel; and the Holy Spirit was upon him.*

26 *And it had been revealed to him by the Holy Spirit that he would not see death before he had seen the Lord's Christ.*

27 *And he came in the Spirit into the temple; and when the parents brought in the child Jesus, to carry out for Him the custom of the Law,*

28 *then he took Him into his arms, and blessed God, and said,*

29 *"Now Lord, Thou dost let Thy bond-servant depart In peace, according to Thy word;*

30 *For my eyes have seen Thy salvation,*

31 *Which Thou hast prepared in the presence of all peoples,*
32 *A light of revelation to the Gentiles,*
And the glory of Thy people Israel."

Another example is Anna:

Luke 2:36–38
36 *And there was a prophetess, Anna the daughter of Phanuel, of the tribe of Asher. She was advanced in years, having lived with a husband seven years after her marriage,*
37 *and then as a widow to the age of eighty-four. And she never left the temple, serving night and day with fastings and prayers.*
38 *And at that very moment she came up and began giving thanks to God, and continued to speak of Him to all those who were looking for the redemption of Jerusalem.*

The redemption of Jerusalem is tied directly to the Kingdom age and the rule of the Messiah. It is synonymous with the Kingdom.

8

WHY DON'T WE KNOW ABOUT THE KINGDOM?

If the Kingdom is such an important theological concept of Christianity and Judaism, why is it that the average Christian has very little knowledge of it and reads it as just another phrase regarding heaven? The average Christian thinks they will go to Heaven when they die, and that's the end of it. They are hoping they don't go to hell, so if they make it to Heaven, all is well.

A very well-known parable explains why. One has to have a desire to learn spiritual truths. Once one comes face to face with the Lord Jesus Christ, that person wants to learn as much as they can about spiritual concepts.

Matthew 13:3–17
3 And He spoke many things to them in parables, saying, "Behold, the sower went out to sow;
4 and as he sowed, some seeds fell beside the road, and the birds came and ate them up.
5 Others fell on the rocky places, where they did not have much soil; and immediately they sprang up, because they had no depth of soil.

6 *But when the sun had risen, they were scorched;*
and because they had no root, they withered away.
7 *Others fell among the thorns, and the thorns came*
up and choked them out.
8 *And others fell on the good soil and yielded a crop,*
some a hundredfold, some sixty, and some thirty.
9 *He who has ears, let him hear."*

An explanation:

10 *And the disciples came and said to Him, "Why do*
You speak to them in parables?"
11 *Jesus answered them, "To you it has been granted*
to know the mysteries of the kingdom of heaven, but
to them it has not been granted.
12 *For whoever has, to him more shall be given, and*
he will have an abundance; but whoever does not
have, even what he has shall be taken away from him.
13 *Therefore I speak to them in parables; because*
while seeing they do not see, and while hearing they
do not hear, nor do they understand.
14 *In their case the prophecy of Isaiah is being*
fulfilled, which says,
'You will keep on hearing, but will not understand;
You will keep on seeing, but will not perceive;
15 *For the heart of this people has become dull,*
With their ears they scarcely hear,
And they have closed their eyes,
Otherwise they would see with their eyes,
Hear with their ears,
And understand with their heart and return,
And I would heal them.'
16 *But blessed are your eyes, because they see; and*
your ears, because they hear.

17 For truly I say to you that many prophets and righteous men desired to see what you see, and did not see it, and to hear what you hear, and did not hear it."

The phrase in verse 9, "ear to hear," basically says that if you want to hear, you will understand. Verse 11 states that the disciples have been granted to know about the kingdom and others have not been granted that understanding. This may lead into a discussion of the doctrine of "Election" but it may also mean that if you really want to understand, you will.

Perhaps verses 14–15 are referring to those who are not really seeking the truth; they are hanging around Jesus to witness His miracles! Could this still be true today? Verse 16 states that those who want to understand will be blessed.

The fact that Jesus is telling a parable about the Word of the Kingdom is not my idea. He goes on to explain exactly what He is talking about.

Matthew 13:18–23
18 "Hear then the parable of the sower.
*19 When anyone hears **the word of the kingdom** and does not understand it, the evil one comes and snatches away what has been sown in his heart. This is the one on whom seed was sown beside the road.*
20 The one on whom seed was sown on the rocky places, this is the man who hears the word and immediately receives it with joy;
21 yet he has no firm root in himself, but is only temporary, and when affliction or persecution arises because of the word, immediately he falls away.
22 And the one on whom seed was sown among the thorns, this is the man who hears the word, and the

worry of the world and the deceitfulness of wealth choke the word, and it becomes unfruitful.
23 *And the one on whom seed was sown on the good soil, this is the man who hears the word and understands it; who indeed bears fruit and brings forth, some a hundredfold, some sixty, and some thirty."*

In Matthew, Jesus explains that the seed is in reference to the word of the Kingdom. The first thing that happens is Satan tries to takes it away. That is the main reason why we have not heard about the Kingdom. Other worldly concerns can choke out the word like affliction, persecution, worry, and the deceitfulness of riches. Luke tells the same story and he reports that Jesus said the seed was the word of God.

Let's look at each type of ground on which the seed falls.

Beside the road: The roads at that time were along farmer's fields. When they sowed seed, some of it fell onto the road side, where it had not been plowed or tilled. The seed that fell on this pathway hardened by traffic never has a chance to even germinate of sprout. In fact, the seeds are usually snatched away by the birds. Those who think the idea of the Kingdom is interesting but don't let it affect their lives or relationships with God will soon forget about it.

The rocky places: Farmers usually pick up the rocks in their fields over the years and throw them in a place off to the side. The soil is not deep enough to support a healthy plant after it sprouts. Affliction, persecution, or, as Luke says, temptation: martyrs have a sure ticket into the Kingdom because they love the Kingdom more than life itself. There are some who receive the word of the Kingdom with great joy but soon afterwards fall away. In the last days, there will be a lot of persecution for those claiming to follow Christ. Affliction or persecution can really "weed out" (no pun intended) those who truly believe. What kind of seed will you be?

Among thorns:

> Literally, *upon* thorns, *i.e.,* upon soil from which thorns were springing. The expression refers to soil from which the thorns had not been removed, and not to thorn bushes.[76]

The thorns choke out the plant.

The deceitfulness of riches is a tough one. It will choke out the word of the Kingdom and it becomes unfruitful. First of all, we can learn here that the word of the Kingdom should bear fruit. We can easily get caught up in "earning a living" and become totally distracted by worldly things. It is so easy to lose our sense of priorities in the business world. Our families can suffer and our walk with God can suffer because our vocations require so much time and effort. The "rat race" and "keeping up with the Joneses" are activities that can cause us to put filling our pocketbooks before the ministry to which Christ has called us. Financial security is a false security the world says must be pursued. It is pure deception. Security can only come from God. The Lord tells us not to worry about tomorrow and He will meet all needs, but we have a different concept of what our needs are. That is much easier to say than to practice. The key is keeping your priorities in the right order.

People pursue riches at least forty hours a week and end up trapped in a lifestyle based on the pursuit of "success." Once a level of financial security is reached, it becomes almost impossible to live on a lower income. Then we are trapped. One must continue to work just to maintain that false security and pursuing it can choke out the word of the Kingdom.

---

[76] (Lange J. P., 2008)

Satan tries to make people forget that they are really forgiven. This can also cause them to lose their hope of the Kingdom. It needs to be remembered. A primary element of the Kingdom is grace, the forgiveness that Christ freely bestowed to all men. If the "evil one" can motivate us to try and please God with our works or our self-discipline, the word of the Kingdom fades away.

Every time you sin, Satan whispers in your ear, "You told God you would not do that again, and you broke your promise. Surely He will not forgive you this time." You must be strong enough in your Faith to know that you are forgiven for all of your sins. Otherwise, that guilty conscience will cause you to hide from God.

Jesus was teaching this so people might know that Satan and the Flesh can cause them to lose the hope of the Kingdom. It must be the focus of their lives. All need to understand it and cling to it as their hope. If they do, it will bear fruit.

The hope is that the one who hears and understands the word regarding the kingdom bears fruit. We have to ask ourselves constantly what kind of ground we are. We need to ask God to prepare our hearts to receive His word.

Good Ground:

> Thank God that the soil is not all hard or shallow or thorny! We have but to turn backward in the history of the growth of the kingdom to assure ourselves of this. "The good and honest hearts" have never been wanting. Again and again it has looked as though there was to be no more harvest. When the leaders of the faith were put to death, its assemblies dispersed, and the word of God was burned and trampled upon, it has seemed to be the end, but there were hearts in which the seed was cherished. In such there sprang up the most shining and unworldly virtues. The Christ-life of love and sacrifice has been reproduced

wherever the seed has fallen. Men receiving the Word have been moved to live and die and spend themselves for others.[77]

The focus of hope is the return of Jesus Christ as King. He is coming back to earth and all should be looking forward to His return. At that time, the saints will be resurrected and have an important role in that Kingdom.

During the reign of Christ upon the earth, the saints will enjoy peace, health, and happiness. The greatest Joy will be their relationship and knowledge of God in the actual presence of the King.

Christians can truly look forward to being reunited with those loved ones that were also followers of Christ. What a wonderful joyous time that will be.

> What joy in the midst of the desert to know that we are soon to meet Him; and what a meeting that will be! We shall see Him as He is, and be like Him. We shall press again to our bosoms the loving and loved ones of whom death has robbed us here. We shall see them and know them again, as the friends we have known on earth. We shall clasp their hands again, as of old, in warmer embraces than earth has ever known, and never again be separated from them.[78]

Martin Luther started the reformation of the church because he read the Bible literally and found that it taught grace instead of penitence. However, he still kept the old ideas of heaven and hell and the kingdom, instead of re-evaluating those doctrines, too. He tried to make them fit a doctrine of grace. The literal interpretation of heaven, hell, and the kingdom is far different than what most people imagine today.

---

[77] (Boteler, 1915)

[78] (Torrey, 1998)

Earlier, I mentioned that the Amillennialists decided the coming of Christ was not going to happen because He had not come yet. They decided they were interpreting the word and prophesy incorrectly, so they changed to an allegorical interpretation. One of the reasons the average Christian does not know about the Kingdom is that Orthodox Christianity does not take the return of Christ literally. Is this because they gave up hope of a physical return? Did they start to question if He was ever coming back?

2nd Peter 3:3–18

3 *Know this first of all, that in the last days mockers will come with their mocking, following after their own lusts,*

4 *and saying, "Where is the promise of His coming? For ever since the fathers fell asleep, all continues just as it was from the beginning of creation."*

5 *For when they maintain this, it escapes their notice that by the word of God the heavens existed long ago and the earth was formed out of water and by water,*

6 *through which the world at that time was destroyed, being flooded with water.*

7 *But by His word the present heavens and earth are being reserved for fire, kept for the day of judgment and destruction of ungodly men.*

8 *But do not let this one fact escape your notice, beloved, that with the Lord one day is like a thousand years, and a thousand years like one day.*

9 *The Lord is not slow about His promise, as some count slowness, but is patient toward you, not wishing for any to perish but for all to come to repentance.*

10 *But the day of the Lord will come like a thief, in which the heavens will pass away with a roar and the elements will be destroyed with intense heat, and the earth and its works will be burned up.*

11 *Since all these things are to be destroyed in this way, what sort of people ought you to be in holy conduct and godliness,*

12 *looking for and hastening the coming of the day of God, because of which the heavens will be destroyed by burning, and the elements will melt with intense heat!*

13 *But according to His promise we are looking for new heavens and a new earth, in which righteousness dwells.*

14 *Therefore, beloved, since you look for these things, be diligent to be found by Him in peace, spotless and blameless,*

15 *and regard the patience of our Lord as salvation; just as also our beloved brother Paul, according to the wisdom given him, wrote to you,*

16 *as also in all his letters, speaking in them of these things, in which are some things hard to understand, which the untaught and unstable distort, as they do also the rest of the Scriptures, to their own destruction.*

17 *You therefore, beloved, knowing this beforehand, be on your guard so that you are not carried away by the error of unprincipled men and fall from your own steadfastness,*

18 *but grow in the grace and knowledge of our Lord and Savior Jesus Christ. To Him be the glory, both now and to the day of eternity. Amen.*

Don't let the good news about the Kingdom fade in your heart, and never, ever give up hope.

Matthew 24:10–14
10 *At that time many will fall away and will betray one another and hate one another.*

11 *Many false prophets will arise and will mislead many.*

12 *Because lawlessness is increased, most people's love will grow cold.*

13 *But the one who endures to the end, he will be saved.*

14 *This gospel of the kingdom shall be preached in the whole world as a testimony to all the nations, and then the end will come.*

9

ABRAHAM'S COVENANT

Between approximately 2100 and 1800 BC during the Bronze Age, a man named Abram was living in the city of Ur of the Chaldeans in Mesopotamia. He was the son of Terah and the brother of Nahor and Haran. Haran was the father of Lot, but died while still in Ur. Abram and his brothers were direct descendants of Shem, one of the sons of Noah. Allegedly, they were a family of high culture and wealth.

Terah, Abram's father, led them to a city called Haran on the upper Euphrates River in northwestern Mesopotamia, about 300 miles from Ur. Several cities in Mesopotamia were named after Abram's predecessors and relatives. His grandfather and brother were named Nahor, and Nahor was a city located close to Haran. It is possible that Haran was named after Abram's dead brother. Terah may have led them to Haran to be close to his father. Terah evidently died in Haran at the age of 205.

I do not believe this is a story or a myth; it actually happened. Archeological research indicates that the story of Abram and his journeys are most likely true.

> Texts from Nuzi, Mari, Boghazköy, and Babylon shed
> light on his life and actions. His name, travels, manner of

life, his barren wife, and his relationship with her slave—
all fit the culture of the Early and Middle Bronze periods.[79]

Abram found favor in the sight of God and eventually received many promises from Him. These promises are very important to Christians, as they apply to us as well.

Genesis 12:1–8

1 *Now the Lord said to Abram,*
"Go forth from your country,
And from your relatives
And from your father's house,
To the land which I will show you;
2 *And I will make you a great nation,*
And I will bless you,
And make your name great;
And so you shall be a blessing;
3 *And I will bless those who bless you,*
And the one who curses you I will curse.
*And **in you all the families of the earth shall be blessed**."*
4 *So Abram went forth as the Lord had spoken to him; and Lot went with him. Now Abram was seventy-five years old when he departed from Haran.*
5 *And Abram took Sarai his wife and Lot his nephew, and all their possessions which they had accumulated, and the persons which they had acquired in Haran, and they set out for the land of Canaan; thus **they came to the land of Canaan**.*
6 *And Abram passed through the land as far as the site of Shechem, to the oak of Moreh. Now the Canaanite was then in the land.*

---

[79] (Elwell, 1988)

7 And the Lord appeared to Abram and said, "__To your descendants I will give this land__." So he built an altar there to the Lord who had appeared to him. 8 Then he proceeded from there to the mountain on the east of Bethel, and pitched his tent, with Bethel on the west and Ai on the east; and there he built an altar to the Lord and called upon the name of the Lord.

Why did God pick Abram? As I mentioned earlier, Abram was a direct descendant of Noah's son Shem. Noah blessed Shem and his brother Japheth but cursed Ham and his son Canaan. Other than that, the Bible never really tells us anything special about Abram that would cause God to favor him. Hebrews 11:8 tells us it was Abram's response to God's call that made him special.

Hebrews 11:8

By faith Abraham, when he was called, obeyed by going out to a place which he was to receive for an inheritance; and he went out, not knowing where he was going.

Abraham obeyed when he "went forth as the Lord had spoken to him." I think there is a lesson to be learned here. Believing God and obeying His call by faith is how we should live.

If we look at Genesis 12:1–8, we see seven promises made to Abram. These promises were based on only one condition: that he leave his home and go where God told him. The seven promises are:

1. God will make Abram a great nation.
2. God will bless Abram.
3. God will make Abram's name great.
4. God will make Abram a blessing.
5. God will bless the friends of Abram.
6. God will curse the enemies of Abram.

7. All of the families of the earth will be blessed through Abram.

To realize that these promises have been fulfilled, remember that Abram's name was changed to Abraham. Abraham was the father of the nation of Israel, and Jesus was a descendant of Abraham. The promises are repeated several times throughout the Old Testament.

> **Genesis 18:18–19**
> **18** *"...since Abraham will surely become a great and mighty nation, and in him all the nations of the earth will be blessed?*
> **19** *For I have chosen him, in order that he may command his children and his household after him to keep the way of the Lord by doing righteousness and justice; in order that the Lord may bring upon Abraham what He has spoken about him."*

> **Genesis 22:17–18**
> **17** *"...indeed I will greatly bless you, and I will greatly multiply your seed as the stars of the heavens, and as the sand which is on the seashore; and your seed shall possess the gate of their enemies.*
> **18** *And in your seed all the nations of the earth shall be blessed, because you have obeyed My voice."*

Now we come to one of the basic themes of the Kingdom: the land. We have heard of the Promised Land all our lives, but have we ever stopped to think of what the promised land really is and what it means to us? We all know that the nation of Israel is based in the Promised Land, but I think it is a lot more than that, and has strong significance to everyone who claims Christ as his or her Savior. Let's examine the land promises.

Genesis 13:14–18

14 *And the Lord said to Abram, after Lot had separated from him, "Now lift up your eyes and look from the place where you are, northward and southward and eastward and westward;*

15 *for **<u>all the land which you see, I will give it to you and to your descendants forever</u>**.*

16 *And I will make your descendants as the dust of the earth; so that if anyone can number the dust of the earth, then your descendants can also be numbered.*

17 *Arise, **<u>walk about the land through its length and breadth; for I will give it to you</u>**."*

18 *Then Abram moved his tent and came and dwelt by the oaks of Mamre, which are in Hebron, and there he built an altar to the Lord.*

The Lord tells Abram that all of the land that he sees will be given to him. The phrase *I will give it to you* is used throughout the entire Old Testament regarding this land. The word *"give"* is used approximately one thousand times in the Old Testament, and most of the time it is in reference to the land God gave to Abram.

The following figures depict maps of Abram's journeys.

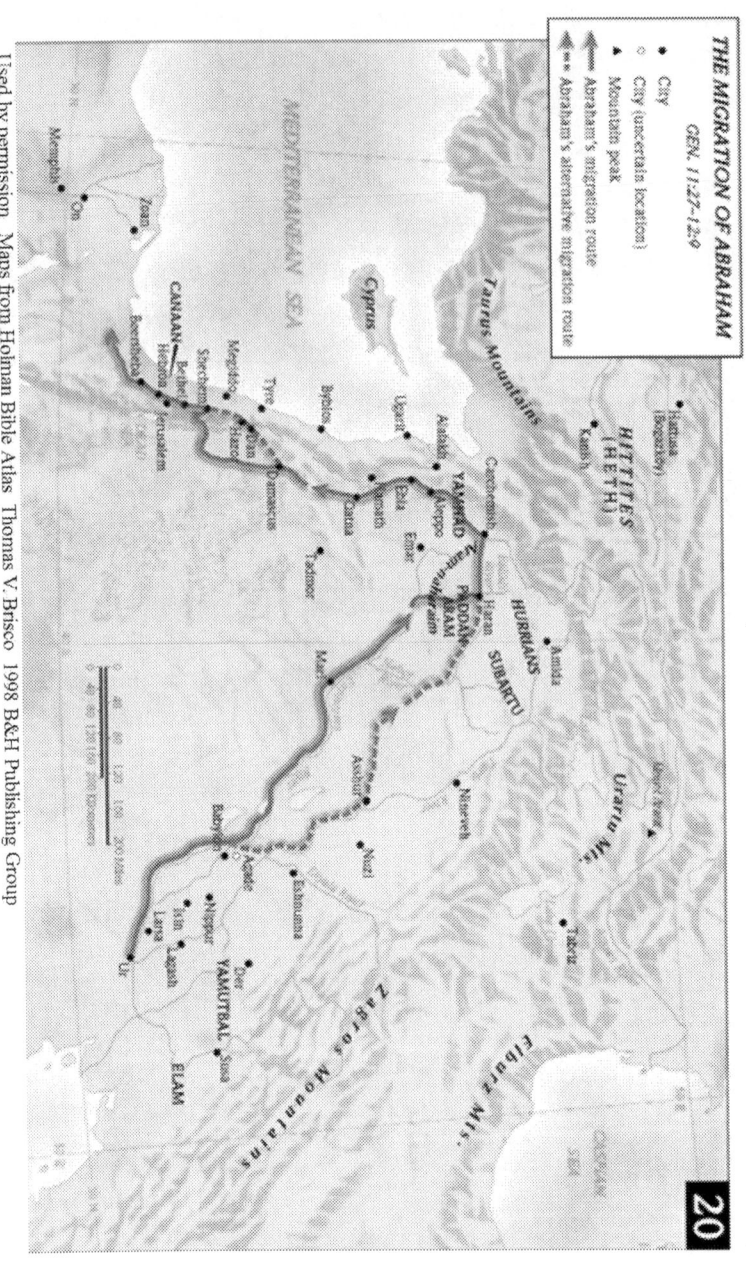

Fig. 1 The Migration of Abraham

Fig. 2 Modern Map of the Mid East

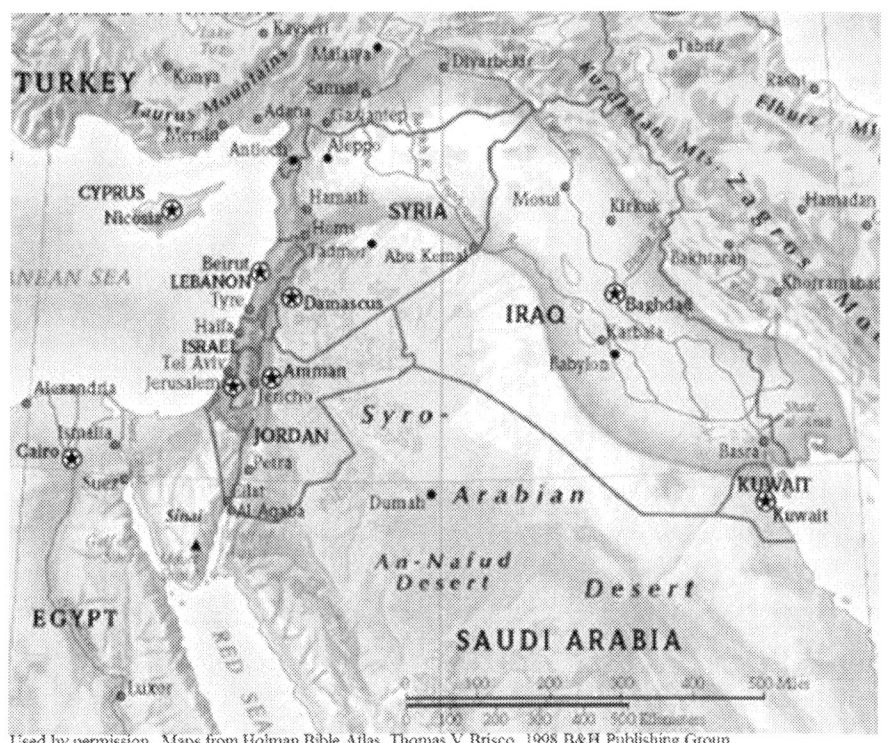

Used by permission Maps from Holman Bible Atlas Thomas V. Brisco 1998 B&H Publishing Group
This map has been cropped from the original map by Ken Stewart to enlarge the area of interest.

Genesis 15:5–8

5 *And He took him outside and said, "Now look toward the heavens, and count the stars, if you are able to count them." And He said to him, "So shall your descendants be."*

6 *Then he believed in the Lord; and He reckoned it to him as righteousness.*

7 *And He said to him, "I am the Lord who brought you out of Ur of the Chaldeans, __to give you this land to possess it__."*

8 *He said, "O Lord GOD, __how may I know that I will possess it?__"*

Notice here that the Lord promises Abram that he will possess the land. Abram responds with, "How do I know I shall possess it?" To answer this question, God didn't just say, "Trust me." Instead, He answers with what seems like a very strange answer.

Genesis 15:9–10

9 *So He said to him, "Bring Me a three year old heifer, and a three year old female goat, and a three year old ram, and a turtledove, and a young pigeon."* **10** *Then he brought all these to Him and cut them in two, and laid each half opposite the other; but he did not cut the birds.*

To understand this answer we have to put this in the proper context of Abram's background. Today if we wanted proof that God had made a promise and would fulfill that promise, we would probably say, "Can I have that in writing?" God's answer to Abram meant the same to him as if He told us, "Go get a lawyer and have him draw up a legally binding contract, I will sign it and even have it notarized."

Israel is unique among ancient Near Eastern peoples in their belief that God entered a covenant with them. While non-Israelites formed covenants with other peoples by invoking the names of their gods, only the God of Israel initiates a covenant and binds himself by oath to his people.[80]

Abram was familiar with the concept of a covenant, which was the same during the Bronze Age as a legal contract is today. In a covenant, an animal is cut in half and the two parties making the legal agreement pass through the pieces. Then, both parties are bound by blood to fulfill their part of the contract. If either party breaks the agreement, that person must be cut in half just like the animals.

---

[80] (Hahn, 2012)

The extra animals listed here emphasized the importance and certainty of the contract. Let's take a close look at how the Lord entered into this contract or covenant.

Genesis 15:12–17

12 *Now when the sun was going down, a deep sleep fell upon Abram; and behold, terror and great darkness fell upon him.*

13 *And God said to Abram, "Know for certain that your descendants will be strangers in a land that is not theirs, where they will be enslaved and oppressed four hundred years.*

14 *But I will also judge the nation whom they will serve; and afterward they will come out with many possessions.*

15 *And as for you, you shall go to your fathers in peace; you shall be buried at a good old age.*

16 *Then in the fourth generation they shall return here, for the iniquity of the Amorite is not yet complete."*

17 *And it came about when the sun had set that it was very dark, and behold, there appeared a smoking oven and a flaming torch which passed between these pieces.*

Normally when a covenant was made and the animals were split in two, the two parties participating in the covenant would pass through the pieces together. Notice here that God put Abram to sleep and passed through the pieces alone. This shows that Abram was a receiver of the covenant, but he had no role in making it come to pass. It was a totally unconditional covenant. Only God was responsible for the fulfillment of the promise. It was truly a gift.

On occasions of great importance, when two or more parties join in a compact, they either observe precisely the same rites as Abram did, or, where they do not, they

125

invoke the lamp as their witness. According to these ideas, which have been from time immemorial engraved on the minds of Eastern people, the Lord Himself condescended to enter into covenant with Abram. **The patriarch did not pass between the sacrifice and the reason was that in this transaction he was bound to nothing**. He asked a sign, and God was pleased to give him a sign, by which, according to Eastern ideas, He bound Himself.[81]

Later, we will see that although the promise of the land is unconditional, the entrance into that land *is* conditional. The condition is that we walk with God and be identified as one of Abraham's descendants. It would not make any sense for anyone who is not willing to obey God, or to be identified with Him, to enter into His Kingdom. It would be God's place, God's rule, but not God's people.

Genesis 15:18
18 *On that day the Lord made a covenant with Abram, saying,*
"To your descendants I have given this land,
From the river of Egypt as far as the great river, the river Euphrates:
19 *the Kenite and the Kenizzite and the Kadmonite*
20 *and the Hittite and the Perizzite and the Rephaim*
21 *and the Amorite and the Canaanite and the Girgashite and the Jebusite."*

The Promised Land is not just a hope of the Kingdom, but Zionists believe that it is their political goal to take over the land promised.

In February 1896, Theodor Herzl, a brilliant Austrian journalist, published a pamphlet *The Jewish State* which swept through the Jewish world like a tornado. Within a few months, Zionist groups were springing up in Jewish

---

[81] (Jamieson, 1997)

communities everywhere. The pamphlet advocated a Jewish nation in a Jewish national land. "We shall live at last as free men on our own soil."[82]

The map below is the area that Theodor Herzl and Rabbi Fischman believed was the Promised Land.

Fig. 3 The Promised Land according to Rabbi Fischmann (1947)

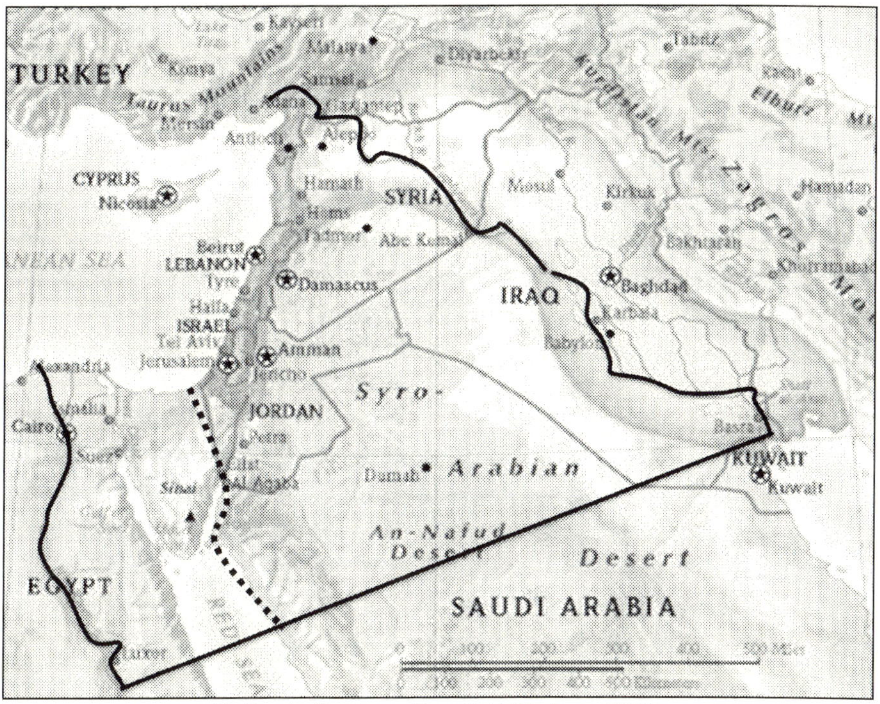

The Promised Land according to Rabbi Fischmann (1947)
Used by permission Maps from Holman Bible Atlas Thomas V. Brisco 1998 B&H Publishing Group
This map has been cropped from the original map by Ken Stewart to enlarge the area of interest.
Dotted Line added by Ken Stewart and was not part of the original map.

In verse 15:18 above, God laid out the southwest boundary of the Promised Land from the "River of Egypt". Rabbi Fischmann and many others mistakenly think this means the Nile River. The River of Egypt (or, according to some translations, the "Brook of Egypt")

---

82 (Tan, 1996)

is east of the Nile. I have added a dotted line to show the approximate location of this river.

> The Hebrew word is *nahal*, denoting a stream flowing rapidly in winter, or in the rainy season. This is a desert stream on the borders of Egypt. It is now called the Wady el-'Arish. The present boundary between Egypt and Palestine is about midway between this wady and Gaza.[83]

A more detailed description of the boundaries of the Promised Land was given to Moses.

Numbers 34:1–12

1 *Then the* LORD *spoke to Moses, saying,*

2 *"Command the sons of Israel and say to them, 'When you enter the land of Canaan, this is the land that shall fall to you as an inheritance, even the land of Canaan according to its borders.*

3 *Your southern sector shall extend from the wilderness of Zin along the side of Edom, and your southern border shall extend from the end of the Salt Sea eastward.*

4 *Then your border shall turn direction from the south to the ascent of Akrabbim and continue to Zin, and its termination shall be to the south of Kadesh-barnea; and it shall reach Hazaraddar and continue to Azmon.*

5 *The border shall turn direction from Azmon to the brook of Egypt, and its termination shall be at the sea.*

6 *As for the western border, you shall have the Great Sea, that is, its coastline; this shall be your west border.*

7 *And this shall be your north border: you shall draw your border line from the Great Sea to Mount Hor.*

---

[83] (Easton, 1893)

8 *You shall draw a line from Mount Hor to the Lebo-hamath, and the termination of the border shall be at Zedad;*

9 *and the border shall proceed to Ziphron, and its termination shall be at Hazar-enan. This shall be your north border.*

10 *For your eastern border you shall also draw a line from Hazar-enan to Shepham,*

11 *and the border shall go down from Shepham to Riblah on the east side of Ain; and the border shall go down and reach to the slope on the east side of the Sea of Chinnereth.*

12 *And the border shall go down to the Jordan and its termination shall be at the Salt Sea. This shall be your land according to its borders all around."'*

Not only was the gift promised and covenanted to Abram, but also to his descendants.

Genesis 17:1–8

1 *Now when Abram was ninety-nine years old, the Lord appeared to Abram and said to him,*
"I am God Almighty;
Walk before Me, and be blameless.
2 *And I will establish My covenant between Me and you,*
And I will multiply you exceedingly."
3 *And Abram fell on his face, and God talked with him, saying,*
4 *"As for Me, behold, My covenant is with you,*
And you shall be the father of a multitude of nations.
5 *No longer shall your name be called Abram,*
But your name shall be Abraham;

For I will make you the father of a multitude of nations.

6 *And I will make you exceedingly fruitful, and I will make nations of you, and kings shall come forth from you.*

7 *And I will establish My covenant between Me and you and your descendants after you throughout their generations for an everlasting covenant, to be God to you and to your descendants after you.*

8 *And I will give to you and to your descendants after you, the land of your sojournings, all the land of Canaan, for an everlasting possession; and I will be their God."*

There are five main points to remember about the Abrahamic covenant.

1. Abraham will receive the land.
2. God will make Abraham's descendants a great nation.
3. They will be given the Promised Land to dwell in.
4. They will be established on a special relationship to God.
5. All the people on earth will be blessed through them.

It seems pretty clear, but there is one thing we must consider in all of this: **Abraham never possessed the land!** You are probably wondering how I can say that after all of these promises. In Acts, Stephen was brought before the Sanhedrin (the religious court or council of Israel) and the high priest to answer charges of blasphemy. What is the message that Stephen thought was so important to share at this moment?

Acts 7:2–5

2 *And he said, "Hear me, brethren and fathers! The God of glory appeared to our father Abraham when he was in Mesopotamia, before he lived in Haran,*

3 *and said to him, 'Depart from your country and your relatives, and come into the land that I will show you.'*
4 *Then he departed from the land of the Chaldeans, and settled in Haran. And from there, after his father died, God removed him into this country in which you are now living.*
5 *<u>**And He gave him no inheritance in it, not even a foot of ground; and yet, even when he had no child, He promised that He would give it to him as a possession, and to his offspring after him**</u>."*

He gave him no inheritance in it, ***not even a foot of ground!*** Yet, He promised it to him as a possession.

I know you are thinking, "Wait a minute. He lived there; what does this mean?" Yes, he lived there, but he did not own or possess it. It was not his. He lived there as a foreigner, as an alien. The writer of Hebrews tells us the same thing.

Hebrews 11:8–10
8 *By faith Abraham, when he was called, obeyed by going out to a place which he was to receive for an inheritance; and he went out, not knowing where he was going.*
9 *<u>**By faith he lived as an alien in the land of promise, as in a foreign land**</u>, dwelling in tents with Isaac and Jacob, fellow heirs of the same promise;*
10 *for he was looking for the city which has foundations, whose architect and builder is God.*

If Abraham was unconditionally promised that he would inherit or possess the land, and yet did not receive it, or lived in it as an alien, then we are confronted with a conundrum. How could this be true?

Did the promise God made go unfulfilled? Does God not keep his covenants? We know that can't be, so we have only one other choice.

Abraham must still be able to receive the land. How can that be? Easy: the resurrection of the dead!

Matthew 8:11

"And I say to you, that many shall come from east and west, and recline at the table with Abraham, and Isaac, and Jacob, in the Kingdom of heaven..."

Jesus explains that Abraham, Isaac, and Jacob will be resurrected and possess the land.

Matthew 22:31–32

31 *"But regarding the resurrection of the dead, have you not read that which was spoken to you by God, saying,*
32 *'I am the God of Abraham, and the God of Isaac, and the God of Jacob'? He is not the God of the dead but of the living."*

I think this is pretty strong evidence that the patriarchs will be resurrected. They will receive the promises that God made to them. Sure, this proves the resurrection, but what about the land? God specifically speaks through Ezekiel regarding the resurrection and the possession of the land.

Ezekiel 37:12–14

12 *"Therefore prophesy, and say to them, 'Thus says the Lord God, "Behold, I will open your graves and cause you to come up out of your graves, My people; and I will bring you into the land of Israel.*

13 Then you will know that I am the Lord, when I have opened your graves and caused you to come up out of your graves, My people.

14 And I will put My Spirit within you, and you will come to life, and I will place you on your own land. Then you will know that I, the Lord, have spoken and done it," declares the Lord.'"

In summary, we see God's people in God's place under God's rule. That is the definition of the Kingdom. At first glance, we might read this and think that this has been fulfilled when the nation of Israel was established. We will see later that this is not the case. To become identified as a descendant of Abraham and a participant in the promises, God gave a sign for them to remember the covenant.

CIRCUMCISION

Genesis 17:9–14

9 God said further to Abraham, "Now as for you, you shall keep My covenant, you and your descendants after you throughout their generations.

10 This is My covenant, which you shall keep, between Me and you and your descendants after you: every male among you shall be circumcised.

11 And you shall be circumcised in the flesh of your foreskin; and it shall be the sign of the covenant between Me and you.

12 And every male among you who is eight days old shall be circumcised throughout your generations, a servant who is born in the house or who is bought with money from any foreigner, who is not of your descendants.

13 *A servant who is born in your house or who is bought with your money shall surely be circumcised; thus shall My covenant be in your flesh for an everlasting covenant.*

14 *But an uncircumcised male who is not circumcised in the flesh of his foreskin, that person shall be cut off from his people; he has broken My covenant."*

God sometimes wants to remind us of his promises. When God promised Noah that it would never rain like it did in the great flood, He gave us a sign as verification of that promise. Whenever we see a rainbow, we are reminded that God is true to His promise and a flood will never again wipe out the earth.

Genesis 9:8–17

8 *Then God spoke to Noah and to his sons with him, saying,*

9 *"Now behold, I Myself do establish My covenant with you, and with your descendants after you;*

10 *and with every living creature that is with you, the birds, the cattle, and every beast of the earth with you; of all that comes out of the ark, even every beast of the earth.*

11 *And I establish My covenant with you; and all flesh shall never again be cut off by the water of the flood, neither shall there again be a flood to destroy the earth."*

12 *And God said, "This is the sign of the covenant which I am making between Me and you and every living creature that is with you, for all successive generations;*

13 *I set My bow in the cloud, and it shall be for a sign of a covenant between Me and the earth.*

14 *And it shall come about, when I bring a cloud over the earth, that the bow shall be seen in the cloud,*

15 *and I will remember My covenant, which is between Me and you and every living creature of all flesh; and never again shall the water become a flood to destroy all flesh.*

16 *When the bow is in the cloud, then I will look upon it, to remember the everlasting covenant between God and every living creature of all flesh that is on the earth."*

17 *And God said to Noah, "This is the sign of the covenant which I have established between Me and all flesh that is on the earth."*

The rainbow was a sign of the covenant made with Noah. God said He would see the rainbow and remember the everlasting covenant. I doubt God needs to be reminded, but it is an assurance on our part that He will remember the promise.

Circumcision is the same type of sign. It was to remind the descendants of Abraham that they were partakers of the covenant. On the eighth day after a male was born, that child was to be circumcised. This celebration served to signify God's promises and that this child was becoming an heir of that promise. I think we can safely assume that God will be reminded of His promise when He sees circumcision. Now, don't run out and become circumcised until we see what the rest of the Bible says about it.

Fascinatingly, when reading about things like circumcision and ceremonial washings that God implemented in His covenants, we now understand the health benefits associated with such practices. If some man had just invented this religion, how would he have had such foresight?

10

ABRAHAM'S DESCENDANTS

Abraham had two sons: Ishmael, the son of Hagar, the Egyptian maid of Sarai (Abram's wife) and Isaac, the son of Sarai. Ishmael was sent away, and God told Abraham,

Genesis 21:12
"Through Isaac your descendants shall be named."

Isaac was given the same promises that God gave to Abraham.

Genesis 26:1–5
1 *Now there was a famine in the land, besides the previous famine that had occurred in the days of Abraham. So Isaac went to Gerar, to Abimelech king of the Philistines.*
2 *And the Lord appeared to him and said, "Do not go down to Egypt; stay in the land of which I shall tell you.*
3 *Sojourn in this land and I will be with you and bless you, for to you and to your descendants I will give all these lands, and I will establish the oath which I swore to your father Abraham.*
4 *And I will multiply your descendants as the stars of heaven, and will give your descendants all these*

lands; and by your descendants all the nations of the
earth shall be blessed;
5 *because Abraham obeyed Me and kept My charge,*
My commandments, My statutes and My laws."

Notice God never tells Isaac that he deserved these promises, but that
it was all because Abraham obeyed God and kept His commandments.
This is Grace. The obedience of Abraham enabled his descendants to
receive the promises. Isaac did nothing to earn this blessing.

Isaac had two twin sons Esau and Jacob. Esau was the first-born and
therefore was the one destined to receive the blessings of his father
Isaac. Their mother helped Jacob deceive Isaac so that he would
receive the blessings instead of Esau. Isaac had become old and blind,
and Jacob dressed up like Esau and fooled his father into giving the
blessing meant for Esau to Jacob.

Genesis 27:18–29

18 *Then he came to his father and said, "My father."*
And he said, "Here I am. Who are you, my son?"
19 *And Jacob said to his father, "I am Esau your first-*
born; I have done as you told me. Get up, please, sit
and eat of my game, that you may bless me."
20 *And Isaac said to his son, "How is it that you have*
it so quickly, my son?" And he said, "Because the
Lord your God caused it to happen to me."
21 *Then Isaac said to Jacob, "Please come close, that*
I may feel you, my son, whether you are really my son
Esau or not."
22 *So Jacob came close to Isaac his father, and he felt*
him and said, "The voice is the voice of Jacob, but the
hands are the hands of Esau."
23 *And he did not recognize him, because his hands*
were hairy like his brother Esau's hands; so he
blessed him.

24 And he said, "Are you really my son Esau?" And he said, "I am."

25 So he said, "Bring it to me, and I will eat of my son's game, that I may bless you." And he brought it to him, and he ate; he also brought him wine and he drank.

26 Then his father Isaac said to him, "Please come close and kiss me, my son."

27 "So he came close and kissed him; and when he smelled the smell of his garments, he blessed him and said,

"See, the smell of my son
Is like the smell of a field which the Lord has blessed;
28 Now may God give you of the dew of heaven,
And of the fatness of the earth,
And an abundance of grain and new wine;
29 May peoples serve you,
And nations bow down to you;
Be master of your brothers,
And may your mother's sons bow down to you.
Cursed be those who curse you,
And blessed be those who bless you."

Did Jacob steal the birthright from Esau? Not really—earlier, Esau came to Jacob hungry and sold the birthright to Jacob for some food.

Genesis 25:29–34

29 And when Jacob had cooked stew, Esau came in from the field and he was famished;

30 and Esau said to Jacob, "Please let me have a swallow of that red stuff there, for I am famished." Therefore his name was called Edom.

31 But Jacob said, "First sell me your birthright."

32 And Esau said, "Behold, I am about to die; so of what use then is the birthright to me?"

33 *And Jacob said, "First swear to me"; so he swore to him, and sold his birthright to Jacob.*

34 *Then Jacob gave Esau bread and lentil stew; and he ate and drank, and rose and went on his way. Thus Esau despised his birthright.*

This still seems deceitful, but God had said that Esau would serve Jacob.

Genesis 25:21–23

21 *And Isaac prayed to the Lord on behalf of his wife, because she was barren; and the Lord answered him and Rebekah his wife conceived.*

22 *But the children struggled together within her; and she said, "If it is so, why then am I this way?" So she went to inquire of the Lord.*

23 *And the Lord said to her,*
"Two nations are in your womb;
And two peoples shall be separated from your body;
And one people shall be stronger than the other;
And the older shall serve the younger."

Notice that Isaac's blessing to Jacob was the same blessing God had given to him and his father Abraham. Jacob received these blessings through lies and deceit—or, rather, *in spite of* his lies and deceit. Again, this undeserved kindness is another example of how grace works: it is given, not earned.

Genesis 28:10–15

10 *Then Jacob departed from Beersheba and went toward Haran.*

11 *And he came to a certain place and spent the night there, because the sun had set; and he took one of the stones of the place and put it under his head, and lay down in that place.*

12 *And he had a dream, and behold, a ladder was set on the earth with its top reaching to heaven; and behold, the angels of God were ascending and descending on it.*

13 *And behold, the Lord stood above it and said, "I am the Lord, the God of your father Abraham and the God of Isaac; the land on which you lie, I will give it to you and to your descendants.*

14 *Your descendants shall also be like the dust of the earth, and you shall spread out to the west and to the east and to the north and to the south; and in you and in your descendants shall all the families of the earth be blessed.*

15 *And behold, I am with you, and will keep you wherever you go, and will bring you back to this land; for I will not leave you until I have done what I have promised you."*

Jacob has now received the promise of the Land directly from God. Notice also that God tells him, "Wherever you go, I will bring you back to this land."

Genesis 35:9–12

9 *Then God appeared to Jacob again when he came from Paddan-aram, and He blessed him.*

10 *And God said to him, "Your name is Jacob; You shall no longer be called Jacob, But Israel shall be your name." Thus He called him Israel.*

11 *God also said to him, "I am God Almighty; Be fruitful and multiply; A nation and a company of nations shall come from you, And kings shall come forth from you.*

12 *And the land which I gave to Abraham and Isaac,*
I will give it to you,
And I will give the land to your descendants after you."

Jacob is now to be called Israel. Israel is promised the land, and God said He would also give the land to Israel's descendants.

We see that Abraham, Isaac, and Jacob were all promised the land. This is mentioned many, many times. There must be some importance to these promises, or they would not be repeated so many times to so many people.

Judaism and Christianity are they only religions that believe in the resurrection of dead people into flesh and bone bodies. All other religions believe in a spiritual life after death, but actual *coming back to life and living in the land* is one of the main themes that separate the Jews and Christians from other religions. That is one of the reasons the test of spirits given in 1st John 4:1-3 stresses that they must confess "that Jesus Christ is coming in the flesh" (has come is a perfect participle—continuous action: has come, still is, and will come in the flesh).

> **Is come**—Greek, "coming." He who denies Christ's coming in the flesh denies the possibility of the incarnation; he who denies that he has come, denies its actuality. They denied the possibility of a Messiah's appearing, or coming, in the flesh [Neander]. I think the Greek present participle implies both the first and the second advent of Christ. He is often elsewhere called the Coming One (Greek), Mt 11:3; Heb. 10:37. The denial of the reality of His manifestation in the flesh, at His first coming, and of His personal advent again, constitutes Antichrist. "The world turns away from God and Christ, busily intent upon its own husks; but to oppose God and Christ is of the leaven of Satan" [Bengel].[84]

---

[84] (Jamieson, 1997)

Almost every Christian I talk to does not believe in a physical resurrection. They have the idea that they will become like ghosts, a spirit form, still recognizable as a physical being. They only have a concept of a spiritual afterlife in heaven. Holograms have been used to display this concept in haunted houses. Those who believe this have lost their hope.

> **Hebrews 6:17–20**
> **17** *In the same way God, desiring even more to show to the heirs of the promise the unchangeableness of His purpose, interposed* [intervened or mediated] *with an oath,*
> **18** *so that by two unchangeable things in which it is impossible for God to lie,* <u>**we who have taken refuge**</u> *would have* <u>**strong encouragement to take hold of the hope set before us**</u>.
> **19** <u>**This hope we have as an anchor of the soul, a hope both sure and steadfast**</u> *and one which enters within the veil,*
> **20** *where Jesus has entered as a forerunner for us, having become a high priest forever according to the order of Melchizedek.*

I would like to make a side comment about the rest of this passage. The heirs of the promise are all that have faith in the accomplishment of Jesus Christ. The two unchangeable things are the promise and the oath. When God made the covenant with Abram, He made a promise bound by a contract and He swore an oath at the same time. The contract was a promise that Abraham would obtain the land; the oath was the promise of blessing and multiplying his family.

> **Hebrews 6:11–14**
> **11** *And we desire that each one of you show the same diligence so as to realize the full assurance of hope until the end,*

12 *so that you will not be sluggish, but imitators of those who through faith and patience inherit the promises.*

13 *For when God made the promise to Abraham, since He could swear by no one greater, He swore by Himself,*

14 *saying, "I WILL SURELY BLESS YOU AND I WILL SURELY MULTIPLY YOU."*

Back in Hebrews 6:18, it says *we who have taken refuge would have strong encouragement to take hold of the hope set before us.* In the Greek interlinear it reads:

We	who	have		taken	refuge
	οἱ	→		καταφυγόντες	←
	hoi			kataphygontes	

The Greek word καταφυγόντες (*kataphygontes*) literally means *flee to safety* as into one of the old cities of refuge.

Numbers 35:11–13

11 *"...then you shall select for yourselves cities to be your cities of refuge, that the manslayer who has killed any person unintentionally may flee there.*

12 *The cities shall be to you as a refuge from the avenger, so that the manslayer will not die until he stands before the congregation for trial.*

13 *The cities which you are to give shall be your six cities of refuge."*

For those who have fled to a safe place, our city of refuge is the presence of God. As Hebrews 6:18-20 says, we *have strong encouragement to take hold of the hope set before us. This hope we have as an anchor of the soul, a hope both sure and steadfast and one which enters within the veil, where Jesus has entered as a forerunner for us...*

THE PROMISE OF THE LAND AND THE
KINGDOM ADDED TO ISRAEL

Ezekiel 37:21–28

21 *Thus says the Lord God, "Behold, I will take the sons of Israel from among the nations where they have gone, and I will gather them from every side and bring them into their own land;*

22 *and I will make them one nation in the land, on the mountains of Israel; and one king will be king for all of them; and they will no longer be two nations, and they will no longer be divided into two Kingdoms.*

23 *And they will no longer defile themselves with their idols, or with their detestable things, or with any of their transgressions; but I will deliver them from all their dwelling places in which they have sinned, and will cleanse them. And they will be My people, and I will be their God."*

<u>The Davidic Kingdom</u>

24 *"And My servant David will be king over them, and they will all have one shepherd; and they will walk in My ordinances, and keep My statutes, and observe them.*

25 *And they shall live on the land that I gave to Jacob My servant, in which your fathers lived; and they will live on it, they, and their sons, and their sons' sons, forever; and David My servant shall be their prince forever.*

26 *And I will make a covenant of peace with them; it will be an everlasting covenant with them. And I will place them and multiply them, and will set My sanctuary in their midst forever.*

27 My dwelling place also will be with them; and I will be their God, and they will be My people.

28 And the nations will know that I am the Lord who sanctifies Israel, when My sanctuary is in their midst forever."

Another heir to the promises made to Abraham is Jesus Christ.

Galatians 3:16

Now the promises were spoken to Abraham and to his seed. He does not say, "And to seeds," as referring to many, but rather to one, "And to your seed," that is, Christ.

WE ARE DESCENDANTS OF ABRAHAM

Millions of people claim to be Descendants of Abraham—of course the Israelites, but also the Muslims through Ishmael, the son of Hagar, Abraham's first son. According to the New Testament, Christians are also children of Abraham.

Galatians 3:6–9

6 Even so Abraham believed God, and it was reckoned to him as righteousness.

7 Therefore, be sure that it is those who are of faith who are sons of Abraham.

8 And the Scripture, foreseeing that God would justify the Gentiles by faith, preached the gospel beforehand to Abraham, saying, "All the nations shall be blessed in you."

9 So then those who are of faith are blessed with Abraham, the believer.

Romans 8:14–17

14 *For all who are being led by the Spirit of God, these are sons of God.*

15 *For you have not received a spirit of slavery leading to fear again, but you have received a spirit of adoption as sons by which we cry out, "Abba! Father!"*

16 *The Spirit Himself bears witness with our spirit that we are children of God,*

17 *and if children, heirs also, heirs of God and fellow heirs with Christ, if indeed we suffer with Him in order that we may also be glorified with Him.*

Galatians 3:26–29

26 *For you are all sons of God through faith in Christ Jesus.*

27 *For all of you who were baptized into Christ have clothed yourselves with Christ.*

28 *There is neither Jew nor Greek, there is neither slave nor free man, there is neither male nor female; for you are all one in Christ Jesus.*

29 *And if you belong to Christ, then you are Abraham's offspring, heirs according to promise.*

Romans 4:3–25

3 *For what does the Scripture say? "And Abraham believed God, and it was reckoned to him as righteousness."*

4 *Now to the one who works, his wage is not reckoned as a favor, but as what is due.*

5 *But to the one who does not work, but believes in Him who justifies the ungodly, his faith is reckoned as righteousness,*

6 *just as David also speaks of the blessing upon the man to whom God reckons righteousness apart from works:*

7 *"Blessed are those whose lawless deeds have been forgiven,*

And whose sins have been covered.

8 *"Blessed is the man whose sin the Lord will not take into account."*

9 *Is this blessing then upon the circumcised, or upon the uncircumcised also? For we say, "Faith was reckoned to Abraham as righteousness."*

10 *How then was it reckoned? While he was circumcised, or uncircumcised? Not while circumcised, but while uncircumcised;*

11 *and he received the sign of circumcision, a seal of the righteousness of the faith which he had while uncircumcised, that he might be the father of all who believe without being circumcised, that righteousness might be reckoned to them,*

12 *and the father of circumcision to those who not only are of the circumcision, but who also follow in the steps of the faith of our father Abraham which he had while uncircumcised.*

13 *For the promise to Abraham or to his descendants that he would be heir of the world was not through the Law, but through the righteousness of faith.*

14 *For if those who are of the Law are heirs, faith is made void and the promise is nullified;*

15 *for the Law brings about wrath, but where there is no law, neither is there violation.*

16 *For this reason it is by faith, that it might be in accordance with grace, in order that the promise may be certain to all the descendants, not only to those who are of the Law, but also to those who are of the faith of Abraham, who is the father of us all,*

17 *(as it is written, "A father of many nations have I made you") in the sight of Him whom he believed, even God, who gives life to the dead and calls into being that which does not exist.*

18 *In hope against hope he believed, in order that he might become a father of many nations, according to that which had been spoken, "So shall your descendants be."*

19 *And without becoming weak in faith he contemplated his own body, now as good as dead since he was about a hundred years old, and the deadness of Sarah's womb;*

20 *yet, with respect to the promise of God, he did not waver in unbelief, but grew strong in faith, giving glory to God,*

21 *and being fully assured that what He had promised, He was able also to perform.*

22 *Therefore also it was reckoned to him as righteousness.*

23 *Now not for his sake only was it written, that it was reckoned to him,*

24 *but for our sake also, to whom it will be reckoned, as those who believe in Him who raised Jesus our Lord from the dead,*

25 He who was delivered up because of our transgressions, and was raised because of our justification.

Verse 11: "Father of all who believe"

...that he might be the father of all who believe without being circumcised, that righteousness might be reckoned to them...

Verses 13–14: "heir of the world"

That he would be heir of the world was not through the Law, but through the righteousness of faith. For if those who are of the Law are heirs, faith is made void and the promise is nullified...

Verse 18: he believed, hoped, kept on believing no matter what

...he believed, in order that he might become a father of many nations...

Romans 9:6–8

6 But it is not as though the word of God has failed. For they are not all Israel who are descended from Israel; 7 neither are they all children because they are Abraham's descendants, but: "through Isaac your descendants will be named." 8 That is, it is not the children of the flesh who are children of God, but the children of the promise are regarded as descendants.

Romans 9:25–26

25 As He says also in Hosea, "I will call those who were not My people, 'My people,' And her who was not beloved, 'beloved.'"

26 *And it shall be that in the place where it was said to them, 'you are not My people,'*
There they shall be called sons of the living God."

Romans 9:30–33

30 *What shall we say then? That Gentiles, who did not pursue righteousness, attained righteousness, even the righteousness which is by faith;*

31 *but Israel, pursuing a law of righteousness, did not arrive at that law.*

32 *Why? Because they did not pursue it by faith, but as though it were by works. They stumbled over the stumbling stone,*

33 *just as it is written,*
"Behold, I lay in Zion a stone of stumbling and a rock of offense,
And he who believes in Him will not be disappointed."

What does this mean? We are heirs of the land! We will be resurrected!

11

Going To Egypt

When the Lord made the covenant with Abraham, He told him that his people would end up in a foreign land for four hundred years.

Genesis 15:13–14

13 *And God said to Abram, "Know for certain that your descendants will be strangers in a land that is not theirs, where they will be enslaved and oppressed four hundred years.*

14 *But I will also judge the nation whom they will serve; and afterward they will come out with many possessions."*

One has to wonder why God would allow the people of Israel to suffer and be enslaved for four hundred years. According to Joseph, the reason the sons of Israel ended up in Egypt was to keep them alive and, as we will see a little later, to make them a great nation.

Genesis 45:4–8

4 *"I am your brother Joseph, whom you sold into Egypt.*

5 *And now do not be grieved or angry with yourselves, because you sold me here; for God sent me before you to preserve life.*

6 For the famine has been in the land these two years, and there are still five years in which there will be neither plowing nor harvesting.

7 And God sent me before you to preserve for you a remnant in the earth, and to keep you alive by a great deliverance.

8 Now, therefore, it was not you who sent me here, but God; and He has made me a father to Pharaoh and lord of all his household and ruler over all the land of Egypt."

Please note a pattern here. Often when God is doing something for the long term good of His people, they may suffer temporarily and that suffering may be intense. When He destroyed the evil population of the earth, He did not take His people (Noah and his family) out of the world to avoid the flood, but He gave them a means to pass through it: the Ark. Building that Ark was no easy chore, and living in it with all those animals and their manure was not exactly a pleasant journey on a cruise ship.

When the children of Israel went to Egypt, they were relieved that they would have enough food to survive and were even given the best of the land. However, after a while they ended up as slaves with a considerable amount of suffering. God had a plan, and sometimes God's plans do not keep us from temporary suffering and pain.

God's plan was to make Israel a great nation. It is plain today that He did exactly that, but they have not avoided trials and tribulations. Don't expect your Christian walk today to be without some pain and suffering or trials. The Lord has a plan, and if we keep our eye on the fact that He is in charge and will see us through, we can keep the faith.

Genesis 46:2–7
2 And God spoke to Israel in visions of the night and said, "Jacob, Jacob." And he said, "Here I am."

3 *And He said, "I am God, the God of your father; do not be afraid to go down to Egypt, for **I will make you a great nation there**.*

4 *I will go down with you to Egypt, and **I will also surely bring you up again**; and Joseph will close your eyes."*

5 *Then Jacob arose from Beersheba; and the sons of Israel carried their father Jacob and their little ones and their wives, in the wagons which Pharaoh had sent to carry him.*

6 *And they took their livestock and their property, which they had acquired in the land of Canaan, and came to Egypt, Jacob and all his descendants with him:*

7 *his sons and his grandsons with him, his daughters and his granddaughters, and all his descendants he brought with him to Egypt.*

God's words to Jacob in the night vision also reiterate the promise to Abraham that from his descendants would come a "great nation" …but they also add that God would do this in Egypt. Egypt was to be the place where the house of Jacob would become the nation of Israel. These words, then, anticipate all the great work of God that was yet to be recounted in the Torah. God would bring his people into Egypt and be with them there; and after they had become a great nation, he would bring them back to the Promised Land.[85]

When these people went into Egypt, they were given the best of the land.

Genesis 47:11

11 So Joseph settled his father and his brothers, and gave them a possession in the land of Egypt, in the best of the land, in the land of Rameses, as Pharaoh had ordered.

---

[85] (Sailhamer, 1990)

According to **Acts 7:14** (*Then Joseph sent word and invited Jacob his father and all his relatives to come to him, seventy-five persons in all*), **75 descendants of Abraham** went into Egypt with Israel.

> **Exodus 12:37**
> *Now the sons of Israel journeyed from Rameses to Succoth, about six hundred thousand men on foot, aside from children.*

In Exodus 12:37, we see that over 600,000 men and their wives and children left with Moses **430 years later**. That means that the number of Israelites who followed Moses out of Egypt was **over 1.5 Million people**.

When Joseph was on his deathbed, he repeated the promise given to him to be the hope of the Israelites.

> **Genesis 50:24**
> *And Joseph said to his brothers, "I am about to die, but God will surely take care of you, and bring you up from this land to the land which He promised on oath to Abraham, to Isaac and to Jacob."*

Approximately 350 years after the Hebrews went into Egypt, a king arose who did not know Joseph and started to fear the Israelites because they had become so numerous. He put them into slavery.

> **Exodus 1:8–14**
> **8** *Now a new king arose over Egypt, who did not know Joseph.*
> **9** *And he said to his people, "Behold, the people of the sons of Israel are more and mightier than we.*
> **10** *Come, let us deal wisely with them, lest they multiply and in the event of war, they also join themselves to those who hate us, and fight against us, and depart from the land."*

11 *So they appointed taskmasters over them to afflict them with hard labor. And they built for Pharaoh storage cities, Pithom and Raamses.*

12 *But the more they afflicted them, the more they multiplied and the more they spread out, so that they were in dread of the sons of Israel.*

13 *And the Egyptians compelled the sons of Israel to labor rigorously;*

14 *and they made their lives bitter with hard labor in mortar and bricks and at all kinds of labor in the field, all their labors which they rigorously imposed on them.*

Exodus 2:23–25

23 *Now it came about in the course of those many days that the king of Egypt died. And the sons of Israel sighed because of the bondage, and they cried out; and their cry for help because of their bondage rose up to God.*

24 *So God heard their groaning; and God remembered His covenant with Abraham, Isaac, and Jacob.*

25 *And God saw the sons of Israel, and God took notice of them.*

When Moses meets God at the burning bush, God told Moses to remove his sandals because he was standing on "Holy Ground."

Exodus 3:5

*Then He said, "Do not come near here; remove your sandals from your feet, for the place on which you are standing is **holy ground**."*

What made that ground holy? Moses may have even walked on that very same spot with his sheep. Since God was now there, it was holy ground. Plain old dirt becomes holy ground when God is present. The only way we can be holy is to have the Lord present in our life.

God told Moses He would lead the people out of Egypt to the Promised Land.

Exodus 3:8–10

8 *"So I have come down to deliver them from the power of the Egyptians, and to bring them up from that land to a good and spacious land, to a land flowing with milk and honey, to the place of the Canaanite and the Hittite and the Amorite and the Perizzite and the Hivite and the Jebusite.*

9 *And now, behold, the cry of the sons of Israel has come to Me; furthermore, I have seen the oppression with which the Egyptians are oppressing them.*

10 *Therefore, come now, and I will send you to Pharaoh, so that you may bring My people, the sons of Israel, out of Egypt."*

The final act of God to get Pharaoh to allow the Israelites to leave was sending the angel of death to kill the firstborn sons of all who did not have blood on their doorposts.

Genesis 12:23–28

23 *"For the Lord will pass through to smite the Egyptians; and when He sees the blood on the lintel and on the two doorposts, the Lord will pass over the door and will not allow the destroyer to come in to your houses to smite you.*

24 *And you shall observe this event as an ordinance for you and your children forever.*

25 *And it will come about when you enter the land which the Lord will give you, as He has promised, that you shall observe this rite.*

26 *And it will come about when your children will say to you, 'What does this rite mean to you?'*

27 that you shall say, 'It is a Passover sacrifice to the Lord who passed over the houses of the sons of Israel in Egypt when He smote the Egyptians, but spared our homes.'" And the people bowed low and worshiped.
28 Then the sons of Israel went and did so; just as the Lord had commanded Moses and Aaron, so they did.

The Passover was an act of salvation. The blood of a lamb saved them. It appears that this whole Egyptian experience was a foretaste of the fact that God's people will need deliverance and will need to be saved by the blood of a lamb so that they may enter into the Promised Land. The deliverance out of Egypt is proof that the covenant made with Abraham is true. If part of the promise is true, we can trust that God will fulfill the rest of it.

Exodus 19:3–6

3 And Moses went up to God, and the Lord called to him from the mountain, saying, "Thus you shall say to the house of Jacob and tell the sons of Israel:
4 'You yourselves have seen what I did to the Egyptians, and how I bore you on eagles' wings, and brought you to Myself.
5 Now then, if you will indeed obey My voice and keep My covenant, then you shall be My own possession among all the peoples, for all the earth is Mine;
6 and __you shall be to Me a Kingdom of priests and a holy nation__.' These are the words that you shall speak to the sons of Israel."

The promise here is that if they obey God, He will make them a Kingdom of priests and a holy nation. This promise has not yet been fulfilled because they did not obey God. The only conditional portion of God's promise is the ___time___ in which He will fulfill it. The promise of becoming a Kingdom of priests and a holy nation is still in effect.

1st Peter 2:9

*But you are a chosen race, a royal priesthood, a holy
nation, a people for God's own possession, that you
may proclaim the excellencies of Him who has called
you out of darkness into His marvelous light...*

The promise will eventually be fulfilled. Verse 10 says we have been
made a Kingdom and priests and **reign on the earth**. This means
we will not be sitting on a cloud playing a harp, but will have a total
priestly relationship with God.

> The oldest manuscripts read, "a Kingdom." One oldest
> manuscript reads the dative, "for us." Another reads "us,"
> accusative: so Vulgate, Syriac, Coptic, and Andreas. This
> seems preferable, "He made us (to be) a Kingdom." So Ex
> 19:6, "a Kingdom of priests"; 1Pe 2:9, "a royal priesthood."
> The saints shall constitute peculiarly a Kingdom of God, and
> shall themselves be kings (Rev 5:10). They shall share His
> King-Priest throne in the millennial Kingdom. The emphasis
> thus falls more on the Kingdom than on priests, whereas in
> English Version reading it is equally distributed between
> both. This book lays prominent stress on the saints' Kingdom.
> They are kings because they are priests: the priesthood is
> the continuous ground and legitimization of their kingship;
> they are kings in relation to man, priests in relation to God,
> serving Him day and night in His temple (Rev 7:15; 5:10).
> The priest-kings shall rule, not in an external mechanical
> manner, but simply in virtue of what they are, by the power of
> attraction and conviction overcoming the heart [Auberlen].[86]

Exodus 23:23–33

23 *"For My angel will go before you and bring you in
to the land of the Amorites, the Hittites, the Perizzites,
the Canaanites, the Hivites and the Jebusites; and I
will completely destroy them.*

---

[86] (Jamieson, 1997)

24 *You shall not worship their gods, nor serve them, nor do according to their deeds; but you shall utterly overthrow them, and break their sacred pillars in pieces.*

25 *But you shall serve the Lord your God, and He will bless your bread and your water; and I will remove sickness from your midst.*

26 *There shall be no one miscarrying or barren in your land; I will fulfill the number of your days.*

27 *I will send My terror ahead of you, and throw into confusion all the people among whom you come, and I will make all your enemies turn their backs to you.*

28 *And I will send hornets ahead of you, that they may drive out the Hivites, the Canaanites, and the Hittites before you.*

29 *I will not drive them out before you in a single year, that the land may not become desolate, and the beasts of the field become too numerous for you.*

30 *I will drive them out before you little by little, until you become fruitful and take possession of the land.*

31 *And I will fix your boundary from the Red Sea to the sea of the Philistines, and from the wilderness to the River Euphrates; for I will deliver the inhabitants of the land into your hand, and you will drive them out before you.*

32 *You shall make no covenant with them or with their gods.*

33 *They shall not live in your land, lest they make you sin against Me; for if you serve their gods, it will surely be a snare to you."*

12

THE MOSAIC COVENANT

The Lord made a covenant with Abraham that was unbreakable, unconditional, and, up to this point, unfulfilled. When the Israelites left Egypt, they came to the Sinai. This is not only the name of the mountain but also the wilderness surrounding the mountain. Sinai is where God gave the Ten Commandments to Moses and where the Israelites built and worshipped the Golden Calf. This is also where we find the origin of the Mosaic Covenant or Sinatic (Sinai) covenant.

The Hebrew word for covenant is בְּרִית (*B'rith*). It appears over 250 times in the Old Testament and over 150 occurrences refer to the Mosaic covenant. This covenant was a conditional covenant, and the obligation from the children of Israel was to follow and obey The Law, consisting of the 10 commandments plus many other laws.

This covenant also initiated the Levitical practices which were God's provision for sins of human weakness. Everything revolved around the tabernacle and, later on, the temple.

> The Mosaic Law detailed the specific functions required of the priests for each sacrifice. First, they caught the blood that gushed from the slain animals and sprinkled it "round about upon the altar" (v. 5), making it possible for God to show mercy to the ones offering the sacrifices.

The priests functioned as mediators between God and the people when they sprinkled the blood on the altar. Likewise Christ, who is the believers' mediating high priest, offered His own blood once to put away sin. [87]

Hebrews 9:11–14

11 *But when Christ appeared as a high priest of the good things to come, He entered through the greater and more perfect tabernacle, not made with hands, that is to say, not of this creation;*

12 *and not through the blood of goats and calves, but through His own blood, He entered the holy place once for all, having obtained eternal redemption.*

13 *For if the blood of goats and bulls and the ashes of a heifer sprinkling those who have been defiled sanctify for the cleansing of the flesh,*

14 *how much more will the blood of Christ, who through the eternal Spirit offered Himself without blemish to God, cleanse your conscience from dead works to serve the living God?*

God had revealed Himself to the children of Israel by miraculously providing passage through the Red Sea, a feast of Quail, Manna every morning, and water from a rock. When Amalek attacked them, the only time the Israelites could win was when Moses held his hands up. There was no possible way they could doubt the existence or the power of God.

At Sinai, God descended in fire and smoke, the mountain quaked violently, and the people were very afraid. After all of that, the first chance they got the people rebelliously turned their backs on the Lord and worshipped a false idol, even while Moses was on the mountain talking directly to God and receiving the Ten Commandments. This

---

[87] (Levy, 1993)

seems incredulous until you think about how easily we ourselves can slip away from God.

Even though the Israelites committed such a grievous sin, God still made a covenant with them. This covenant was not one sided but was dependent upon obedience to the law. The condition of this covenant was to receive God's blessings and to be a blessing to other nations. The Abrahamic Covenant had more to do with eternity, while the Mosaic Covenant was a works-based covenant that had to do with one's earthly existence. I suggest you read all of Leviticus 26 to understand the entirety of this covenant, though the highlights are quoted below:

> **Exodus 24:3–8**
>
> **3** *Then Moses came and recounted to the people all the words of the Lord and all the ordinances; and all the people answered with one voice and said, "All the words which the Lord has spoken we will do!"*
>
> **4** *Moses wrote down all the words of the Lord. Then he arose early in the morning, and built an altar at the foot of the mountain with twelve pillars for the twelve tribes of Israel.*
>
> **5** *He sent young men of the sons of Israel, and they offered burnt offerings and sacrificed young bulls as peace offerings to the Lord.*
>
> **6** *Moses took half of the blood and put it in basins, and the other half of the blood he sprinkled on the altar.*
>
> **7** *Then he took the book of the covenant and read it in the hearing of the people; **and they said, "All that the Lord has spoken we will do, and we will be obedient!"***
>
> **8** *So Moses took the blood and sprinkled it on the people, and said, **"Behold the blood of the covenant,***

which the Lord has made with you in accordance with all these words."

The people all said that they would obey the law given to them as part of this covenant. It is like us saying, "I promise, Lord, I will not sin again." We can't do it, and neither could they.

Leviticus 26:3–4
Blessings of Obedience

3 *If you walk in My statutes and keep My commandments so as to carry them out,*
4 *then I shall give you rains in their season, so that the land will yield its produce and the trees of the field will bear their fruit.*

Leviticus 26:11–13

11 *Moreover, I will make My dwelling among you, and My soul will not reject you.*
12 *I will also walk among you and be your God, and you shall be My people.*
13 *I am the Lord your God, who brought you out of the land of Egypt so that you would not be their slaves, and I broke the bars of your yoke and made you walk erect.*

Leviticus 26:14–18
Penalties of Disobedience

14 *But if you do not obey Me and do not carry out all these commandments,*
15 *if, instead, you reject My statutes, and if your soul abhors My ordinances so as not to carry out all My commandments, and so break My covenant,*
16 *I, in turn, will do this to you: I will appoint over you a sudden terror, consumption and fever that will waste away the eyes and cause the soul to pine*

*away; also, you will sow your seed uselessly, for your
enemies will eat it up.*

17 *I will set My face against you so that you will be
struck down before your enemies; and those who hate
you will rule over you, and you will flee when no one
is pursuing you.*

18 *If also after these things you do not obey Me, then
I will punish you seven times more for your sins.*

Leviticus 26:40–46

40 *If they confess their iniquity and the iniquity of
their forefathers, in their unfaithfulness which they
committed against Me, and also in their acting with
hostility against Me—*

41 *I also was acting with hostility against them, to
bring them into the land of their enemies—or if their
uncircumcised heart becomes humbled so that they
then make amends for their iniquity,*

42 *then I will remember My covenant with Jacob, and
I will remember also My covenant with Isaac, and My
covenant with Abraham as well, and I will remember
the land.*

43 *For the land will be abandoned by them, and will
make up for its sabbaths while it is made desolate
without them. They, meanwhile, will be making
amends for their iniquity, because they rejected My
ordinances and their soul abhorred My statutes.*

44 *Yet in spite of this, when they are in the land of
their enemies, I will not reject them, nor will I so
abhor them as to destroy them, breaking My covenant
with them; for I am the Lord their God.*

45 *But I will remember for them the covenant with
their ancestors, whom I brought out of the land of*

*Egypt in the sight of the nations, that I might be their
God. I am the Lord."'*

46 *These are the statutes and ordinances and laws
which the Lord established between Himself and the
sons of Israel through Moses at Mount Sinai.*

This is the law that we are no longer under according to Paul.

Galatians 3:16–19

16 *Now the promises were spoken to Abraham and to
his seed. He does not say, "And to seeds," as referring
to many, but rather to one, "And to your seed," that
is, Christ.*

17 *What I am saying is this: **the Law, which came four
hundred and thirty years later, does not invalidate a
covenant previously ratified by God,** so as to nullify
the promise.*

18 *For if the inheritance is based on law, it is no
longer based on a promise; but **God has granted it
to Abraham by means of a promise**.*

19 *Why the Law then? It was added because of
transgressions, having been ordained through angels
by the agency of a mediator, until the seed would
come to whom the promise had been made.*

The relationship between the unconditional Abrahamic and the
conditional Mosaic covenants can be summarized thus:

1. The Abrahamic covenant takes precedence over the Mosaic
   covenant;
2. The Mosaic covenant did not void the Abrahamic covenant
   (cf. Gal. 3:17);
3. The Abrahamic covenant is unconditional, while the Mosaic
   covenant was conditional (v. 12);

4. The Mosaic covenant was instituted because of human sinfulness (v. 19), whereas the Abrahamic covenant was given because of God's graciousness;

5. The Mosaic covenant was temporary (v. 19); the Abrahamic covenant is forever.[88]

In the front of the temple was a sanctuary, also called the holy place, containing the altar of incense, the candlesticks, and the showbread table. Inside the sanctuary was a room called the Holy of Holies that contained the Ark of the Covenant. The Mosaic Covenant prohibited anyone except the high priests to enter, and then only after they had offered a sacrifice for their own sins. The Holy of Holies was separated from the sanctuary by a veil made of blue, purple, scarlet, and fine twisted linen. On it were figures of cherubim to represent the presence and un-approachableness of Jehovah.

This covenant ended as Christ died and the veil in the temple separating the Holy of Holies from the rest of the temple was torn in half. This signified the barrier between God and man being taken away. Sin, or breaking of the law, no longer separates us from God.

Matthew 27:51
And behold, the veil of the temple was torn in two from top to bottom; and the earth shook and the rocks were split.

Hebrews 10:19–22
A New and Living Way
19 *Therefore, brethren, since we have confidence to enter the holy place by the blood of Jesus,*
20 *by a new and living way which He inaugurated for us through the veil, that is, His flesh...*

---

[88] (Geisler N. L., Systematic Theology, Volume Four: Church, Last Things, 2005)

This compares the destruction of Jesus Christ's human body to the Veil in the temple which separated all but the priests from the Holies of Holies.

21 *and since we have a great priest over the house of God,*

22 *let us draw near with a sincere heart in full assurance of faith, having our hearts sprinkled clean from an evil conscience and our bodies washed with pure water.*

Portions of verse 22 in the Greek Interlinear are shown below to emphasize the depth of meaning in this passage.

sprinkled	*clean*	from	an	evil	conscience
ῥεραντισμένοι	•	ἀπὸ		πονηρᾶς	συνειδήσεως
rherantismenoi		apo		ponēras	syneidēseōs

The ἀπὸ means that we are so sprinkled *as to be removed from* the evil conscience (Winer, p. 736). The words mean "having our souls—our inmost consciousness—sprinkled as it were with the blood of Christ (9:14, 12:24, 1 Pet. 1:2) and so cleansed from the consciousness of guilt." So the Jewish priests were purified from ceremonial defilement by being sprinkled with blood (Ex. 29:21; Lev. 8:30).[89]

and	our	bodies		washed	with	pure	water	.
καὶ	→	τὸ σῶμα		λελουσμένοι		καθαρῷ	ὕδατι	
kai		to sōma		lelousmenoi		katharō	hydati	

λελουμένοι. The perfect participles in these clauses— *"having been sprinkled," "having been washed"*—imply that it is to be done once and for ever. All Christians are priests to God (Rev. 1:5, 6); and therefore Christian

---

[89] (Farrar, 1893)

Priests, before being permitted to approach God, must, like the Jewish Priests (Ex. 30:20), be *sprinkled* with the blood of Christ, and bathed in the water of baptism (Eph. 5:26; Tit. 3:5; 1 Pet 3:21).

ὕδατι καθαρῷ. "I will sprinkle clean water upon you, and ye shall be clean" (Ezek. 36:25).[90]

This reference is not to Baptism, but refers to Christ washing the church clean with His word. We are totally free from sin to freely and boldly approach our Father in heaven. This happened at the Cross when Christ died. It cannot be improved on or supplemented by anything we do.

---

[90] (Farrar, 1893)

13

THE DAVIDIC COVENANT

One might think that the promises involving the land and the Kingdom were fulfilled when David became the King of Israel. There are a number of reasons that cannot be true. First of all, the land was promised directly to Abraham. Abraham was not resurrected during David's rule. Second, David had most of the land, but not all of it, and third, if it was fulfilled, why was the promise of a future Kingdom still made?

Again the Land is a critical part of the promise of the Kingdom, and David never possessed all of the Promised Land. The following maps show this. (Maps show approximate locations.)

Fig. 4 The Land Possessed by David and Solomon

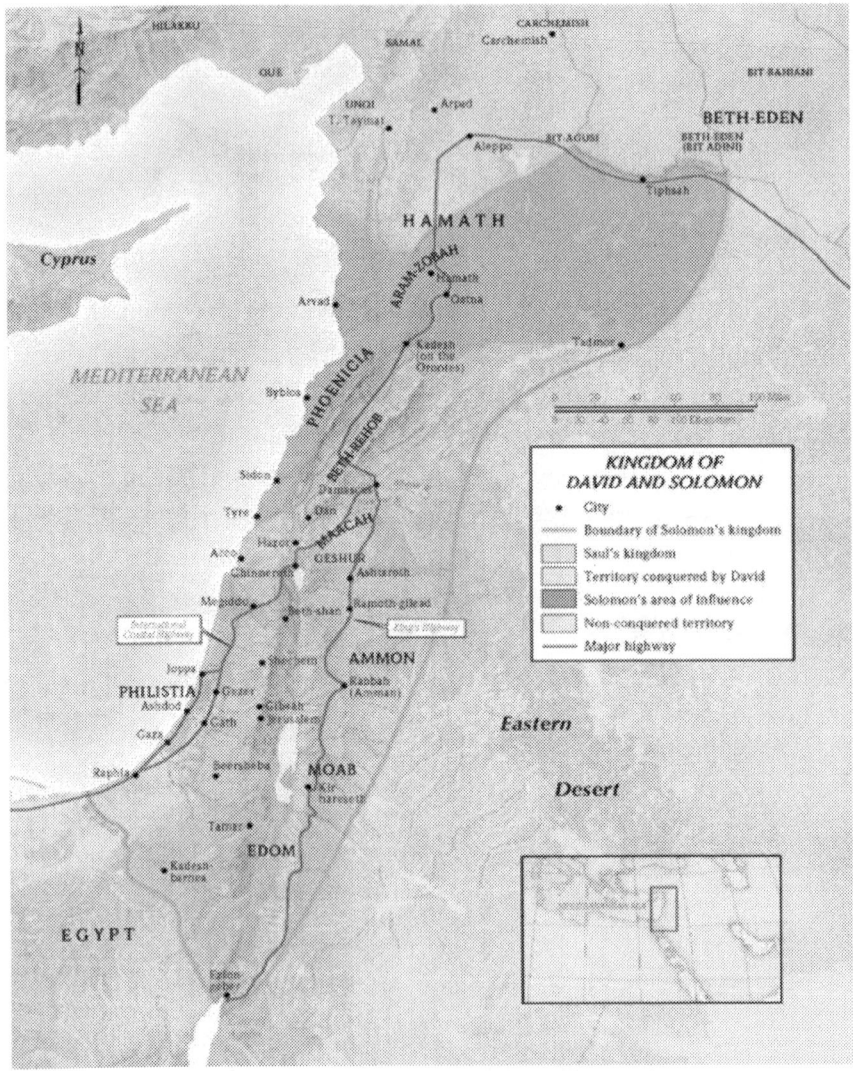

Fig. 5 The Land where the Kingdom of God will Reside

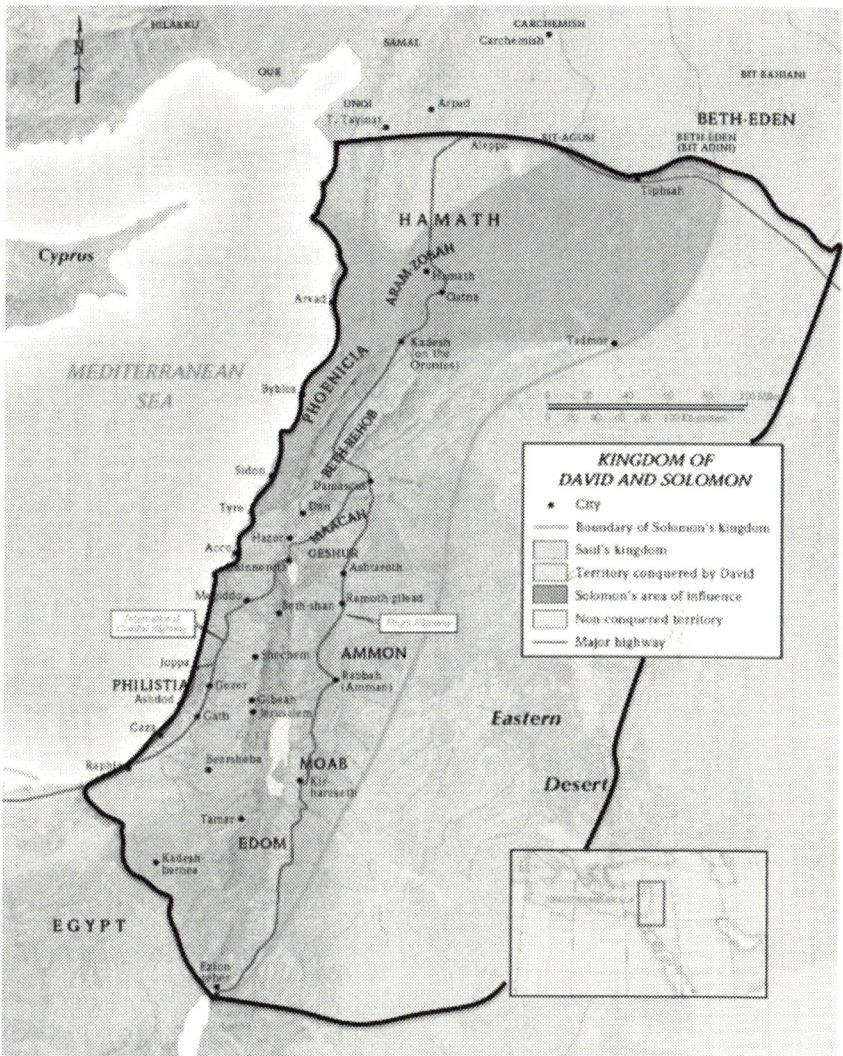

Used by permission Maps from Holman Bible Atlas Thomas V. Brisco 1998 B&H Publishing Group
Dark Line shows where I believe the Kingdom of Jesus Christ will be located. This "line" was added by
Ken Stewart and not part of the original map.

2nd Samuel 7:8–17

8 *"Now therefore, thus you shall say to My servant David, 'Thus says the Lord of hosts, "I took you from the pasture, from following the sheep, that you should be ruler over My people Israel.*

9 *And I have been with you wherever you have gone and have cut off all your enemies from before you; and I will make you a great name, like the names of the great men who are on the earth.*

10 *I will also appoint a place for My people Israel and will plant them, that they may live in their own place and not be disturbed again, nor will the wicked afflict them any more as formerly,*

11 *even from the day that I commanded judges to be over My people Israel; and I will give you rest from all your enemies. The Lord also declares to you that the Lord will make a house for you.*

12 *When your days are complete and you lie down with your fathers, I will raise up your descendant after you, who will come forth from you, and I will establish his Kingdom.*

13 *He shall build a house for My name, and I will establish the throne of his Kingdom forever.*

14 *I will be a father to him and he will be a son to Me; when he commits iniquity, I will correct him with the rod of men and the strokes of the sons of men,*

15 *but My loving kindness shall not depart from him, as I took it away from Saul, whom I removed from before you.*

16 *And your house and your Kingdom shall endure before Me forever; your throne shall be established forever."'"*

17 *In accordance with all these words and all this vision, so Nathan spoke to David.*

We need to understand the provisions of this covenant:

- *God said that He would make David's name a great name.*
  We know this came true; everyone is aware of David, if only from the story of David and Goliath.
- *God will appoint a place for His people where they will not be disturbed again, and they will have rest from all of their enemies.*
  This proves that the nation of Israel has never fulfilled this promise. Every time they have possessed any of the land, they were contending with their neighbors. Even today, the terrorism in Israel shows that this promise is yet to be fulfilled.
- *The Lord will make a house for David.*
  This is different than Solomon making a house for God. I think that the term "house" used here is not a physical house, but the line of David always being a royal line. The House of Windsor has the same type of connotation. On the other hand, this may be fulfilled as a physical house when Jesus returns with the new city of Jerusalem. See Rev. 21:10.
- *God will raise his descendant and establish his Kingdom.*
  It is tempting to interpret all of these promises as being meant for Solomon. While Solomon's reign is part of this prophesy, it was never fulfilled during his reign. The conditional part of the promises is time: when it will take place. Perhaps if Solomon had not turned his back on God, it may have been fulfilled at that time. However, we also know that God knew beforehand how that would take place; His plan calls for a Savior as well as a Messiah. I am convinced that the descendant referred to here is Jesus. That is why the long genealogies are listed when the birth of Christ is told in the Gospels—to prove that Jesus was the descendant of David.
- *This descendant will build a house for the name of God.*
  Solomon did build a temple for the Lord. I think this portion of the prophecy refers to Solomon, mostly because of the

reference, "When he commits iniquity, I will correct him with the rod of men and the strokes of the sons of men." I don't think God could be referring to Jesus at this point.

- *God will establish the throne of David forever.*
  - The word throne does not refer to a physical chair but more to the right to rule.
  - The Hebrew word translated as "forever" does not necessarily mean for eternity, but rather as "a long time." Forever and forever means a longer time. It is possible in this context that God is referring to the length of time that David actually ruled over Israel, but it is likely that God is referencing a much longer time to include the one thousand year reign of Jesus Christ upon the earth. This is clarified in the Psalms.

Psalms 89:34–37

34 *My covenant I will not violate,*
Nor will I alter the utterance of My lips.
35 *Once I have sworn by My holiness;*
I will not lie to David.
36 *His descendants shall endure forever,*
And his throne as the sun before Me.
37 *It shall be established forever like the moon,*
And the witness in the sky is faithful. [Selah].

The throne of David will last forever like the moon. Many times in the summer evenings when I gaze upon a full moon, I am reminded of this verse and my hope of the Kingdom is rekindled.

> As the Abrahamic covenant centers around the land, the Davidic covenant centers around the throne. The former provides the land and the nation; the latter provides a king

to rule over the kingdom. *Both* involve literal, national, unconditional, and perpetual blessings.[91]

2nd Samuel 7:11–16

11 *The Lord also declares to you that the Lord will make a house for you.*

12 *When your days are complete and you lie down with your fathers, I will raise up your descendant after you, who will come forth from you, and I will establish his Kingdom.*

13 *He shall build a house for My name, and I will establish the throne of his Kingdom forever.*

14 *I will be a father to him and he will be a son to Me; when he commits iniquity, I will correct him with the rod of men and the strokes of the sons of men,*

15 *but My loving kindness shall not depart from him, as I took it away from Saul, whom I removed from before you.*

16 *And your house and your Kingdom shall endure before Me forever; your throne shall be established forever.*

Though David desired to build a house for the Lord, God instead declared that He would build David's house for him, a dynasty from which the Messiah would come and reign on David's throne.[92]

Like the Abrahamic covenant, the Davidic covenant, which expanded God's blessings to Israel, was irrevocable— "everlasting," based on "the sure mercies of David" (Isa. 55:3 NKJV). While much of this prophecy refers to David's son Solomon (cf. v. 14), the use of *forever* clearly reveals that further Davidic descendants were also in mind. Other

---

[91] (Geisler N. L., Systematic Theology, Volume Four: Church, Last Things, 2005)
[92] (Geisler N. L., Systematic Theology, Volume Four: Church, Last Things, 2005)

passages confirm that this text is a prediction that Messiah would come through David's line and reign on David's throne. Indeed, at His triumphal entry, Jesus was heralded by the Jerusalem crowd with shouts of "Hosanna to the Son of David" (Matt. 21:15), "Blessed is the coming kingdom of our father David!" (Mark 11:10). They expected the beginning of the promised messianic kingdom.[93]

Isaiah 9:6–7

6 *...for a child will be born to us, a son will be given to us;*
And the government will rest on His shoulders;
And His name will be called Wonderful Counselor, Mighty God,
Eternal Father, Prince of Peace.
7 *There will be no end to the increase of His government or of peace,*
On the throne of David and over his Kingdom,
To establish it and to uphold it with justice and righteousness
From then on and forevermore.

Verse 6 should have a familiar ring to it; at every Christmas Eve Service that I have attended, and at other occasions around that time, someone reads this verse. I don't think I ever heard anyone read Verse 7.

---

[93] (Geisler N. L., Systematic Theology, Volume Four: Church, Last Things, 2005)

14

THE NEW COVENANT

The old covenant spoke of a great physical deliverance
from Egypt through the blood of lambs and the power
of God; the new covenant proclaims a great spiritual
deliverance from sin and death through the efficacious
blood of the Lamb of God and the power of God. The
Passover Feast memorialized the first, the Lord's Supper
memorializes the second.[94]

The children of Israel constantly disobeyed the laws of the Mosaic
Covenant. They strayed from the law and God. The Pharisees turned
it into an opportunity to suppress the masses and arrogantly set
themselves up above everyone else as pious and godly people.

2nd Kings 21:1–6

1 *Manasseh was twelve years old when he became
king, and he reigned fifty-five years in Jerusalem; and
his mother's name was Hephzibah.*

2 ***He did evil in the sight of the LORD,*** *according
to the abominations of the nations whom the LORD
dispossessed before the sons of Israel.*

---

[94] (Feinberg, 1986)

> **3** *For he rebuilt the high places which Hezekiah his father had destroyed; and __he erected altars for Baal__ and made an Asherah, as Ahab king of Israel had done, and worshiped all the host of heaven and served them.*
> **4** *He built altars in the house of the LORD, of which the LORD had said, "In Jerusalem I will put My name."*
> **5** *For he built altars for all the host of heaven in the two courts of the house of the LORD.*
> **6** *He made his son pass through the fire, __practiced witchcraft and used divination, and dealt with mediums and spiritists. He did much evil in the sight of the LORD provoking Him to anger.__*

This law was given, but there was no spiritual guidance or transformation. So, it did not give life; it lead to death. So many people today still try to live according to the law without the help of the Spirit. This leads to a "dos and don'ts" concept of religion. The new covenant is different.

In 586 BC, the Babylonian army destroyed Jerusalem, burned down the Temple, and took its precious vessels. The city lay in ruins and the land was no longer Israel's. The Mosaic Covenant was broken.

Jeremiah (628–523 BC) and Ezekiel (594–535 BC) were prophets of God and both lived during this time. Jeremiah was in Jerusalem, while Ezekiel was in exile at Babylon. Both of these men were given prophesies regarding the new covenant, for which the New Testament is named.

Jeremiah was a prophet during a very tempestuous time for Judah, the reign of many kings who ruled, including:

- Manasseh
- Amon
- Josiah
- Jehoahaz

- Jehoiakim
- Jehoiachin
- Zedekiah

Earlier king Ahaz had made a deal with the king of Assyria, which led to Judah becoming a vassal state of Assyria. (A vassal state means that they were subordinate to that country and had to pay an annual tribute and bow down to the king of that country.) Judah remained a vassal state of Assyria until Josiah won Judah's independence from them. He was killed in a battle against Egypt, and then Israel became a vassal state of Egypt, who made Jehoiakim king. Babylon then defeated Egypt, and made Zedekiah king. Zedekiah rebelled against Babylon ten years later, and that led to Babylon destroying Jerusalem, and the nation of Judah.

The Hebrew word for covenant occurs twenty-three times in Jeremiah and covenantal concepts, such as obedience, are common. Jeremiah 11:1–17 accuses Judah of a breach of covenant with the Lord—and the oracles of judgment against Judah and Jerusalem (Jer. 1–25) relate to aspects of the Sinai Covenant (Mosaic Covenant). Furthermore, Jeremiah often mentions the exodus event, which marked Israel's special relationship to the Lord (Jer. 2:2–7; 7:21–22; 31:31–34). **Jeremiah 31 states that the Lord will make a new covenant with the people of Israel** who survive the current judgment. As part of the new covenant, the Lord will gather the exiles and place His law in their hearts so that they will keep the covenant.[95]

Jeremiah 31:31–34

31 *"Behold, days are coming,"* declares the Lord, *"when I will make a **new covenant** with the house of Israel and with the house of Judah,*

---

[95] (Meek, 2012)

32 *not like the covenant which I made with their fathers in the day I took them by the hand to bring them out of the land of Egypt, My covenant which they broke, although I was a husband to them," declares the Lord.*

33 *"But this is the covenant which I will make with the house of Israel after those days," declares the Lord,* **"*I will put My law within them and on their heart I will write it; and I will be their God, and they shall be My people*.**

34 *They will not teach again, each man his neighbor and each man his brother, saying, 'Know the Lord,' for they will all know Me, from the least of them to the greatest of them," declares the Lord, "for I will forgive their iniquity, and their sin I will remember no more."*

Jeremiah 23:5–6

5 *"Behold, the days are coming," declares the Lord, "When I shall raise up for David a righteous Branch; And He will reign as king and act wisely And do justice and righteousness in the land.*

6 *In His days Judah will be saved, And Israel will dwell securely; And this is His name by which He will be called, 'The Lord our righteousness.'"*

This is definitely a prophecy regarding the future reign of Jesus in the Promised Land.

Ezekiel 36:24–28

24 *For I will take you from the nations, gather you from all the lands, and bring you into your own land.*

25 *Then I will sprinkle clean water on you, and you will be clean; I will cleanse you from all your filthiness and from all your idols.*

26 *Moreover, I will give you a new heart and put a new spirit within you; and I will remove the heart of stone from your flesh and give you a heart of flesh.*

27 *And I will put My Spirit within you and cause you to walk in My statutes, and you will be careful to observe My ordinances.*

28 *And you will live in the land that I gave to your forefathers; so you will be My people, and I will be your God...*

Ezekiel 37:24–28

24 *And My servant David will be king over them, and they will all have one shepherd; and they will walk in My ordinances, and keep My statutes, and observe them.*

25 *And they shall live on the land that I gave to Jacob My servant, in which your fathers lived; and they will live on it, they, and their sons, and their sons' sons, forever; and David My servant shall be their prince forever.*

26 *And I will make a covenant of peace with them; it will be an everlasting covenant with them. And I will place them and multiply them, and will set My sanctuary in their midst forever.*

27 *My dwelling place also will be with them; and I will be their God, and they will be My people.*

28 *And the nations will know that I am the Lord who sanctifies Israel, when My sanctuary is in their midst forever.*

This was written by Ezekiel in 573 BC. David reigned as King of Israel from 1011 BC to 971 BC. **Three hundred ninety-eight years**

later, Ezekiel prophesized that David shall be their prince forever. Again, the Resurrection is implied. David will be the Prince, Jesus will be the King!

> **Luke 22:19–20**
> *19 And when He had taken some bread and given thanks, He broke it and gave it to them, saying, "This is My body which is given for you; do this in remembrance of Me."*
> *20 And in the same way He took the cup after they had eaten, saying, "This cup which is poured out for you is the **new covenant** in My blood."*

Whenever a covenant is made with God and His people, blood is involved.

> **Hebrews 9:13–15**
> *13 For if the blood of goats and bulls and the ashes of a heifer sprinkling those who have been defiled sanctify for the cleansing of the flesh,*
> *14 how much more will the blood of Christ, who through the eternal Spirit offered Himself without blemish to God, cleanse your conscience from dead works to serve the living God?*
> *15 For this reason He is the mediator of a new covenant, so that, since a death has taken place for the redemption of the transgressions that were committed under the first covenant, those who have been called may receive the promise of the eternal inheritance.*

These are the provisions of the new covenant:

- The Nation of Israel will have a converted heart
- This covenant provides for restoration to the favor of God
- Forgiveness of sins

- The Indwelling of the Holy Spirit
- God will be present with them in a visible way
- Israel will be re-gathered as one nation, ruled by one king, and will dwell in the Promised Land forever
- The Sanctuary will be rebuilt in Jerusalem

This covenant is literal, unconditional, and eternal. As you can see, parts of the new covenant have been fulfilled, while other parts remain in the future.

> The Gospels, especially Matthew and Luke, clearly depict Jesus as the Son (heir) of David and thus the one to restore the Davidic kingdom covenant (Matt. 1:1–25; Luke 1:31–33, 69; 2:4). At the Last Supper, Jesus explicitly identifies His body and blood as the new covenant promised by the Prophets (Jer. 31:31; Luke 22:20; 1st Cor. 11:25), fulfilling the oracle of Isaiah regarding the Servant of the Lord, who would not simply make a covenant but would become one (Isa. 42:6; 49:8).[96]

> Seventeen of the 33 occurrences of "covenant" in the New Testament are found in Hebrews. The author of Hebrews argues for the superiority of the new covenant over the old (i.e. broken Mosaic) covenant, based on the "better" promises, mediator, sacrifice, high priesthood, oath, sanctuary etc. (Heb. 1–9). All of this is the result of the royal high priestly work of Christ as God's firstborn Son (Heb. 1:6).[97]

> The new covenant also fulfills the other covenants of salvation history. Jesus is a new Adam (Rom 5:12–19) who makes us a new creation (2nd Cor. 5:17; Gal. 6:15). He fulfills the sworn promises of the Abrahamic covenant (Luke 1:72–73; Rom. 4; Gal. 3–4). Christ also fulfills the

---

[96] (Hahn, 2012)

[97] (Hahn, 2012)

Mosaic covenant with his new Passover and new exodus (Luke 9:31; 22:14–20). For Paul, it is by the power of the Holy Spirit that the divine law, which was given to Israel in the Mosaic covenant, is fulfilled in the new covenant (Rom. 8:3–4; 10:4; 13:8–10). The notion of covenant reaches its zenith in Christ, who fulfills the divine covenants not only in who He is, as the eternal Son of the Father, but by what He accomplishes in causing us to share in the grace of His own divine sonship (1st John 3:1–2). The new covenant of Christ ends up fulfilling the old covenant in a way that surpasses the greatest hopes of ancient Israelites, even as it will exceed our own expectations.[98]

---

[98] (Hahn, 2012)

15

SALVATION

There are many different doctrines regarding salvation and eternal life. So many of the conflicting doctrines are because the Kingdom is not understood. One common belief says your sins are not forgiven until you believe; some say once you do believe, you can never lose that salvation. They call it *eternal security*. Others say you can lose your salvation and still others say you are not forgiven until you are baptized. It can go on and on.

Anytime anyone tells you that you have to do something to be forgiven, they are trampling on the blood of Christ. Christ performed a complete work at the cross, and when He said, "It is finished," He meant it. The confusion starts with the belief that the forgiveness of sin is what enables us to inherit eternal life or enter into heaven. It is only the first step. The fact that a judgment will occur causes people to just assume that they will be judged for sin. What they don't understand is the judgment for sin has already taken place. 2,000 years ago at the cross, the world was judged, found guilty, and the price was paid by the death of Jesus Christ.

All sin was judged, for **all** time, for **all** people! Even you! We were **all** found guilty, and condemned to death. Jesus Christ took your place and died in your stead—not just for the believer, but also for the unbelievers as well.

> Christ, by parting with his life, made atonement for sin,
> and so rescued ours; he was made sin, and a curse for us,
> and died, not only for our good, but in our stead...[99]

Is this scriptural? It certainly is, but since it does not fit their doctrines, denominations have changed the interpretation of the word "all." They will tell you that "all" does not mean "all." They have to say this because they think that unforgiven sin is what keeps you from salvation. In their minds, if you don't believe, you are not forgiven. Because they do not understand the Kingdom and Outer Darkness, they would call the previous paragraph universalism.

I am not a Universalist. Even though I believe all sins are forgiven at the cross, all that does is enable us to have access to God with a clear conscience. Once we accept this fact, we can freely approach God without a guilty conscience. We should want to start walking with Him, and allow the Holy Spirit to influence our actions leading us to exhibit the Love of God and placing us on the path to sanctification.

When we realize that Grace is a true gift **_to all_**, and not something we earned, or received because we did something, then we will recognize that everyone else is a recipient of that Grace as well, and we are not superior to them. This understanding should purge all condemnation of others from a believer.

If ones salvation is a result of our actions or beliefs, then it is easy to condemn anyone whose actions are different than ours.

Let's examine why I believe all sins are forgiven. John the Baptist said the world's sins would be taken away.

---

[99] (Henry, 1996, c 1991)

John 1:29

*...Behold the Lamb of God who **<u>takes away the sin</u>** **<u>of the world</u>**.*"

Did Jesus do that, or didn't He?

2nd Corinthians 5:14–21

*One died for **<u>all</u>**, therefore **<u>all</u>** died; and **<u>He died</u>** **<u>for all</u>**, that they who lived should no longer live for themselves, but for Him. Therefore from now on we recognize no man according to the flesh...God reconciled us to himself through Christ, and gave us the ministry of reconciliation, namely, that God was in Christ reconciling **<u>the world</u>** to Himself, not counting their trespasses against them.*

Because Christ died for all of the sins for all, not counting their trespasses against them, we cannot judge people by their flesh. Our ministry is to tell the world that Christ has reconciled them to God. They will no longer be judged for sin. They can freely approach the throne of Grace, knowing they are forgiven for every evil deed they have ever committed.

Let's take a good look at Romans 5.

Romans 5:6–19

6 *For while we were still helpless, at the right time **<u>Christ died for the ungodly</u>**.*

<u>Who did He die for?</u>

7 *For one will hardly die for a righteous man; though perhaps for the good man someone would dare even to die.*
8 *But God demonstrates His own love toward us, in that **<u>while we were yet sinners, Christ died for us</u>**.*

When did He die for us?

> **9** *Much more then, having now been justified by His blood, we shall be saved from the wrath of God through Him.*
>
> **10** *For if while we were enemies we were reconciled to God through the death of His Son, much more, having been reconciled, we **shall** be saved by His life.*

The word "shall" is future salvation into the Kingdom.

> **11** *And not only this, but we also exult in God through our Lord Jesus Christ, through whom we have now received the reconciliation.*
>
> **12** *Therefore, **just as through one man sin entered into the world, and death through sin, and so death spread to all men, because all sinned—** (Adam)*
>
> **13** *for until the Law sin was in the world, but sin is not imputed when there is no law.*
>
> **14** *Nevertheless death reigned from Adam until Moses, even over those who had not sinned in the likeness of the offense of Adam, who is a type of Him who was to come.*
>
> **15** *But the free gift is not like the transgression. **For if by the transgression of the one the many died, much more did the grace of God and the gift by the grace of the one Man, Jesus Christ, abound to the many**.*

Special care should be taken to note that Paul repeated the words "the many." The definite article was used here, just as it was when he said "the many" died. The many who died were "all men;" the many to whom this grace did abound was the same group, "all men."

Green's Handbook to The Grammar of the Greek Testament, Section 227 on Page 212 states that the use of the Article with πολλοὺς (pollous - many) "to which it gives the significance of the many, the generality, the whole mass of the particular objects of thought". One "the many" is equal to the other "the many." It is the same group of people. All men died in Adam, and all men received this gift of grace of the one man Jesus Christ.[100]

16 *The gift is not like that which came through the one who sinned; for on the one hand the judgment arose from one transgression resulting in condemnation, but on the other hand the free gift arose from many transgressions resulting in justification.*

17 *For if by the transgression of the one, death reigned through the one, much more* ___those who receive the abundance of grace and of the gift of righteousness will reign in life through the One, Jesus Christ___.

18 *So then as* ___through one transgression there resulted condemnation to all men, even so through one act of righteousness there resulted justification of life to all men___.

19 *For as through the one man's disobedience the many were made sinners, even so through the obedience of the One the many will be made righteous.*

Titus 2:11
The grace of God has appeared, bringing salvation ___to all men___.

The wages of sin is death, which is ultimate separation from God. Man will no longer be separated or die this death because of sin, **but only because he chooses not to believe** in Christ.

---

[100] (Kenison F., The Truth Revealed in Romans, 1999)

Romans 3:23–25

All have sinned and fall short of the Glory of God, being justified as a gift by His grace through the redemption which is in Christ Jesus; whom God displayed publicly as a propitiation in His blood through Faith. This was to demonstrate His righteousness, because in the forbearance of God He passed over the sins previously committed.

Until the cross, sin had only been covered, not taken away. The Old Testament sacrifices did not take away sins. Above where it says "in the forbearance of God, He passed over sins previously committed" displays God's tolerance knowing that Christ's death was coming to remove all sin.

Now that sin has been judged, and removed, taken away, can one be judged again for sin?

Look at all of the scriptures regarding the Judgment seat of Christ and see if it ever mentions sin. He separates the sheep from the goats based on their beliefs and resulting works. These are not our works, but works that the Holy Spirit inspires in us when we yield to Him. When we die to ourselves, then the Lord can use us.

Hopefully, by now you understand the Kingdom and realize that the Judgment that evaluates who gets into the kingdom does not look at sin, but your relationship with Christ. Did you trust that He died for all of your sins and did you wash your robes in the blood of the lamb?

Romans 10:9–13

9 *...that if you confess with your mouth Jesus as Lord, and believe in your heart that God raised Him from the dead, you will be saved;*

10 *for with the heart a person believes, resulting in righteousness, and with the mouth he confesses, resulting in salvation.*

11 *For the Scripture says, "Whoever believes in Him will not be disappointed."*

12 *For there is no distinction between Jew and Greek; for the same Lord is Lord of all, abounding in riches for all who call on Him;*

13 *for "Whoever will call on the name of the Lord will be saved."*

Understanding the gospel of the Kingdom sheds light on the topic of salvation. As simple as salvation may seem, it is often misunderstood and causes a lot of confusion among believers. I think it is easier to understand the complete concept of salvation if you think of it as if there are three tenses: past tense, present tense, and future tense.

- **Past Tense**- Jesus died 2,000 years ago for all sins for all time. Everyone is saved from the punishment for sin.
- **Present Tense**- If you believe that Jesus died for your sins, then you are able to boldly approach the Throne of God, have fellowship with Him, and experience the abundant life. That occurs now, or "in the now."
- **Future Tense**- If you believe that Jesus died for your sins with a belief that changes your life, then you will inherit eternal life and enter into the Kingdom of our Lord Jesus Christ! This will happen in the future when Christ returns.

It is important to understand what was accomplished at the cross 2,000 years ago and what the judgment will be based upon in the future. When Jesus was nailed to the cross, He was the total atonement for sin. He was the sacrifice for the sins of mankind. He died in our place as a substitute for the whole world. Isaiah foretold of the death of Christ and what it would accomplish.

Isaiah 53:4–12

4 *Surely our griefs He Himself bore, and our sorrows He carried; yet we ourselves esteemed Him stricken, Smitten of God, and afflicted.*

5 *But He was pierced through for our transgressions, He was crushed for our iniquities; the chastening for our well-being fell upon Him, and by His scourging we are healed.*

6 *All of us like sheep have gone astray, each of us has turned to his own way; but the Lord has caused the **iniquity of us all To fall on Him**.*

7 *He was oppressed and He was afflicted, yet He did not open His mouth; like a lamb that is led to slaughter, and like a sheep that is silent before its shearers, so He did not open His mouth.*

8 *By oppression and judgment He was taken away; and as for His generation, who considered that He was cut off out of the land of the living for the transgression of my people, to whom the stroke was due?*

9 *His grave was assigned with wicked men, yet He was with a rich man in His death, because He had done no violence, nor was there any deceit in His mouth.*

10 *But the Lord was pleased to crush Him, putting Him to grief; if He would render Himself as a guilt offering, He will see His offspring, He will prolong His days, and the good pleasure of the Lord will prosper in His hand.*

11 *As a result of the anguish of His soul, He will see it and be satisfied; by His knowledge the Righteous*

*One, My Servant, will justify the many, as He will
bear their iniquities.*

12 *Therefore, I will allot Him a portion with the great,
and He will divide the booty with the strong; because
He poured out Himself to death, and was numbered
with the transgressors; yet He Himself bore the sin of
many, and interceded for the transgressors.*

The outstanding element of this chapter is the vicarious,
substitutionary sufferings of the Messiah. "Marvelous
chapter," comments A. T. Pierson, "containing only twelve
verses, yet fourteen times announcing the doctrine of
the **vicarious sacrifice for all human sin**." The whole
section (Isa. 52:13-53:12) overflows with this concept, and
the mystery was never solved until the Lord Jesus was
"made ... sin for us" (2nd Cor. 5:21) and "died for our
sins" (1st Cor. 15:3).

Jehovah "hath caused to meet with overwhelming force
in Him the iniquity of us all" (Heb.). The Messiah was
the divine Redeemer on whom fell "all the fiery rays
of judgment which would have fallen on mankind"
(Baron). How wonderful is God's grace through Christ's
substitutionary atonement! The cross became Christ's
deepest humiliation and His highest glory—the appointed
means of bringing salvation to men.

When the Lord Jesus came, He fulfilled these messianic
predictions by His atoning death on the cross: "Who his
own self bore our sins in his own body on the tree, that
we, being dead to sins, should live unto righteousness; by
whose stripes ye were healed" (1st Pet. 2:24).[101]

When Jesus was about to die, He cried out to God, "Why have you
forsaken me?"

---

[101] (Meldau, 1988)

Matthew 27:46

About the ninth hour Jesus cried out with a loud voice, saying, "Eli, Eli, lama sabachthani?" that is, "My God, My God, why have You forsaken Me?"

This was followed by His declaration, "It is finished."

John 19:30

Therefore when Jesus had received the sour wine, He said, "It is finished!" And He bowed His head and gave up His spirit.

The word translated as "it is finished" is the Greek word Τετέλεστα from the root word τελέω (*teleō*) meaning completed, fulfilled, to bring to an end. It is important to note that this word is in the perfect tense.

> The perfect tense in Greek corresponds to the perfect tense in English, and describes an action which is viewed as having been completed in the past, once and for all, not needing to be repeated.

> Jesus' last cry from the cross, TETELESTAI ("It is finished!"), is a good example of the perfect tense used in this sense, namely "It [the atonement] has been accomplished, completely, once and for all time."[102]

Most Christians understand that at that point in time, Jesus paid the penalty for sin. He was the sacrifice for all sin. He died in your stead. When Jesus sensed God had forsaken Him, He knew then that God was applying the punishment for the sins of mankind to Him. God judged the sins of mankind and found them guilty. The penalty for that sin was death and separation from God. This was the first sign of the separation. When Jesus declared that it was finished, He was referring to His mission as a sacrificial lamb. He had completed His

---

[102] (Pierce)

mission. He had finished what He had to do for forgiveness of sins. Then He died, which was the final payment.

At that point in time, God applied our punishment to Christ and our debt was paid—*in full*! One popular hymn expresses the words, "Amazing love, how can it be, that thou my God should'st die for me." The forgiveness of sins happened at that time, before anyone alive today was born. That is when the sacrifice for sins was performed.

When people pray the "prayer of salvation" and invite Christ to come into their lives or hearts, they usually experience a dramatic change. What really happens at that point in time? Does Jesus come back, climb back on the cross, and die again just for that person at that time? No, but many teach that it is at that point in time when that person was forgiven for his or her sins. How could this be true if He died for all sins 2,000 years ago?

The foundation of the Christian Faith is that Jesus Christ died for **all** sins at the cross and at that time, all sins—I repeat—**ALL SINS were paid for and forgiven**. The greatest sin ever committed, or ever will be committed by anyone, was paid for at the cross. Remember the first rule of interpretation? The most obvious meaning is true. When the Bible says that all sins were forgiven at the cross, it means all. Even if they could prove that argument, they would still have to deal with the expression, "the sins of the world." That means all sins.

John 12:47
If anyone hears My sayings and does not keep them, I do not judge him; for I did not come to judge the world, but to save the world.

John said that Jesus didn't come to judge or condemn the world (12:47), but elsewhere we clearly read that Jesus will function as Judge on the last day… This is scarcely a contradiction, since John himself recorded that Jesus had all judgment entrusted to Him (John 5:22). The purpose of the incarnation was to offer a plan of salvation for all who would receive it.[103]

Incidentally, we would point out that there is manifestly a vast difference between the place of "weeping and gnashing of teeth" (which speaks merely of sore disappointment—Matt. 24:51; 25:30), and the place of "everlasting fire, prepared for the devil and his angels" (Matt. 25:41).[104]

Jesus said all sins:

Mark 3:28
Truly I say to you, all sins shall be forgiven the sons of men, and whatever blasphemies they utter...

Note that Jesus said this talking about the future of his death at the cross.

Paul said all:

2nd Corinthians 5:14–15
14 *For the love of Christ controls us, having concluded this, that one died for all, therefore all died;*
15 *and He died for all, so that they who live might no longer live for themselves, but for Him who died and rose again on their behalf.*

This is referring to past tense salvation. John the apostle said the whole world:

1st John 2:2
...and He Himself is the propitiation for our sins; and not for ours only, but also for those of the whole world.

---

[103] (Nash, 2007)
[104] (Mauro, 1918)

Jesus has redeemed every person that has ever lived. In God's eyes, we are now faultless, pure, and as innocent as a newborn babe.

This does not mean that everyone will be saved. Jesus paid the price for all sins. Does that mean that everyone will go to heaven or enter the Kingdom? **The answer is <u>NO</u>!** Entrance into the Kingdom is not based on sin or forgiveness of sins, but only on having a relationship with Jesus Christ. Everyone has been saved from the punishment for sin. They are not going to be judged for any of their sins; that has already happened. The world was judged, the verdict was *guilty*, the sentence was death, and Jesus stepped in and served that sentence for all. In the future, all will be judged to see if they rejected that which Christ did for them on the cross and if they have a relationship with God through Christ and have made Him Lord.

You were saved (past tense) at the cross, and so was every man, woman, and child. If you believe that (not just acknowledge it but really understand it), then you will experience an abundant life. This is present tense salvation because you are receiving that forgiveness, you make it yours, and you believe that it applies specifically to you. That changes you, because you then know how much God loves you unconditionally. That changes your entire attitude about God and life in general. This is the peace that surpasses all understanding.

The ramifications of this are many. Think about how this changes the message when witnessing. Instead of telling people, "If you do this and this, God will forgive you," you can tell them, "God has already forgiven you, and He just wants you to know it and believe it."

Hal Lindsey (the author of *The Late Great Plant Earth, Satan is Alive and Well on Planet Earth,* and many other Christian books) gave a good analogy of this, somewhat as follows (with much of my own embellishment). Let's say you borrowed fifty thousand dollars from a friend (let's call him Guido). You spent all of the money and now you will never be able to pay him back. You imagine that Guido is very upset, and you have heard that he can be merciless and very violent towards someone who owes him money. Every time you think you might run into Guido, you take a different route. You run and hide when you see him.

Let's say another friend (we will call him Joe) paid Guido back all of the money you owed him. If you did not know this, you would still run and hide every time you saw Guido coming. You would take all the precautions you could to avoid him. Then someone else, one of the guys at work named Bernie, tells you that Joe paid Guido back the fifty thousand dollars plus the interest you owed, and now Guido just wants to be your friend again and invite you to a big party. You have two choices. You could believe that Joe paid Guido your debt, or you could believe that Bernie was lying to you and that Guido still wants to extract payment from you.

Let me ask, if you believed Bernie, would that change Guido's attitude toward you? No, but it would change your attitude about Guido and Joe. In fact, you would probably really want to get to know Joe and would want to do anything you could for him.

If you did **not** believe Bernie, would that change Guido's attitude toward you? No, but you would never become friends again with Guido, and you would miss out on the big party that Guido was getting ready to throw.

This analogy may fall short, but it does describe the effect past forgiveness has on people and their relationship with God. Jesus has paid your debt. If you believe it, you will feel free to approach God because you no longer think He holds you accountable for sin. You will really want to get to know Christ and do whatever He wants you to do.

Accepting Christ does not change your status with God in His role as judge. As a judge, He still sees you as forgiven, but as a Father,

He welcomes you back home as the prodigal son. This is when you can become an obedient son of God. This is your adoption. Sinners can know that they are forgiven, and that will change their lives if they really believe it. This is why lives change so dramatically when someone accepts Christ and His forgiveness. Our faith doesn't change God; our faith changes us. It will also change your relationship with your Father who is in Heaven.

Romans 5:17–19

17 *For if by the transgression of the one, death reigned through the one, much more those who receive the abundance of grace and of the gift of righteousness will reign in life through the One, Jesus Christ.*
18 *So then as through one transgression there resulted condemnation to all men, even so through one act of righteousness there resulted justification of life to all men.*
19 *For as through the one man's disobedience the many were made sinners, even so through the obedience of the One the many will be made righteous.*

Verse 17 shows that those who receive or accept God's grace and His gift of righteousness will reign in Life. This points to the Kingdom and only to those that receive His Grace. That means they believe in it.

Verse 18 says that the one sin of Adam resulted in condemnation for all men, and the one act of righteousness of Jesus (His death on the cross) resulted in justification for all men.

Understanding the three tenses of salvation solves the argument regarding eternal security. Those who teach eternal security say that one can never lose their salvation, pointing to the scriptures referring to past tense salvation. Others believe you can lose your salvation, and they point to scriptures that refer to future tense salvation.

When someone denounces their faith, and many do (they sometimes even join an organization called "Evangelicals Anonymous"), the *eternal security* people simply say those people were never saved in the first place. The others say they lost their salvation (meaning their forgiveness). Neither is correct because they are confused about the three tenses of salvation.

Those who teach *eternal security* believe they caused God to change His attitude toward them when they believed. If that were the case, then belief would be the same as works. If God forgave us for our sins when we believed, then we could not lose that forgiveness later. We cannot lose the forgiveness of sins through Christ, because it was finished at the cross. They also believe that future salvation is determined by obtaining forgiveness of sins. Not understanding the Kingdom involves not understanding the basis on which we will be judged. That basis is not sin; it is a relationship with Christ.

Many who believe you can lose your salvation also think that when you accept Jesus into your heart, you are forgiven for all of your sins, but only up to that point in time. Any sins committed afterwards must be confessed in order for them to be forgiven. If they sin enough and do not confess them, they will lose their salvation. What a terrible bondage! What a terrible slap in Christ's face, denying the work He gave His life for.

Sin is never the reason that you could lose your past or future salvation, at least not directly. Continued, un-repented sin will cause one to quit believing or lose faith, but you must always remember that sins have been taken care of at the cross. If people quit believing, or forget that they are forgiven, then they lose their present tense salvation. If they continue in that state until death, they will lose their future tense salvation. These are the ones who do not hold firm until the end. They quit believing, turn their backs on God, and walk away. This takes an active act of rebellion. It is shaking your fist into the face of God and saying, "I don't want your grace." This is the same action we take when we try to achieve what Christ did on the cross through grace by our works. Works or legalism is a lack of faith or trust in Christ. It is taking control of your own destiny, and, in essence, telling God that you now deserve to be forgiven or loved. This is worse than apostasy.

Galatians 3:3

Are you so foolish? Having begun by the Spirit, are you now being perfected by the flesh?

Do Christians need to be concerned about continuing the walk with Christ? The writer of Hebrews seemed to think so.

Hebrews 3:12–14

12 *Take care, brethren, that there not be in any one of you an evil, unbelieving heart that falls away from the living God.*

13 *But encourage one another day after day, as long as it is still called "today," so that none of you will be hardened by the deceitfulness of sin.*

14 *For we have become partakers of Christ, if we hold fast the beginning of our assurance firm until the end..."*

Why would they need to encourage each other if they were guaranteed an entrance into the Sabbath rest that God offers in His Kingdom?

The deceitfulness of sin is that it causes you to forget that you are forgiven. That is why the writer of Hebrews instructs them to encourage one another day after day, to remind each other that they are forgiven, not to condemn each other for sinning as is the habit of some.

2nd Timothy 4:7–8

7 *I have fought the good fight, I have finished the course, I have kept the faith;*

8 *in the future there is laid up for me the crown of righteousness, which the Lord, the righteous Judge, will award to me on that day; and not only to me, but also to all who have loved His appearing.*

Paul declares that he has kept the faith. He has continued to believe after all of his trials and suffering.

One can never lose or undo what Jesus did at the Cross. His work is eternal. You cannot lose your forgiveness of sins. You cannot lose your past tense salvation. You can rebel against God, and if you do, you will not enter into the Kingdom. Entrance into the Kingdom is based upon believing and continuing to believe. This is future tense salvation.

Matthew 10:22 (also Mark 13:13)
You will be hated by all because of My name, but it is the one who has endured to the end who will be saved.

Luke 8:13
Those on the rocky soil are those who, when they hear, receive the word with joy; and these have no firm root; they believe for a while, and in time of temptation fall away.

1st Timothy 4:1–4
1 *But the Spirit explicitly says that in later times some will fall away from the faith, paying attention to deceitful spirits and doctrines of demons,*
2 *by means of the hypocrisy of liars seared in their own conscience as with a branding iron,*

3 *men who forbid marriage and advocate abstaining from foods which God has created to be gratefully shared in by those who believe and know the truth.*
4 *For everything created by God is good, and nothing is to be rejected if it is received with gratitude...*

2nd Peter 2:20–21

20 *For if, after they have escaped the defilements of the world by the knowledge of the Lord and Savior Jesus Christ, they are again entangled in them and are overcome, the last state has become worse for them than the first.*

21 *For it would be better for them not to have known the way of righteousness, than having known it, to turn away from the holy commandment handed on to them.*

John 3:16

For God so loved the world, that He gave His only begotten Son, that whoever believes in Him shall not perish, but have eternal life.

The word "believes" is in the present tense in the Greek. That means that it signifies a continuous action: believes and keeps on believing. Once someone has believed and tasted the joy of present tense salvation, they will normally not have any reason to stop believing. There are some people who at one time were very sincere believers but have forgotten that they were forgiven and have stopped believing. They have several excuses, but they no longer believe. Some might say that those individuals were never saved in the first place, but then how hard is it to be truly saved? If these people sincerely believed, thought they had it, but were wrong? If it is that hard to be saved, then it really puts the act of salvation back on to the believer. It becomes works-based.

When one does not understand the three tenses of salvation, they start to wonder if they are truly saved. They start to ask questions like, "Was I sincere enough? Did I truly repent? Did I do it right?" People walk up the aisle to receive Christ every Sunday service because they are not sure if they got it right. They are convinced they had to do something to have God forgive them. They hear they are saved by faith. How do they know their faith was good enough? Satan is constantly trying to get believers to strive in the flesh and to make "getting saved" a result of one's actions. They end up thinking that their faith saved them. This is called having faith in faith. Faith then becomes a work.

16

FAITH

Faith is not something that we manufacture within ourselves. It is a gift of God's grace. Since it is a gift, we certainly cannot claim any accomplishment for having faith.

> The power to walk worthy of the Lord is bestowed through that portion of holy spirit God granted every man through his grace. Faith, or believing, releases that power in our lives by allowing God to control our actions.

> We can believe only through the grace of God's gift of faith, and, therefore, believing is not of ourselves but of God. **The only thing about faith that comes from us is faithlessness, or unbelief,** which causes us to be in rebellion. We can always claim the act of rebellion for ourselves, although many still fall back on the old excuse, "the devil made me do it." The devil is a convenient whipping post; it is easier to blame the devil than to blame our own fleshly lusts.

> Before losing the thought of this scripture, let us point out again that Paul was not eulogizing Abraham for his faith, but showing the effects of faith upon someone's life. For this He chose Abraham, a person well known to the Jews and many Gentiles.[105]

---

[105] (Kenison F., The Truth Revealed in Romans, 1999)

Our goal in this life is not to drum up more faith, but to quit rebelling and surrender to His Holy Spirit.

When someone becomes a believer in Christ, they become excited and full of joy and all they know is that they are forgiven. As time goes by, they hear that they should be baptized with water, baptized with the Holy Spirit, speak in tongues, and tithe. They hear that they shouldn't get divorced, shouldn't have abortions, shouldn't be gay, shouldn't dance, shouldn't drink, shouldn't go to movies, and on and on it goes. They can start to lose that joy. They go to church and everyone seems to have it all together, yet they are struggling with a lot of doubt and questions. It is hard to admit this because then you fear that they will all think you are not a good Christian. It seems true believers don't have any problems. What they don't know is that most of the people there are putting on a face and hiding their problems and struggles with the faith as well.

In the beginning of their walk, they are not tempted by sin because they are on such a high. They are not distracted. This is walking by the spirit. They have been crucified with Christ and have died to the law. Eventually, they do sin and the legalists start to tell them what they "must now do as a Christian," putting them back under the law. They regress and begin to live again through the flesh and not by the power of the Spirit.

2nd Corinthians 10:3–4
3 *For though we walk in the flesh, we do not war according to the flesh,*
4 *for the weapons of our warfare are not of the flesh, but divinely powerful for the destruction of fortresses.*

Galatians 5:16–18
16 *But I say, walk by the Spirit, and you will not carry out the desire of the flesh.*

17 *For the flesh sets its desire against the Spirit, and the Spirit against the flesh; for these are in opposition to one another, so that you may not do the things that you please.*
18 *But if you are led by the Spirit, you are not under the Law.*

Galatians 5:24–26

24 *Now those who belong to Christ Jesus have crucified the flesh with its passions and desires.*
25 *If we live by the Spirit, let us also walk by the Spirit.*
26 *Let us not become boastful, challenging one another, envying one another.*

All of the verses above talk about walking by the Spirit. What you must remember is that if you do sin, even repeatedly, as long as you turn back to God, you can still walk by the Spirit. It is never too late!

Once you sin, the guilty conscience causes you to want to hide from God. That is your first reaction. If you forget that you are forgiven and feel that you have let God down, it will become more and more difficult to come into His presence. That is when you must re-focus on what was done at the cross for you. Remind yourself again and again that all sin has been paid for. God wants you to come back to Him. Fellowship, reading the word, prayer, music, worship, and praise all help to bring your focus back onto what Christ did instead of what you did.

As you learn to do this repeatedly, you will be overwhelmed with His unfailing love and you will find it easier to walk with Him in the Spirit for longer and longer periods of time. You will fail again, but do not let Satan tell you that you have sinned too much. Before God created you, He knew how often you would repeatedly sin, and He sent Jesus to die just for you. You cannot disappoint God, because He already knew all of your failures and has declared His love for you anyway. He has provided for your shortcomings through the blood of Jesus Christ.

The flesh is always striving to overcome the spirit. That is part of the sinful nature. If you try to live the Christian life by the power of your flesh, you will lose, and Satan is winning the battle.

Just as muscles that are used become strong, those that are not used become weak. If you live by the flesh, then your flesh becomes strong, stronger than your spirit. If you needed to respond in a spiritual crisis, you would automatically use the stronger flesh. If you live by the spirit, you deny the power of the flesh and strengthen your spiritual relationship with God. Christians must learn to put the flesh to death.

Romans 7:5
For while we were in the flesh, the sinful passions, which were aroused by the Law, were at work in the members of our body to bear fruit for death.

Romans 8:13–14
13 *...for if you are living according to the flesh, you must die; but if by the Spirit you are putting to death the deeds of the body, you will live.*
14 *For all who are being led by the Spirit of God, these are sons of God.*

Galatians 3:3
Are you so foolish? Having begun by the Spirit, are you now being perfected by the flesh?

When you live the Christian life by the power of the flesh, you can start to gain pride in your works and start to condemn anyone who does not appear to have these works. People have a tendency to ignore any weaknesses they might have and focus on everyone else's weakness. Fleshly work leads to condemning others. It leads to the attitude, "God loves me more than He does them, because I live a good life and they are filthy sinners."

If living the Christian life seems impossible, then you are striving in the flesh. You are trying to stop sinning and have lost your focus that God has forgiven you and loves you unconditionally. You will soon start to think that God will not tolerate your repeated sinning. This is when you will lose your faith that Christ died for your sins. To say I have sinned so much I am not going to make it into the Kingdom is denying Christ. It is denying that His death was sufficient.

The thief on the cross was forgiven even though he believed at the last moments of his life. He did not have time to stop believing. That is how simple it is: just believe.

John 11:25–26

25 *Jesus said to her, "I am the resurrection and the life; he who believes in Me will live even if he dies,* **26** *and everyone who lives and believes in Me will never die. Do you believe this?"*

Jesus was talking to Martha in this verse, but the question applies to everyone. Do you believe this?

Walking in the Sprit, relishing in the taste of God's Grace and Love, bathing in the forgiveness He has poured out for you—all of this is present tense salvation. Your heart will shout with joy, and you will automatically start to exhibit the fruits of the spirit. Present tense salvation will lead to future tense salvation.

If the saints are to rule and reign with Christ, then they must be responsible and knowledgeable of the way to live the life that Christ wants them to live. They must know how to walk by the Spirit. They will be ministering to those who are outside of the Kingdom but under its rule. When Jesus comes to set up His Kingdom, the first thing He will do is determine who can enter. This is known as the Judgment Seat of Christ.

The Bible is clear on what this Judgment will entail, and I have written a complete chapter on this judgment later in this book. I do imagine that many people will be shocked at who they will see enter into the Kingdom. Many who think they deserve to enter will be denied.

Be aware that not all who call Jesus Master or preach in the name of Jesus will enter the Kingdom.

> ### Matthew 7:21–23
> **21** *"Not everyone who says to Me, 'Lord, Lord,' will enter the Kingdom of heaven, but he who does the will of My Father who is in heaven will enter.*
> **22** *Many will say to Me on that day, 'Lord, Lord, did we not prophesy in Your name, and in Your name cast out demons, and in Your name perform many miracles?'*
> **23** *And then I will declare to them, 'I never knew you; depart from Me, you who practice lawlessness.'"*

It appears from the scripture above that the requirements for entrance into the Kingdom are doing the will of the Father, Christ knowing you, and not practicing lawlessness.

> ### 2nd Timothy 2:19
> ...*"The Lord knows those who are His," and, "Everyone who names the name of the Lord is to abstain from wickedness."*

Obviously, it is absolutely necessary to have a personal relationship with God through Jesus Christ, and if you have that relationship with Him, you are to abstain from wickedness. Just professing to have a relationship with Christ is not enough. Calling yourself a Christian and professing to believe in Christ is not enough. Saying the prayer at the end of a tract is not enough. Going forward at a Billy Graham Crusade is not enough. Even prophesizing (preaching) and performing miracles is not enough. If the relationship with Christ is true, it will be demonstrated in your works. True faith is a life-changing faith, and it will endure throughout your life. You may stray from it for a time, but you will come back once you are reminded of God's love.

Good works performed for the wrong reason will not provide you an entrance into the Kingdom. Your entrance into the Kingdom is only through the grace of God and you responding to that grace by believing, and continuing to believe, that Jesus died for all of your sins. The confusing aspect of grace is that it has nothing to do with performing good works, but believing in God's grace will result in good works. It is the motivation behind your works that will be judged, and if your motivation is to earn God's approval, it is the same as filthy rags. Why is this wrong? It demonstrates that you do not really believe that Christ did it all. It is denying Christ and relying on the flesh to earn your favor with God.

If you love God because you know how much He loved you and that it is purely by His Grace that you have His approval, then you will naturally start to love others, which will result in works that show the evidence of your faith.

This was the insight that caused Martin Luther to take issue with the Roman Church, and he said it this way: "We are saved by faith alone, but the faith that saves is never alone." James said it best:

James 2:14–26
14 What use is it, my brethren, if someone says he has faith but he has no works? Can that faith save him?

15 *If a brother or sister is without clothing and in need of daily food,*

16 *and one of you says to them, "Go in peace, be warmed and be filled," and yet you do not give them what is necessary for their body, what use is that?*

17 *Even so faith, if it has no works, is dead, being by itself.*

18 *But someone may well say, "You have faith and I have works; show me your faith without the works, and I will show you my faith by my works."*

19 *You believe that God is one. You do well; the demons also believe, and shudder.*

20 *But are you willing to recognize, you foolish fellow, that faith without works is useless?*

21 *Was not Abraham our father justified by works when he offered up Isaac his son on the altar?*

22 *You see that faith was working with his works, and as a result of the works, faith was perfected;*

23 *and the Scripture was fulfilled which says, "And Abraham believed God, and it was reckoned to him as righteousness," and he was called the friend of God.*

24 *You see that a man is justified by works and not by faith alone.*

25 *In the same way, was not Rahab the harlot also justified by works when she received the messengers and sent them out by another way?*

26 *For just as the body without the spirit is dead, so also faith without works is dead.*

Attempting to live the Christian life by the power of your flesh demonstrates a lot of "dos and don'ts" but does not demonstrate love. Sometimes, what appears to be love can show up as selfish works. Giving to the poor or helping someone can appear to be loving actions, but whenever they say, "They never even said thanks," or,

"I just want a little appreciation," their motivation was not love but selfishness.

1st Corinthians 13:3

And if I give all my possessions to feed the poor, and if I surrender my body to be burned, __but do not have love, it profits me nothing__.

If you are seeking thanks, praise, appreciation, or payback, then your motives are not out of love, but to receive these things. This is not the evidence of the love of God in your life.

Luke 6:32–33

32 *If you love those who love you, what credit is that to you? For even sinners love those who love them.*
33 *If you do good to those who do good to you, what credit is that to you? For even sinners do the same.*

Jesus will determine those who will enter into the Kingdom when He returns.

John 5:22

For not even the Father judges anyone, but He has given all judgment to the Son...

But more importantly, Jesus will judge people's motives. What may appear as love is not the same love that God wants you to exhibit. All love is from God, but the Agape love that is described in 1st Corinthians 13 can only be achieved by experiencing and accepting the love of God as your own. A non-believer cannot demonstrate Agape love. The love that God demands is humanly impossible. You cannot do it by the power of the flesh. It can only be by knowing His love and yielding to the Holy Spirit.

1st John 4:10–16

10 *In this is love, not that we loved God, but that He loved us and sent His Son to be the propitiation for our sins.*

11 *Beloved, if God so loved us, we also ought to love one another.*

12 *No one has seen God at any time; if we love one another, God abides in us, and His love is perfected in us.*

13 *By this we know that we abide in Him and He in us, because He has given us of His Spirit.*

14 *We have seen and testify that the Father has sent the Son to be the Savior of the world.*

15 *Whoever confesses that Jesus is the Son of God, God abides in him, and he in God.*

16 *We have come to know and have believed the love which God has for us. God is love, and the one who abides in love abides in God, and God abides in him.*

Verse 10 says *"In this is love, that He first loved us"*! To love, you must dwell in the depth of God's Love. We can only love, because He first loved us. Love is the commandment Christ meant when He said, "Keep my commandments."

John 14:15

If you love Me, you will keep My commandments.

John 15:10

If you keep My commandments, you will abide in My love; just as I have kept My Father's commandments and abide in His love.

If you are living the Christian life by the power of the Holy Spirit, and asking Him to show His love to others through you, then you will be successful.

Love is <u>THE MOST IMPORTANT</u> quality of a Christian. Many Christians do not believe this. They think it is important, but they think it is more important to stop sinning. If you could stop sinning, then Jesus would not have had to die on the cross. That is what the law tried to do: get us to stop sinning. It did not work, but what the law could not do...

Romans 8:3–8

3 *For what the Law could not do, weak as it was through the flesh, God did: sending His own Son in the likeness of sinful flesh and as an offering for sin, He condemned sin in the flesh,*

4 *so that the requirement of the Law might be fulfilled in us, who do not walk according to the flesh but according to the Spirit.*

5 *For those who are according to the flesh set their minds on the things of the flesh, but those who are according to the Spirit, the things of the Spirit.*

6 *For the mind set on the flesh is death, but the mind set on the Spirit is life and peace,*

7 *because the mind set on the flesh is hostile toward God; for it does not subject itself to the law of God, for it is not even able to do so,*

8 *and those who are in the flesh cannot please God.*

Some of the most judgmental and condemning people claim to be Christians. If they understood the Gospel of the Kingdom, maybe they would realize the gravity of their error.

Romans 13:10

Love does no wrong to a neighbor; therefore love is the fulfillment of the law.

True love, the love God wants His children to demonstrate, the Love commanded by Christ, will be exhibited by the act of putting someone else's needs before yours. This is an impossible task to perform in the flesh. Only by living by the spirit can one consistently put others first.

The greatest love is laying down your life for someone else. All people think that if the time came they would do that, but you don't have to die to exhibit this love. You just have to die to your own selfish desires and what you think are your individual needs.

This can be harder than taking a bullet for someone. This means letting people have their way, letting them cut in line in front of you, and letting them cut you off in traffic. This is truly dying to yourself. People rebel against this concept because the flesh screams, "ME, ME, ME!" Looking out for number one is a popular concept, but is not what Christ demands from us. This love, putting others first, is commanded; in fact, it is the only commandment that Christ gave, other than loving God with all of your heart. You cannot love God if you do not love your neighbor.

> **1st John 4:17–21**
> **17** *By this, love is perfected with us, so that we may have confidence in the Day of Judgment; because as He is, so also are we in this world.*
> **18** *There is no fear in love; but perfect love casts out fear, because fear involves punishment, and the one who fears is not perfected in love.*
> **19** *We love, because He first loved us.*
> **20** *If someone says, "I love God," and hates his brother, he is a liar; for the one who does not love his brother whom he has seen, cannot love God whom he has not seen.*
> **21** *And this commandment we have from Him, that the one who loves God should love his brother also."*

When you try to live this kind of love, the first question becomes, "What about **my** needs?" God knows your needs and will take care of them. Christians need to let God love others freely through them. They have to become the arms of God's Love.

FAITH VS. WORKS

One of the main doctrinal differences the reformers had with the Roman Church is this entire concept of works versus faith. The Pharisees and the Sadducees during the time of Christ were the religious people of that day. They surround us again today. They may go by a different name, but they are trying to earn God's approval by works or the law of dos and don'ts.

R.C. Sproul explains this with the following formula:

> Faith + Works = Salvation (Roman Catholic)
> Faith = Salvation + Works (Reformed)

Many times I find Christians treat faith as a work. They can become proud of their faith.

Romans 12:3
I say to everyone among you not to think more highly of himself than he ought to think; but to think so as to have sound judgment, as God has allotted to each a measure of faith.

Many put faith in their belief, thinking that is what changes God's attitude towards them. It was the faith of Christ driving Him to willfully give His life for us on the Cross that saved us, not our faith.

The Faith that God now apportions to us, enables us to walk with Him.

Our faith in God, does not affect God, it only affects us.

I think the formula then becomes:

217

Grace (Free gift from God) = Forgiveness of sins. (Past Tense Salvation)

Grace = Faith (Not of ourselves, it is the gift of God).

Faith = Love and Works (Not our works but God acting through us)

Love and Works = Future Tense Salvation

Understanding Christ's work at the cross (even that comes from God) allows you to accept the Faith that He has given you. The only thing you can do on your own is reject this.

Ephesians 2:8–9
8 *For by grace you have been saved through faith; and that not of yourselves, it is the gift of God;*
9 *not as a result of works, so that no one may boast.*

Aquinas held that faith and reason intertwine. Faith uses reason, and reason cannot succeed in finding truth without faith. Reason Cannot Produce Faith. Reason accompanies, but does not cause, faith. Faith is consent without inquiry in that faith's assent is not caused by investigation. Rather, it is produced by God.[106]

All people have been given a portion of faith by which they are enabled to believe. Unbelief, rebellion to God and Jesus, fails to bring about good fruit. The gift of faith and the portion of Holy Spirit given to each person makes them accountable to God for what they do with his gifts. [107]

Faith will result in works, and the only way anyone can truly exhibit love in the way that Christ commanded us is to know Him and His

---

[106] (Geisler N. L., 1999)
[107] (Kenison F., The Truth Revealed in Romans, 1999)

love for us. Any other love is a counterfeit, and the motivation is a selfish motivation.

Works do not justify; they only testify. They are a testimony that we have the Love of God in us and that we know Him. He is the object of our faith. True faith produces the fruit of the spirit.

Galatians 5:22–26

22 *But the fruit of the Spirit is love, joy, peace, patience, kindness, goodness, faithfulness,*

23 *gentleness, self-control; against such things there is no law.*

24 *Now those who belong to Christ Jesus have crucified the flesh with its passions and desires.*

25 *If we live by the Spirit, let us also walk by the Spirit.*

26 *Let us not become boastful, challenging one another, envying one another.*

It is important to point out that the fruits demonstrated by one who has a personal relationship with Christ are not tied to obeying the law. Religious people stress the don'ts of the law and even add more requirements. Commands such as *do not handle, do not taste*, and *do not touch* are manmade restrictions that appear to be religious but have no benefit in living the life Christ wants us to live.

Colossians 2:20–23

20 *If you have died with Christ to the elementary principles of the world, why, as if you were living in the world, do you submit yourself to decrees, such as,*

21 *"Do not handle, do not taste, do not touch!"*

22 *(which all refer to things destined to perish with use)—in accordance with the commandments and teachings of men?*

23 *These are matters which have, to be sure, the appearance of wisdom in self-made religion and self-abasement and severe treatment of the body, but are of no value against fleshly indulgence.*

All too often, the church stresses these decrees, and you may find yourself judging your own walk with Christ based on these rules. Worse, you could end up condemning those who fall short of your "works based" standards. People need to be aware of what harm they are doing to others when they judge or condemn those who are truly desiring to serve God but are struggling with sin. It has been said, "The Christian Army is the only army that shoots its wounded."

It is ironic, but those who are trying to please God by these works end up disobeying God by not loving anyone who does not live up to their standards. You might say, "I love them, but hate the sin." Love does not condemn. When the woman caught in adultery was brought before Jesus, He did not condemn her. They must learn that if they know Christ, then they will have this same attitude toward sinners. This cannot be stressed enough. Many people that think they are godly because they exhibit good works and act as if they have no sin in their life, but they are very often the most judgmental people in the world. This is not the humble attitude of a servant, yet that is what they should be striving for.

Matthew 20:26–27

26 *It is not this way among you, but whoever wishes to become great among you shall be your servant,*
27 *and whoever wishes to be first among you shall be your slave...*

Matthew 23:11–12

11 *But the greatest among you shall be your servant.*
12 *Whoever exalts himself shall be humbled; and whoever humbles himself shall be exalted.*

Mark 9:35

*Sitting down, He called the twelve and said to them,
"If anyone wants to be first, he shall be last of all and
servant of all.*

They know that they are supposed to love their neighbor as
themselves, so when they don't, they have to justify their actions.
You might hear things like, "I am judging them by their fruits," or
"Am I supposed to love children of the devil?" How many times have
so-called Christians shown racial prejudices? They are unmerciful,
condemning, and non-loving. Those who belong to Christ would not
exhibit this type of fruit. Yet, these very people will tell you they are
very godly Christians.

James 1:26–27

26 *If anyone thinks himself to be religious, and yet
does not bridle his tongue but deceives his own heart,
this man's religion is worthless.*
27 *Pure and undefiled religion in the sight of our
God and Father is this: to visit orphans and widows
in their distress, and to keep oneself unstained by the
world.*

In verse 26, the phrase "religion is worthless" is translated as "religion
is vain" in the King James Version of the Bible. Matthew Henry
writes:

> In a vain religion there is much censuring, reviling, and
> detracting of others. The not bridling the tongue here
> is chiefly meant of not abstaining from these evils of
> the tongue. When we hear people ready to speak of the
> faults of others, or to censure them as holding scandalous
> errors, or to lessen the wisdom and piety of those about
> them, that they themselves may seem the wiser and
> better, this is a sign that they have but a vain religion.
> The man who has a detracting tongue cannot have a

truly humble gracious heart. He who delights to injure his neighbour in vain pretends to love God; therefore a reviling tongue will prove a man a hypocrite...This has ever been a leading sin with hypocrites, that the more ambitious they have been to seem well themselves the more free they have been in censuring and running down others; and there is such quick intercourse between the tongue and the heart that the one may be known by the other. On these accounts it is that the apostle has made an ungoverned tongue an undoubted certain proof of a vain religion. There is no strength nor power in that religion which will not enable a man to bridle his tongue...In a vain religion a man deceives his own heart; he goes on in such a course of detracting from others, and making himself seem somebody, that at last the vanity of his religion is consummated by the deceiving of his own soul. When once religion comes to be a vain thing, how great is the vanity!

...False religions may be known by their impurity and un-charitableness; according to that of John, He that doeth not righteousness is not of God neither he that loveth not his brother, 1 Jn. 3:10. But, on the other hand, a holy life and a charitable heart show a true religion. Our religion is not (says Dr. Manton) adorned with ceremonies, but purity and charity...Compassion and charity to the poor and distressed from a very great and necessary part of true religion: Visiting the fatherless and widow in their affliction. Visiting is here put for all manner of relief which we are capable of giving to others; and fatherless and widows are here particularly mentioned, because they are generally most apt to be neglected or oppressed: but by them we are to understand all who are proper objects of charity, all who are in affliction. It is very remarkable that if the sum of religion be drawn up to two articles this is one-to be charitable and relieve the afflicted. Observe, (4.) An unspotted life must accompany an unfeigned love and charity: To keep himself unspotted from the world. The world is apt to spot and blemish the soul, and it is hard to live in it, and have to do with it, and not be defiled; but this must be our constant endeavour. Herein consists pure and undefiled religion. The very things of the world too much taint our spirits, if we are much conversant with them; but the sins and lusts of the world deface and defile them very woefully indeed. John comprises all that is in the world, which we are not to love, under three heads: the lust of the flesh, the lust of the eyes, and the pride of life; and to keep ourselves unspotted from all these is to keep ourselves unspotted from the world. May God by his grace keep both our hearts and lives clean from the love of the world, and from the temptations of wicked worldly men.[108]

People who are living by works or act religious but have a religion that is vain are not going to enter into the Kingdom. The Pharisees were such people. Jesus told them they would not be a part of the Kingdom. Christ determines if you enter the Kingdom based on your knowing Him (or Him knowing you) and believing in His substitutionary death for your sins. When you try to live the Christian life by works, then you are saying to Christ, "I do not believe you did it all. I have to add more." Jesus will say, "Depart from me for I never knew you."

It is for this reason the hope of the Kingdom is so important and such a motivator, not to try and do good works but to put to death our selfish desires and fully accept the love and forgiveness of God. Allowing Him to produce true godly love into your life will in turn produce good works and fulfill the law.

If you are concerned whether or not your faith is producing the works that are important, note what Peter says after he describes the qualities one should have as a Christian.

---

[108] (Henry, 1996, c 1991)

2nd Peter 1:5–9

5 *Now for this very reason also, applying all diligence,* ***in your faith supply moral excellence****, and in your moral excellence,* ***knowledge****,*

6 *and in your knowledge,* ***self-control****, and in your self-control,* ***perseverance****, and in your perseverance,* ***godliness****,*

7 ***and in your godliness, brotherly kindness, and in your brotherly kindness, love.***

8 ***For if these qualities are yours and are increasing****, they render you neither useless nor unfruitful in the true knowledge of our Lord Jesus Christ.*

9 ***For he who lacks these qualities is blind or short-sighted, having forgotten his purification from his former sins****.*

Many people interpret this passage to indicate that if you don't work to add these qualities to your Christian walk, you have turned your back on your purification from sin. Religious people (those striving to please God by the power of the flesh) always want to put the work back on you. They deny the truth: the Holy Spirit will empower you to live the life God desires for you. I believe that this verse is saying that if you do not have these qualities, it is because you have forgotten that you have been purified. Remembering what Christ did on the cross because of God's unconditional love motivates believers to allow the Holy Spirit to impart these qualities into their lives. Don't focus on the works; focus on the relationship.

If you want better works, don't strive harder in the flesh; concentrate on Jesus Christ and what He did for you on the cross. This will produce in your heart rejoicing and gratitude, creating a responsive love of a magnitude that will spill out into your actions. You will want to obey the commandment to love your neighbor as yourself. You will be so filled with His love that you will strongly desire to put the needs of others before your own needs. Let us remind each other of the forgiveness and purification that He has given us and not condemn our brothers when they fall short of our expectations.

To put to death the desires of the flesh, you must learn that selfishness is the root of rebellion against God. Christians must constantly remind themselves to put others' needs before their own desires. They must become servants. You cannot do this by the power of the flesh; it is humanly impossible. That is why you must die to self and let the Holy Spirit live and love through you. The only way you can do that is to fully understand the great and marvelous love that God has for you. This is the only way one can enter into the Kingdom.

1st Peter 3:8–9

8 *To sum up, all of you be harmonious, sympathetic, brotherly, kindhearted, and humble in spirit;*
9 *not returning evil for evil or insult for insult, but giving a blessing instead; for you were called for the very purpose that you might inherit a blessing.*

Paul says—"My determination is to be my utmost for His Highest." To get there is a question of will, not of debate nor of reasoning, but a surrender of will, an absolute and irrevocable surrender on that point. An overweening [overconfident] consideration for ourselves is the thing that keeps us from that decision, though we put it that we are considering others. When we consider what it will cost others if we obey the call of Jesus, we tell God He does not know what our obedience will mean. Keep to the point; He does know. Shut out every other consideration and keep yourself before God for this one thing only—"My Utmost for His Highest." I am determined to be absolutely and entirely for Him and for Him alone.[109] [comments mine]

---

[109] (Chambers, 1986)

225

17

THE CONSCIENCE

The conscience is very important in your relationship with God. Before doing an act, the conscience can help you know to do the right thing. After doing something you know is wrong, the guilty conscience can be very destructive to your life. Suicides have been blamed on a guilty conscience.

The *Dictionary of Bible Themes* defines "conscience" as an:

> innate ability to discern the difference between right and wrong, which Scripture describes as having its origin in God himself.[110]

And the "*nature* of conscience" as:

> The faculty, given to every individual, that is capable of producing guilt, or reassurance in the case of innocence. Though never wholly reliable, the conscience is cleansed when the individual turns to God for forgiveness. It is possible for the conscience to become deadened through lack of use.[111]

> Some things never change. The problem of a dirty conscience is as old as Adam and Eve. As soon as they

---

[110] (Manser, 2009)
[111] (Manser, 2009)

sinned, their conscience was defiled. Their sense of guilt was ruinous. It ruined their relationship with God—they hid from him. It ruined their relation to each other—they blamed. It ruined their peace with themselves—for the first time they saw themselves and felt shame.[112]

All through the Old Testament, conscience was an issue. But the animal sacrifices themselves could not cleanse the conscience. "Gifts and sacrifices are offered that cannot perfect the conscience of the worshiper, but deal only with food and drink and various washings, regulations for the body imposed until the time of reformation" (Hebrews 9:9–10). As a foreshadowing of Christ, God counted the blood of the animals as sufficient for cleansing the flesh— the ceremonial uncleanness, but not the conscience.[113]

No animal blood could cleanse the conscience. They knew it (see Isaiah 53 and Psalm 51). And we know it. So a new high priest comes—Jesus the Son of God—with a better sacrifice: himself. "How much more will the blood of Christ, who through the eternal Spirit offered himself without blemish to God, **purify our conscience from dead works to serve the living God**" (Hebrews 9:14). The animal sacrifices foreshadowed the final sacrifice of God's Son, and the death of the Son reaches back to cover all the sins of God's people in the old time period, and forward to cover all the sins of God's people in the new time period.[114]

So here we are in the modern age—the age of science, Internet, organ transplants, instant messaging, cell phones—and our problem is fundamentally the same as always: **Our conscience condemns us.** We don't feel good enough to come to God. And no matter how distorted our

---

[112] (Piper, 2006)

[113] (Piper, 2006)

[114] (Piper, 2006)

consciences are, this much is true: We are not good enough
to come to him.[115]

Did this tree of knowledge of good and evil bear the fruit that would
give man a conscience? God had told Adam not to eat from the tree
of knowledge of good and evil (one of the meanings of the word
conscience), because if he did, he would surely die. The knowledge
of good and evil is what kills—not immediately, but spiritually and,
eventually, physically. It is an evil conscience that has the same result
on Christians today as it did on Adam and Eve. Think about what
happened. First of all, Satan tempted Eve to eat the fruit. This is how
the Bible tells it in Genesis 3:

> **Genesis 3:1–5**
> **1** *Now the serpent was more crafty than any beast of
> the field which the* LORD *God had made. And he said
> to the woman, "Indeed, has God said, 'You shall not
> eat from any tree of the garden'?"*
> **2** *And the woman said to the serpent, "From the fruit
> of the trees of the garden we may eat;*
> **3** *but from the fruit of the tree which is in the middle
> of the garden, God has said, 'You shall not eat from
> it or touch it, lest you die.'"*
> **4** *And the serpent said to the woman, "You surely
> shall not die!*
> **5** *For God knows that in the day you eat from it
> your eyes will be opened, and you will be like God,
> knowing good and evil."*

Satan confirms that they will learn what is good and what is evil, the
difference between right and wrong. It does not appear God wanted
Mankind to know right from wrong. Read on and you will see why.

---

[115] (Piper, 2006)

Genesis 3:6–7

6 When the woman saw that the tree was good for food, and that it was a delight to the eyes, and that the tree was desirable to make one wise, she took from its fruit and ate; and she gave also to her husband with her, and he ate.

7 Then the eyes of both of them were opened, and they knew that they were naked; and they sewed fig leaves together and made themselves loin coverings.

As soon as they ate it, they realized that they were naked. Big deal! They had been naked all of the time before this and didn't even realize it. It had never hurt their relationship with God before this, so why the sudden change? It was because they now had consciences.

Look what it made them do. They hid from God!

Genesis 3:8

And they heard the sound of the LORD God walking in the garden in the cool of the day, and the man and his wife hid themselves from the presence of the LORD God among the trees of the garden.

This new knowledge caused them to hide from God, because they now knew they were naked. They covered themselves with fig leaves, but it was not enough. They now realized that God knew everything about their inner most thoughts, and they felt guilty in front of God. This started a trend of man hiding from God. Because he has a conscience—the knowledge that he did wrong—it kills him and his relationship with God.

They covered themselves with fig leaves, and it did not do any good. You could say this is analogous to man trying to cover his nakedness before God with good works. That does not work, either. Let's see what God did with Adam and Eve to solve this problem with a conscience.

Genesis 3:9

Then the LORD God called to the man, and said to him, "Where are you?"

Just a note: if God is all-knowing (He is), then why did He ask, "Where are you"? God wanted them to confront what they did wrong in His presence. Confession of your sinful state to God is the first step toward relieving a guilty conscience.

Genesis 3:10–13

10 *And he said, "I heard the sound of Thee in the garden, and I was afraid because I was naked; so I hid myself."*
11 *And He said, "Who told you that you were naked? Have you eaten from the tree of which I commanded you not to eat?"*
12 *And the man said, "The woman whom Thou gavest to be with me, she gave me from the tree, and I ate."*
13 *Then the LORD God said to the woman, "What is this you have done?" And the woman said, "The serpent deceived me, and I ate."*

Notice how the first reaction was to blame their sin on someone else. They wanted God to think they were victims, not taking responsibility for their actions. Here comes the punishment.

Genesis 3:17–19

17 *Then to Adam He said, "Because you have listened to the voice of your wife, and have eaten from the tree about which I commanded you, saying, 'You shall not eat from it';*
Cursed is the ground because of you;
In toil you shall eat of it
All the days of your life.
18 *Both thorns and thistles it shall grow for you;*

And you shall eat the plants of the field;
19 *By the sweat of your face*
You shall eat bread,
Till you return to the ground,
Because from it you were taken;
For you are dust,
And to dust you shall return."

Eating the fruit of the tree of knowledge of good and evil caused all mankind to die. Before this, there was no mention of death. Satan was a liar. It is interesting to note here that the curse is not on Adam and Eve, but upon the ground and the creation.

Genesis 3:21
And the LORD God made garments of skin for Adam and his wife, and clothed them.

This is the first time in the Bible that an animal was killed. Blood was spilled so that an animal's skin could be used to cover the nakedness of mankind. You could say that the animal whose skin was used gave his life for the sin of Adam and Eve. This is prophetical, because from this point on, blood is used as the sacrifice for sin; first the lambs in the Old Testament, and then the final completion of all sacrifices: the life of Jesus Christ. He gave his life for your sins.

When I first became a Christian, I was taught that God hated sin so much that He couldn't fellowship with sinful man. To look on man, or to have fellowship with him, He had to cover us with the blood of Christ. I am now convinced that it is not God that has the problem, but man. People require a blood sacrifice in order to believe that they have been forgiven. From the first blood sacrifice in the Garden to all of the blood sacrifices in the temple, blood appears to be required for mankind to believe they are forgiven. Man's guilty conscience is the reason that God had to send Jesus to die on the cross, so that man could and would believe that God loved him.

Genesis 3:22

Then the LORD God said, "Behold, the man has become like one of Us, knowing good and evil; and now, lest he stretch out his hand, and take also from the tree of life, and eat, and live forever."

The word "Us" above has been the cause of a lot of discussion. Many theologians will try to use this verse to say that God was talking to Jesus, others think He was talking to the angels.

> ...the use of "we" or "us" of God is another literary form known as a royal or regal plural. It is used of royalty and of God in Semitic cultures. Even in a rigid monotheism such as Islam, where there is only one person in the Godhead, there are still references in the Qur'an to God as "we" or "us."[116]

I had always thought that God threw Adam and Eve out of the Garden as punishment for their sin. Looking at this last verse, it appears that He took Adam and Eve out of the Garden so that they would not eat from the Tree of Life. Eating from the Tree of Life would cause them to live forever, but to live forever with a guilty or an evil conscience would not be pleasant. God now had to take care of the evil conscience that man obtained through his selfish desire to be like God.

The other side of this is that God in His wisdom developed a way to use the knowledge of right and wrong for the good of man. There is a good side of the conscience that can provide a guide for living. Knowing right from wrong can keep you from doing things that are harmful to you or others. It also convicts you of your inability to live according to the law, and this can drive you to repentance and to seek God's forgiveness.

---

[116] (Geisler N. L., Systematic Theology, Volume Two: God, Creation, 2003)

God has provided mankind a way to cleanse an evil, guilty conscience: Christ's atoning death on the cross. By believing that Christ's death truly took care of all sin, one can then believe they are forgiven and now are judicially innocent of all sin. Relationally, God our Father knows we sin, but He is not angry, just concerned, as any good father would be. He is concerned because sin drives mankind away from a close relationship, and sin is harmful to those involved. This close relationship will allow you to enter into Paradise where the Tree of Life will be.

Revelation 2:7

*"He who has an ear, let him hear what the Spirit says to the churches. To him who overcomes, I will grant to **eat of the tree of life, which is in the Paradise of God**."*

God did not want man to get back to that Tree of Life, so He guards the Tree of Life.

Genesis 3:23–24

23 *...therefore the LORD God sent him out from the Garden of Eden, to cultivate the ground from which he was taken.*
24 *So He drove the man out; and at the east of the Garden of Eden He stationed the cherubim, and the flaming sword which turned every direction, to guard the way to the tree of life.*

God removed man from the garden and the Tree of Life until His plan could be fulfilled. His plan was to develop a holy nation, a royal priesthood, and a people for God's own possession. To do that, He would first have to show mankind how much He loved them and that He had forgiven them. He would have to cleanse their conscience.

Hebrews 9:13–14

13 *For if the blood of goats and bulls and the ashes of a heifer sprinkling those who have been defiled, sanctify for the cleansing of the flesh,*
14 *how much more will the blood of Christ, who through the eternal Spirit offered Himself without blemish to God, cleanse your conscience from dead works to serve the living God?*

After this cleansing, God's plan is to bring you back into a face-to-face relationship with Him in His Kingdom, the literal, physical reign of Jesus Christ upon the earth.

> The story is not devoid of hope. God was merciful even then. He made them garments of skin to cover their bodies and promised that someday the power of Satan behind the serpent would be crushed by the woman's "seed" (Gen. 3:15; compare Rom. 16:20). Many scholars consider that promise to be the first biblical mention of redemption.[117]

Christ died for all sins, for all, and for all time. Sin has been taken away, and death has been conquered.

No one can stop sinning. If we could, then Christ would not have had to die. We will continue to sin as long as we live, but hopefully it will not be willful, deliberate rebellion against God, because we want to be Holy just as He is Holy. The only thing that is Holy is God, or where He is, and if He is in us, then we are Holy.

Trying to stop sinning by the power of the flesh is futile. It is not being obedient to God.

---

[117] (Elwell, 1988)

Galatians 5:4

You have been severed from Christ, you who are seeking to be justified by law; you have fallen from grace.

Legalism is fuel to sin, not a way to stop sinning. If I tell you not to scratch your nose, it will suddenly begin to itch.

Romans 7:7–9

7 *...for I would not have known about coveting if the Law had not said, "You shall not covet."*
8 *But sin, taking opportunity through the commandment, produced in me coveting of every kind; for apart from the Law sin is dead.*
9 *I was once alive apart from the Law; but when the commandment came, sin became alive and I died..."*

Repentance does not mean you decide to quit sinning, nor to be sorry for your sins. It means to change your mind. The Greek word for sin is ἁμαρτία (*harmatia*). Literally, it means to "miss the mark." It would be used by an archer who missed the target with his arrow. The target in this case is a relationship with God. Sin is rejecting or walking away from God. The consequence of sin is guilt.

Repentance means changing your mind about your sins, realizing that they are forgiven and wiped clean, and turning back to God. The Greek word translated as repent, or repentance, is μετάνοια (*metanoya*).

> μετάνοια: To change one's way of life as the result of a complete change of thought and attitude with regard to sin and righteousness—'to repent, to change one's way, repentance.'

> 'do you fail to understand that God is kind because he wants to lead you to repent?' Ro 2:4.

235

Though in English a focal component of repent is the sorrow or contrition that a person experiences because of sin, **the emphasis in μετάνοια seems to be more specifically the total change, both in thought and behavior, with respect to how one should both think and act.**[118]

In the Old Testament, the Hebrew word *nacham* is translated as either **repent** (41 times) or **comfort** (69 times). Of the 41 translated repent, 35 indicate that it is the Lord who repents; and only six times does it refer to men repenting. The Lord certainly has no sin to feel sorry about.[119]

Translating *nacham* as **repentance**, **comfort**, and **comforter** vividly illustrates an important use of this word in the Old Testament. Repentance is a change of mind which manifests itself as comfort.[120]

I have now realized that repentance also means to **change your mind about what God thinks of your sin**. When we sin, we think that He either now hates us, is disappointed in us, or wants to punish us. That is just not true. God is love, and there is no room in His love for any of the opinions just mentioned. The only reason God does not like sin is that sin hurts us, or someone else, and He does not want that for us. Part of that includes the "hurt" of having our relationship with our Father negatively affected. Sin does that, not because of our guilty conscience, but God's reaction.

I am not advocating antinomianism, the idea that Christians should have no regard for the moral obligations of the law. On the contrary, I am advocating that if you are free from guilt, you will see the unconditional love of God. You will respond and allow Him to

---

[118] (Louw, 1996)

[119] (Kenison F., The Truth Revealed in Romans, 1999)

[120] (Kenison F., The Truth Revealed in Romans, 1999)

sanctify you and help you to die to worldly desires and live for Him. If you are obeying the law of win the favor of God, it is wrong. It should spring forth from the fountain of love. That is why the greatest commandment is to love both God and others.

> The moment we are regenerated, the Spirit of God comes to dwell in our hearts to motivate us, to give us an obedient heart. Now we love the law of God, not because it is the means by which we are redeemed, but because it reveals to us what pleases our Father whom we love. The moment we embrace Jesus as Saviour, we bow to him as Lord, and seek to show our love for him by obeying his commandments.[121]

Using the word "works" can cause some confusion in understanding how we should walk with God. If we die to the law, will we still perform works? It seems that Paul says works are in vain, yet James says that if you have faith, you will exhibit works.

> When Paul and James speak of "works," they speak of different concepts. Paul is speaking of works of the Law; that is, works as an expression of the Law, or what might be called "law-works" (Rom. 3:20). **James, on the other hand, never speaks of works of the Law but rather of works that give expression to faith, or what might be called "faith-works."** James regards faith without works as dead; that is, as no faith at all (James 2:17). For him faith is expressed and perfected by works. Paul and James both affirm that one comes into, and continues in, living relationship to God through faith—apart from the Law but not without the love and obedience that is born of faith.[122]

It all depends on your motivation. If your works are meant to please God or earn favor, then they are in vain and you need to change

---

[121] (Sproul, The Purpose of God: Ephesians, 1994)
[122] (Elwell, 1988)

your motives. When you walk with God in love, your love in turn will result in good works that are of the right motive. To do this you need to die to the law, die to your own selfish desires, and die to your guilty conscience.

> I have been crucified with Jesus Christ, representatively. In God's sight my evil nature is dead. My sin was put to death on the cross of Jesus Christ and my sins were paid for. I was released from the bondage to sin.[123]

Romans 6:11–23

11 *Even so consider yourselves to be dead to sin, but alive to God in Christ Jesus.*

12 *Therefore do not let sin reign in your mortal body so that you obey its lusts,*

13 *and do not go on presenting the members of your body to sin as instruments of unrighteousness; but present yourselves to God as those alive from the dead, and your members as instruments of righteousness to God.*

14 *For sin shall not be master over you, for you are not under law but under grace.*

15 *What then? Shall we sin because we are not under law but under grace? May it never be!*

16 *Do you not know that when you present yourselves to someone as slaves for obedience, you are slaves of the one whom you obey, either of sin resulting in death, or of obedience resulting in righteousness?*

17 *But thanks be to God that though you were slaves of sin, you became obedient from the heart to that form of teaching to which you were committed,*

18 *and having been freed from sin, you became slaves of righteousness.*

---

[123] (Sproul, The Gospel of God: An Exposition of Romans, 1994)

19 *I am speaking in human terms because of the weakness of your flesh. For just as you presented your members as slaves to impurity and to lawlessness, resulting in further lawlessness, so now present your members as slaves to righteousness, resulting in sanctification.*

20 *For when you were slaves of sin, you were free in regard to righteousness.*

21 *Therefore what benefit were you then deriving from the things of which you are now ashamed? For the outcome of those things is death.*

22 *But now having been freed from sin and enslaved to God, you derive your benefit, resulting in sanctification, and the outcome, eternal life.*

23 *For the wages of sin is death, but the free gift of God is eternal life in Christ Jesus our Lord.*

1st Corinthians 15:56

The sting of death is sin; and the strength of sin is the law.

Law only causes one to sin, so that in desperation they will be led to Christ. Why?

Romans 7:4

Wherefore, my brethren, ye also are become dead to the law by the body of Christ; that ye should be married to another, even to him who is raised from the dead, that we should bring forth fruit unto God.

Paul unequivocally stated that we are dead to the law, not because of our faith, but by the body, or sacrifice, of Christ.

In **Galatians 5:18** Paul points out, *"But if ye be led of the Spirit, ye are not under the law."*

Cleansing from besetting (continually recurring) sins requires agreement that the law is good and that the practiced sin is not. Paul's message was that we are not in control of ourselves; that either flesh or spirit controls us. **What good we will to do, we cannot do, and what we will not to do, that is what we end up doing.**

The old man, or old nature, is always under control of the body of the sin, but it can be brought into submission by the spirit of God. Since God bestowed a portion of holy spirit upon each person, we have everything we need to overcome the practice of sin in our lives. This, too, is salvation.

Freedom from the power of sin comes by assenting to the law and recognizing that the death of Christ freed everyone from being subject to law and thereby also subject to sin. When we come to knowledge of the complete salvation wrought by God in Christ, the real "us" stands out as a separate entity apart from the law and sin. This salvation resulted in our participating in Christ's death. When we died, we were no longer married to the law and were now free to be married to Christ. Only when we fail to recognize this liberty from law is it possible for sin to have power over our lives.

The words "now then" set the time: now then since the sacrifice of Jesus Christ, "it is no more I that do it." The new man is set apart from the guilt and penalty of sin when he gives assent to the law that it is right. This is experiential salvation. Confession, agreeing with God that it is sin, sets us apart and lays the acts at the door of sin. The guilt and penalty are then laid at the door of the "sin that dwelleth in me."

Paul was recognizing the constant power sin has over the old man, or the Adamic nature. It is inherently evil because it is in constant rebellion to God, although it may resort to manifold subterfuges to mask this innate rebellion. One form of mask is in practicing an outward form of religion which doesn't affect the heart. The Israelites were constantly reproved and punished for this very thing. Although they had the form, their worship did not come from the heart.[124]

Romans 7:18

For I know that nothing good dwells in me, that is, in my flesh; for the willing is present in me, but the doing of the good is not.

These verses prove the uselessness of sermons telling people to exercise their will when it comes to sinning. It does not work like that, and that is what Paul was saying here.

Paul was telling of his own experience in attempting to will to do good, which was the desire of his heart. He willed this above anything else, yet he was also subject to the whims of the old nature. Finally, Paul recognized that operating his life on the basis of right and wrong was continuing in subjection to law and was actually empowering the old nature to continue in sin.

How could he operate without being under law? Paul knew Christ and believed his sins were forgiven. He desired to serve Christ. What did he lack? He was missing the knowledge of how grace can work. He learned that he must look outside himself for the ability to do the good he desired. Instead of concentrating on right and wrong, Paul learned to allow the Holy Spirit to operate his life according to the will of God. In **Philippians 2:13** he wrote, *"For it is God which worketh in you both to will and to do of his good pleasure."*

We can only bring forth good that is pleasing to God by submitting ourselves to the power of God in our lives. We, too, must come to

---

[124] (Kenison F., The Truth Revealed in Romans, 1999)

the awful realization that within us—which is in our flesh, or old nature—dwells no good thing. Our natural person is opposed to everything which God desires.

This is an awful truth, but until we face it we will continue operating under right and wrong rather than under love. The issue is no longer whether something is right or wrong, but whether or not it is Christlike. What is the spirit? The spirit is the truth, evidenced by deeds of love. When we completely submit ourselves to God, then He is able to "will and do" through us.

Paul had built up to this point by the "knowing, reckoning, and yielding" of the sixth chapter. These things must undergird the submission of our members for God to operate as He desires in and through our lives. If all deeds are done on the basis of love, this fulfills all law. This also frees us from domination of the old nature, or flesh.

The inability to will to do good is an extremely difficult admission. This is a complete repudiation of our old nature. It completely rejects the idea that we can be "good" people without being dominated by the Holy Spirit. We think we can work out our own problems, but attempting to do so means continuing to wallow in captivity to sin.

This is probably the condition of most believers today, because there is very little teaching on this subject. Also, what little *is* taught is often rejected because of our pride or our love of some particular practiced sin that we have never really confessed as sin. It is easy to justify our actions and pretend they are good instead of evil. That's where the law excels. The law is God's statement about what is and is not evil. Law reveals evil. If God's word says something is sin, *it is sin*, and no amount of rationalizing will change that fact.

A common excuse for continuing to practice some sin is that it does not hurt anyone else, but sin always produces evil results, hurting the one committing the sin and often those close to the person sinning. At the very least, continuing to sin adds to "the body of the sin," which indirectly affects us all. Good law works and being a likeable person is not a substitute for godliness. Acting in love is the way out, and this can only be done by yielding to the Holy Spirit to be used for the purposes of God.

Romans 7:21

I find then the principle that evil is present in me, the one who wants to do good.

The realization of verse 7:21 must have surprised even Paul, the Pharisee among Pharisees, who had looked with such favor on the law in the past. All of his willing to do good had not accomplished much for him. Paul said that evil was present with him.

Too many followers today have never learned this, and still try to operate in their own strength. Evil is not only present, but still dominates the life of anyone who has not learned what Paul taught in Chapters 6-7-8 of Romans.

Many people believe Jesus died for them, that he bore the punishment for their sins, but they do not reckon that they also died together with him and are, therefore, no longer subject to law. Because they do not understand this, they slip back under the bondage of denominational rules and regulations, and never experience liberty in their lives. Not liberty to sin or to live in sin, but the liberty to live a life of love and service to God. They worry about fulfilling all the rules and regulations, rather than allowing themselves to be led by the portion of Holy Spirit which God gave them for guidance and enablement.

Without reckoning that we died together with, and at the same time as, Jesus Christ (in the mind of God) we are unable to live in liberty from the law. To use Paul's example, we still feel married to law, and not to Jesus Christ. The result is living under the domination of sin, while trying unsuccessfully to live for God and feeling defeated in the process. Living with sin does not make a complete or happy person. Sin debilitates the soul.[125]

---

[125] (Kenison F., The Truth Revealed in Romans, 1999)

18

HOLY COMMUNION

Matthew 26:26–28

26 *While they were eating, Jesus took some bread, and after a blessing, He broke it and gave it to the disciples, and said, "Take, eat; this is My body."*
27 *And when He had taken a cup and given thanks, He gave it to them, saying, "Drink from it, all of you;*
28 *for this is My blood of the covenant, which is poured out for many for forgiveness of sins."*

All Christian denominations celebrate the Lord's Supper or Holy Communion. Some use grape juice and some use wine, some use wafers and others unleavened bread, but it is basically the same procedure. The Roman Catholic Church offers daily Mass, while some protestant churches only celebrate it quarterly or on Easter. The Disciples of Christ celebrate communion every Sunday. Some churches have open communion that everyone can participate in, and some have closed or "close" communion for only baptized believers or members of that church or denomination.

The thinking behind partaking of the Lord's Supper is more important and probably more divisive. Many protestant denominations believe that the wine and the bread only represent the blood and body of

Christ. While this seems to be a more rational concept, I find a beautiful significance in the other doctrines.

The Roman Catholic Church believes in "Transubstantiation," that though the wine and bread still have the same appearance, the actual *substance* becomes the blood and body of Christ when the Priest consecrates the elements by the words, *In persona Christi* (In the person of Christ). They believe that Christ Himself is now present during their Mass.

The Catechism of the Catholic Church item 1377 says,

> The Eucharistic presence of Christ begins at the moment of the consecration and endures as long as the Eucharistic species subsist. Christ is present whole and entire in each of the species and whole and entire in each of their parts, in such a way that the breaking of the bread does not divide Christ.[126]

The thought of the very presence of Christ is the reason many genuflect when they are about to sit in the pew, or when they leave. It is honoring Christ.

The Lutheran Church holds to "Consubstantiation," which means that it becomes the body and blood of Christ with the taking of the elements. They have the understanding that Christ is present "in, with, and under" the elements.

John Calvin taught the doctrine of Christ's spiritual presence in the elements. The Presbyterians still hold this belief.

I have no strong opinion on which is right. I lean toward Consubstantiation, because when I take communion, I take it with the sincere belief that I am celebrating yet honoring the death of

---

[126] (Cf. Council of Trent DS 1641)

Christ for me personally. I also partake of this with an extremely strong Hope. Jesus told us to take communion in remembrance of Him. He told us that someday He would join us to drink the cup in the Kingdom.

Matthew 26:28–29

28 *"...for this is My blood of the covenant, which is poured out for many for forgiveness of sins.*
29 *But I say to you, <u>__I will not drink of this fruit of the vine from now on until that day when I drink it new with you in My Father's Kingdom__</u>."*

This cup was probably the fourth cup of the Passover. It signified the coming of the Messiah and His Kingdom. Jesus refused to take the fifth cup at that specific time because the Kingdom had not yet begun.

> Just as the first Passover looks forward not only to deliverance but to settlement in the land, so also the Lord's Supper looks forward to deliverance and life in the consummated kingdom. The disciples will keep this celebration till Jesus comes (cf. 1st Cor. 11:26); but Jesus will not participate in it with them till the consummation, when he will sit down with them at the messianic banquet (Isa. 25:6; 1 Enoch 72:14; see on 8:11; cf. Luke 22:29–30) in his Father's kingdom, which is equally Jesus' kingdom (cf. Luke 22:16, 18, 29–30; see on 16:28; 25:31, 34). This point is greatly strengthened if we assume that Jesus speaks after drinking the fourth cup (see on 26:17).

> The four cups were meant to correspond to the fourfold promise of Exodus 6:6–7. The third cup, the "cup of blessing" used by Jesus in the words of institution, is thus associated with redemption (Exod. 6:6); but the fourth cup corresponds to the promise "I will take you as my own people, and I will be your God" (Exod. 6:7; cf. Daube, New Testament, pp. 330–31; Lane, Mark, pp. 508–9). Thus Jesus is simultaneously pledging that he will drink the

"bitter cup" immediately ahead of him and vowing not to drink the cup of consummation, the cup that promises the divine presence, till the kingdom in all its fullness has been ushered in. Then he will drink the cup with his people. This is a veiled farewell and <u>implies a sustained absence</u> (see on 24:14, 25:5, 19). The Lord's Supper therefore points both to the past and to the future, both to Jesus' sacrifice at Calvary and to the messianic banquet.[127]

1st Corinthians 11:26
For as often as you eat this bread and drink the cup, you proclaim the Lord's death until He comes.

We need to take communion often. **We need to participate often enough to keep our walk on track**; however, if it is becoming a meaningless ritual, then something needs to change. Communion is a memorial service for Christ. It should be undertaken with solemn respect the same way you would conduct yourself at a memorial service for a loved one. When participating in this holy sacrament, you should thoughtfully focus on the crucifixion of Christ and that He suffered and died for you.

Jesus said "Do this in remembrance of Me." A reminder of God's love and forgiveness is something that will keep our walk on track.

2nd Peter 1:9–13
9 *<u>For he who lacks these qualities is blind or short-sighted, having forgotten his purification from his former sins</u>.*
10 *Therefore, brethren, be all the more diligent to make certain about His calling and choosing you; for as long as you practice these things, you will never stumble;*

---

[127] (Carson, 1984)

11 *for in this way the entrance into the eternal kingdom of our Lord and Savior Jesus Christ will be abundantly supplied to you.*

12 *Therefore,* **<u>I will always be ready to remind you of these things</u>,** *even though you already know them, and have been established in the truth which is present with you.*

13 *I consider it right, as long as I am in this earthly dwelling,* **<u>to stir you up by way of reminder</u>**...

Communion should remind us of our purification from sins, and fellowship should also remind us the same way. Sometimes, people focus on reminding you of your sins rather than your forgiveness, and that does not help us generate the qualities expressed in the verses above.

The Lord's Supper should also remind us of the coming Kingdom and resurrection.

Luke 22:14–18

14 *When the hour had come, He reclined at the table, and the apostles with Him.*

15 *And He said to them, "I have earnestly desired to eat this Passover with you before I suffer;*

16 *for I say to you,* **<u>I shall never again eat it until it is fulfilled in the kingdom of God</u>.*"*

17 *And when He had taken a cup and given thanks, He said, "Take this and share it among yourselves;*

18 *for I say to you,* **<u>I will not drink of the fruit of the vine from now on until the kingdom of God comes</u>.*"*

Jesus told his disciples to take communion in remembrance of Him. When you participate in the Lord's Supper, you should be aware and hopeful that one day you will celebrate the event with Jesus and your loved ones who have passed on. The resurrected saints will also fellowship with Abraham, Isaac, and Jacob.

> **Matthew 8:10–12**
> **10** *Now when Jesus heard this, He marveled and said to those who were following, "Truly I say to you, I have not found such great faith with anyone in Israel.*
> **11** *I say to you that many will come from east and west, and recline at the table with Abraham, Isaac and Jacob in the kingdom of heaven;*
> **12** *but the sons of the kingdom will be cast out into the outer darkness; in that place there will be weeping and gnashing of teeth."*

I hate to chase rabbit trails, but an explanation is required after citing the passage above to indorse the statement I made about the saints having fellowship with Abraham and his family. In verse 10 above, Jesus was talking to a centurion who was not a Jew and had asked Jesus to heal his servant. The centurion told Jesus that if He would just say the word, the healing would take place. Jesus was amazed at the man's faith. Verse 12 states that the sons of the kingdom, who are the Israelites who rejected Christ, will be sent to outer darkness. This is one of the earliest indications that the Messiah was come to save the Gentiles as well as the Israelites.

> **Luke 22:29–30**
> **29** *"...and just as My Father has granted Me a Kingdom, I grant you*
> **30** *that you may eat and drink at My table in My Kingdom, and you will sit on thrones judging the twelve tribes of Israel."*

What a glorious Hope, to sit at the Lord's table and participate in communion with Jesus, the Disciples, Abraham, Isaac, Jacob, and, perhaps even more exciting to us, our loved ones, our friends and family who had a relationship with Him. All of this will take place in the Land promised to Abraham, Isaac, and Jacob. If you want to see your loved ones there, share your faith with them. Tell them that you want to see them sitting at this table and feast.

These verses help one to understand the hope that is involved with the Kingdom. If we dilute that hope by teaching that it is some metaphysical mystical concept in our hearts now, then where is the hope? If we teach the spiritualization of this, then how is our hope any different than any other religion that believes in a spiritual existence after death? We are looking for a real, physical resurrection for ourselves and our loved ones. This is another reason to be sure that your loved ones will be there.

I can't help but become excited when I read these verses, because we have the hope that we will one day be with Jesus and the Disciples, take communion, and sit at a table and eat with them and our loved ones. What a joy that will be!

1st Corinthians 11:23–26

23 *For I received from the Lord that which I also delivered to you, that the Lord Jesus in the night in which He was betrayed took bread;*

24 *and when He had given thanks, He broke it and said, "This is My body, which is for you;* <u>**do this in remembrance of Me.**</u>*"*

25 *In the same way He took the cup also after supper, saying,* <u>**"This cup is the new covenant in My blood; do this, as often as you drink it, in remembrance of Me.**</u>*"*

26 *For* as often as you eat this bread and drink the cup, you proclaim the Lord's death <u>**until He comes**</u>.

251

19

THE COMING OF THE
LORD JESUS CHRIST

The Kingdom of God begins with the return of Jesus Christ to Earth. Jesus announced it, the Apostle Paul proclaimed it, the Old Testament prophesized it, John revealed it, and all over and over again in plain easy-to-understand language. There are more prophesies in the Old Testament regarding the second coming of the Messiah than His first coming.

> The concept of the second coming originally derived from the OT teachings about a coming Messiah. Therein, the prophets foretold the Lord would send One from within the nation of Israel (Num. 24:17; Jer. 23:5–6) who would not only be God's anointed but would in fact be God Himself (Isa. 9:6; Mic. 5:2). As **various descriptions** of this Messiah developed, **two portraits emerged**. **One described Him as a mighty redeemer** who would destroy Israel's enemies, bring salvation, and restore peace (Jer. 33:15; Zech. 9:9–10) while **the other portrayed Him as a servant who would suffer and be rejected** (Isa. 53; Zech. 13:7). These contrasting descriptions of Messiah, however, would not be delineated into two separate comings until the NT.[128]

---

[128] (Berry, 2003)

The NT clearly distinguishes between two comings of Jesus Christ, the Messiah: the first in the incarnation and the second at the end of this present age. The earliest instructions of this second coming are recounted in the Gospels where **Christ Himself explicitly claimed He would come again**. For example, He urged people to be prepared because He would come unexpectedly, like a thief (Matt. 25:1–13; Mark 13:35–36; Luke 21:34–36). He also promised to return in order to claim His own and reward them (Matt. 25:31–46; John 14:1–3). Furthermore, **at His ascension angels declared that He would return to the earth in the same manner in which He left** (Acts 1:10–11).[129]

After the crucifixion, Jesus had arisen from the grave and for forty days had been telling the Apostles about the Kingdom. He told them they would soon receive the Holy Spirit and then go and share the Gospel worldwide.

He was then taken up into the sky.

Acts 1:9–11

9 *And after He had said these things, He was lifted up while they were looking on, and a cloud received Him out of their sight.*

10 *And as they were gazing intently into the sky while He was departing, behold two men in white clothing stood beside them;*

11 *and they also said, "Men of Galilee, why do you stand looking into the sky? This Jesus, who has been taken up from you into heaven, will* <u>come</u> *in just the same way as you have watched Him go into heaven."*

---

[129] (Berry, 2003)

Presumably, the two men in white clothing were messengers from God, and they said the Christ would return the same way he was taken up. His return is to be a real, physical, and visibly observable event, and he will come from the clouds.

Revelation 1:5–9

5 *To Him who loves us and **released us from our sins by His blood**—*

6 *and He has made us to be a kingdom, priests to His God and Father—to Him be the glory and the dominion forever and ever. Amen.*

7 ***Behold, He is coming with the clouds, and every eye will see Him**, even those who pierced Him; and all the tribes of the earth will mourn over Him. So it is to be. Amen.*

8 *"I am the Alpha and the Omega," says the Lord God, "who is and who was and who is to come, the Almighty."*

Matthew 24:27

For just as the lightning comes from the east, and flashes even to the west, so shall the <u>coming</u> of the Son of Man be.

Matthew 24:29–31

29 *But immediately after the tribulation of those days* THE SUN WILL BE DARKENED, AND THE MOON WILL NOT GIVE ITS LIGHT, AND THE STARS WILL FALL *from the sky, and the powers of the heavens will be shaken.*

30 *and then the sign of the Son of Man will appear in the sky, and then all the tribes of the earth will mourn, and **they will see the Son of Man coming on the clouds of the sky with power and great glory.***

31 *And He will send forth His angels with a great trumpet and they will gather together His elect from the four winds, from one end of the sky to the other.*

He is coming! When He comes, He will come in the glory of His Father and the Angels. What most Christians do not realize is that when He comes, He will come as a man, just the way He left—in a glorified body, but still a man. That is why the term "Son of Man" is used. Jesus was the son of a man, but also the Son of God. He is a true descendant of Abraham, Isaac, Jacob, and David.

Daniel 7:13–14
13 *"I kept looking in the night visions, and behold, with the clouds of heaven **one like a Son of Man was coming**, and He came up to the Ancient of Days and was presented before Him.*
14 *And to Him was given dominion, glory and a kingdom, that **all the peoples, nations and men of every language might serve Him**. His dominion is an everlasting dominion which will not pass away; and His kingdom is one which will not be destroyed.*

Matthew 16:27
*For the **Son of Man is going to come in the glory of His Father** with His angels, and will then repay every man according to his deeds.*

Mark 8:38
*For whoever is ashamed of Me and My words in this adulterous and sinful generation, the **Son of Man** will also be ashamed of him when He comes in the glory of His Father with the holy angels.*

THE SIGNS OF HIS COMING:

Now that we have seen what the Second Coming is, we should take a look at what the signs of His coming are. In **Matthew 24:3**, the

255

disciples asked Jesus, "What is the sign of Your coming and the end of the age?" Jesus said the Kingdom is not to be observed with signs.

Luke 17:22–24

22 *And He said to the disciples, "The days shall come when you will long to see one of the days of the Son of Man, and you will not see it.*

23 *And they will say to you, 'Look there! Look here!' Do not go away, and do not run after them.*

24 *For just as the lightning, when it flashes out of one part of the sky, shines to the other part of the sky, so will the Son of Man be in His day."*

Don't follow after false Christs, no matter what they claim; when He comes, there will be no question, just like the lightning.

Matthew 24:4–14

4 *And Jesus answered and said to them, "See to it that no one misleads you.*

5 *For many will come in My name, saying, 'I am the Christ,' and will mislead many.*

6 *And you will be hearing of wars and rumors of wars; see that you are not frightened, for those things must take place, but that is not yet the end.*

7 *For nation will rise against nation, and Kingdom against Kingdom, and in various places there will be famines and earthquakes.*

8 *But all these things are merely the beginning of birth pangs.*

9 *Then they will deliver you to tribulation, and will kill you, and you will be hated by all nations on account of My name.*

10 *And at that time many will fall away and will deliver up one another and hate one another.*

11 And many false prophets will arise, and will mislead many.

12 And because lawlessness is increased, most people's love will grow cold.

13 But the one who endures to the end, he shall be saved.

14 And this gospel of the Kingdom shall be preached in the whole world for a witness to all the nations, and then the end shall come."

Things that will happen, but that are not yet the end:

- Wars and rumors of war
- Nations against nations
- Famines and earthquakes
  - Global warming and perhaps the thousands of windmills erected lately have changed the weather patterns in the United States. It seems like every storm is the worst one in recorded history.
- These things are merely the beginning of birth pangs
  - Birth pangs or contractions start slowly at first, but when they get closer together, the big event is about to happen. The more rapid and severe they get, the closer we are to His coming.
- They will deliver you to tribulation
  - I would be thrilled if the Pre-Tribulation rapture happens, but it doesn't sound like it here. Why warn us and indicate that it is a sign if we aren't going to be here?
- They will kill you
- You will be hated by all nations
- Many will fall away
  Does that mean you do not have eternal security?
- They will deliver up one another and hate one another
  - It appears here that they are talking about people in a group. Perhaps churches?
- Many false prophets will arise

- People's love will grow cold
- This gospel of the Kingdom shall be preached in the whole world
  - If you want to advance His time for coming, preach the Kingdom.

Mark adds some details:

- They will deliver you to the courts
- You will be flogged in the synagogues
- You will stand before governors and kings

This is nothing that our Lord, or Paul, did not suffer. Are you prepared to go through this? Are you fanatic enough to carry it this far? If we go to church every Sunday and sing in the choir, God will still love us even if we deny Him—right? How serious are you about taking up your cross, leaving everything, and following Christ?

> Am I prepared to let God grip me by His power and do a work in me that is worthy of Himself? Sanctification is not my idea of what I want God to do for me; sanctification is God's idea of what He wants to do for me, and He has to get me into the attitude of mind and spirit where at any cost I will let Him sanctify me wholly.[130]

This is the kind of attitude we need for God to enable us to go through whatever trials we may have if we happen to be here during the tribulation. To live the life that Christ demands of us is humanly impossible; we have to die to self and let the Holy Spirit live in us.

Luke 9:57–62

57 *As they were going along the road, someone said to Him, "I will follow You wherever You go."*

---

[130] (Chambers, 1986)

58 *And Jesus said to him, "The foxes have holes and the birds of the air have nests, but the Son of Man has nowhere to lay His head."*

59 *And He said to another, "Follow Me." But he said, "Lord, permit me first to go and bury my father."*

60 *But He said to him, "Allow the dead to bury their own dead; but as for you, **go and proclaim everywhere the kingdom of God."***

61 *Another also said, "I will follow You, Lord; but first permit me to say good-bye to those at home."*

62 *But Jesus said to him, "No one, after putting his hand to the plow and looking back, is fit for the kingdom of God."*

Maybe it's true what Jesus said in **Matthew 22:14**: *"For many are called, but few are chosen."*

Get alone with Jesus and either tell Him that you do not want sin to die out in you; or else tell Him that at all costs you want to be identified with His death. Immediately you transact in confident faith in what Our Lord did on the Cross, a supernatural identification with His death takes place, and you will know with a knowledge that passeth knowledge that your 'old man' is crucified with Christ. The proof that your 'old man' has been crucified with Christ is in the **amazing ease with which the life of God in you enables you to obey** the voice of Jesus Christ.

Every now and again, Our Lord lets us see what we would be like if it were not for Himself; it is a justification of what He said—"Without Me ye can do nothing." That is why the bedrock of Christianity is personal, passionate devotion to the Lord Jesus. We mistake the ecstasy of our first introduction into the Kingdom for the purpose of God in getting us there; His purpose in getting us there is so we realize all that identification with Jesus Christ means.[131]

Mark 13:10–13

10 *"The gospel must first be preached to all the nations.*

11 *When they arrest you and hand you over, do not worry beforehand about what you are to say, but say whatever is given you in that hour; for it is not you who speak, but it is the Holy Spirit.*

12 *Brother will betray brother to death, and a father his child; and children will rise up against parents and have them put to death.*

13 *You will be hated by all because of My name, but the one who endures to the end, he will be saved."*

No matter which events you interpret as signs, or which events don't seem to happen, always be prepared.

BE READY FOR HIS COMING

Matthew 24:42–44

42 *"Therefore be on the alert, for you do not know which day your Lord is coming.*

43 *But be sure of this, that if the head of the house had known at what time of the night the thief was coming, he would have been on the alert and would not have allowed his house to be broken into.*

44 *For this reason you be ready too; for the Son of Man is coming at an hour when you do not think He will."*

---

[131] (Chambers, 1986)

Luke 17:34–35

34 *"I tell you, on that night there will be two men in one bed; one will be taken, and the other will be left.* **35** *There will be two women grinding at the same place; one will be taken, and the other will be left."*

1st Thessalonians 4:13–18

13 *"But we do not want you to be uninformed, brethren, about those who are asleep, so that you will not grieve as do the rest who have no hope.* **14** *For if we believe that Jesus died and rose again, even so God will bring with Him those who have fallen asleep in Jesus.* **15** *For this we say to you by the word of the Lord, that we who are alive and remain until the coming of the Lord, will not precede those who have fallen asleep.* **16** *For the Lord Himself will descend from heaven with a shout, with the voice of the archangel and with the trumpet of God, and the dead in Christ will rise first.* **17** *Then we who are alive and remain will be caught up together with them in the clouds to meet the Lord in the air, and so we shall always be with the Lord.* **18** *Therefore comfort one another with these words.*

We do not grieve as those who have no hope. These are words of tremendous comfort to someone who has lost a loved one. We are assured of a reunion with loved ones. Some will not even have to experience death, but will be caught up alive.

1st Thessalonians 5:1–8

1 *Now as to the times and the epochs, brethren, you have no need of anything to be written to you.* **2** *For you yourselves know full well that the day of the Lord will come just like a thief in the night.*

261

3 *While they are saying, "Peace and safety!" then destruction will come upon them suddenly like labor pains upon a woman with child, and they will not escape.*
4 *But you, brethren, are not in darkness, that the day would overtake you like a thief;*
5 *for you are all sons of light and sons of day. We are not of night nor of darkness;*
6 *so then let us not sleep as others do, but let us be alert and sober.*
7 *For those who sleep do their sleeping at night, and those who get drunk get drunk at night.*
8 *But since we are of the day, let us be sober, having put on the breastplate of faith and love, and as a helmet, the hope of salvation.*

You know that the coming of the Lord will be a surprise. A thief in the night doesn't tell you he's coming, and events can happen very fast once they start. All attempts to identify signs to this point have proved wrong, which doesn't stop the speculation. Such teaching and preaching tends to make the Word of God an object of curiosity, which it is not. Such teaching causes us to waste time which might better be spent on other things (Acts 1:11—"why stand ye gazing up?"). The hope of second coming (if it is more than speculation) should produce a response in the believer. It produces personal holiness.

1st John 3:3
And everyone who has this hope fixed on Him purifies himself, just as He is pure.

Jesus is coming again! That knowledge should affect our lives significantly. It should cause us to perfect holiness. It should give us a burden for souls—getting people to Jesus. If you are not working on personal holiness and bringing people to Jesus, your belief in the second coming is questionable.[132]

---

[132] (Wood C. R., 1994)

The above quote needs some explanation from my point of view. Wood may have not meant exactly as I am about to explain it, but I would suspect it is close. To perfect holiness, or working on personal holiness, is not a carnal or law based effort. No one is Holy except God. Nothing is Holy unless God is present, such as the Holy Bible (the living word). When Moses was walking in the desert and saw the burning bush, God said to him, "Take off your sandals as you are standing on Holy ground." The ground wasn't holy earlier when the sheep were grazing there, but now it was holy because God was there. The only way you can become holy is to let God be present in your life. Working on personal holiness is constantly dying to self and letting God take over your life. The joy that comes from this, and the blessed love for others that starts to permeate your soul, gives you the strongest, purest desire to share this joy with others.

> Christ's coming will be a dramatic rescue for believers who have survived the Tribulation. It will also, however, bring judgment for unbelievers who are still alive (see, e.g., Ps. 96:13). The Bible tells us that both surviving Gentiles (Mt. 25:31–46) and Israel (Ez. 20:35–38) will be judged at this time, and those who were martyred for their faith during the Tribulation will be raised to participate in the kingdom (Rev. 20:4). The Old Testament saints will also be raised at the second coming (Dan. 12:2; although this verse also says that the wicked will be raised as well, the wording of the Hebrew text suggests that this will occur at a later time—cf. Rev. 20:5).[133]

I will address this argument (regarding the resurrection of the wicked) in the chapter "Our Resurrection."

---

[133] (Hardman, 1996)

20

WHY I BELIEVE IN THE POST-TRIBULATION RAPTURE

I first heard about the concept of the "born again" Christians being "raptured" or taken up to heaven from Hal Lindsey at a Campus Crusade function in Lee Summit, Missouri around 1968. Hal was a great speaker, and all of us college students were enthralled by his teaching. Many students had placed the old fashioned reel to reel tape recorders around the stage and were recording his talk. Just as he said, "Everything in prophesy that needs to be fulfilled has taken place, and Jesus Christ could return at any moment!" one of the tape players started playing instead of recording. We all could hear a loud voice coming from the front of the stage. Hal lifted his hand with a shocked look on his face, as if Christ indeed had returned, and we all gasped, expecting to see Christ appear at that moment. It scared me to death. It certainly burned the idea of the return of Christ into my memory. I remained a firm believer in the Pre-Tribulation "rapture" until I studied the second coming of Christ.

The reason people cling to the idea of the rapture of the church is that it hopefully means that God's church will not have to go through the great tribulation prophesized by Christ.

By the Lord's own prophecy, found in Matthew 24, we learn that during the closing period, called the "end" (or "consummation") of the age, there shall be *"great tribulation, such as was not since the beginning of the world, no, nor ever shall be"*; and that *"immediately after the tribulation of those days ... shall appear the sign of the Son of man in heaven ... and they shall see the Son of man coming in the clouds of heaven with power and great glory"* (Matt. 24:21, 29, 30).[134]

The Great Tribulation. The Bible speaks of a time of great anguish or tribulation, which will come upon the earth, exceeding anything that has ever occurred before. Some, identifying this with the 70th week of Daniel 9:24-27, believe it will be of seven years duration. Some believe the church will be present to experience this, the Lord not returning until the end of the period. These are termed post-tribulationists. Others, known as pre-tribulationists, believe that the Lord's second coming will be in two stages, or phases—that, in addition to his public second coming, Christ will come for his church, to remove them from the world, or "rapture" them, before the great tribulation. Still others, known as mid-tribulationists, believe that the church will be present for the first half of the seven years but will be removed before the severe part of the tribulation begins.[135]

The tribulation is not brought about by God; it is Satan's people against God's people. Let's look at Matthew 24 again.

Matthew 24:9–13

9 *"Then **they will deliver you to tribulation, and will kill you**, and you will be hated by all nations because of My name.*

---

[134] (Mauro, 1918)
[135] (Elwell, 1988)

10 *At that time **many will fall away** and will betray one another and hate one another.*
11 *Many false prophets will arise and will mislead many.*
12 *Because lawlessness is increased, most people's love will grow cold.*
13 *But **the one who endures to the end, he will be saved.***"

The New Revised Standard Bible translates verse 9 above as: "*They will hand you over to be tortured and will put you to death.*" Exactly who it is that delivers us up is not clear, but the idea Christ is trying to convey here is that you may be turned in to some authority that will perhaps kill you.

Revelation 2:10

Do not fear what you are about to suffer. Behold, the devil is about to cast some of you into prison, so that you will be tested, and you will have tribulation for ten days. Be faithful until death, and I will give you the crown of life.

In Revelation 13, it says that the "beast" will make war against the saints.

Revelation 13:4–10

4 *...they worshiped the dragon because he gave his authority to the beast; and they worshiped the beast, saying, "Who is like the beast, and who is able to wage war with him?"*
5 *There was given to him a mouth speaking arrogant words and blasphemies, and authority to act for forty-two months was given to him.*
6 *And he opened his mouth in blasphemies against God, to blaspheme His name and His tabernacle, that is, those who dwell in heaven.*

> **7** *It was also given to him to **make war with the saints and to overcome them**, and authority over every tribe and people and tongue and nation was given to him.*
> **8** *All who dwell on the earth will worship him, everyone whose name has not been written from the foundation of the world in the book of life of the Lamb who has been slain.*
> **9** *If anyone has an ear, let him hear.*
> **10** *If anyone is destined for captivity, to captivity he goes; if anyone kills with the sword, with the sword he must be killed. **Here is the perseverance and the faith of the saints**.*

I understand this as saying, "Don't fight against them; if you want to persevere, let your actions be as one totally walking in the love of God. Trust in Him to deliver you, even unto death." We saw this example in Christ when they came and arrested Him in the Garden of Gethsemane. We also saw this example in all of the Martyrs of the early church who were burned alive at Nero's parties. Peter was crucified upside down, so as not to die the same way Christ had.

We have to possess a faith that is stronger than the fear of pain and death. May the Lord grant us the strength and the faith to overcome this if we indeed have to go through it. Know beforehand how you will react to this before it happens. It's better to be prepared and not have to go through it than to not be prepared if this happens.

Daniel 7:25

And he will speak out against the Most High and wear down the saints of the Highest One, and he will intend to make alterations in times and in law; and they will be given into his hand for a time, times, and half a time.

Most theologians interpret this as the Anti-Christ, and *time* as one period, *times* as two periods, and *a half time* as half a period. They assume that a period is a year, so the timing is three and a half years.

> The reference to a time, times, and half a time identifies this activity as taking place during the Great Tribulation (Dan. 7:25; 12:7; cf. Rev. 11:2; 12:6; 13:5). "Times" refers to years as is clear from the Hebrew of Daniel 11:13 that reads "at the end of times, even years." No one will be able to buy or sell during the Great Tribulation without the mark of the beast (13:17), so perhaps God's provisions will again be miraculous.[136]

Daniel 8:24–25

24 *His power will be mighty, but not by his own power, and he will destroy to an extraordinary degree and prosper and perform his will; He will destroy mighty men and the holy people.*
25 *And through his shrewdness He will cause deceit to succeed by his influence; and he will magnify himself in his heart, and he will destroy many while they are at ease. He will even oppose the Prince of princes, but he will be broken without human agency.*

> When the abomination of desolation appears, the Jews living in Jerusalem and Judea should flee immediately (cf. Luke 17:31; Rev. 12:14). His influence would extend far beyond Jerusalem. They must seek refuge in places where they can escape his persecution. They must not even take time to retrieve possessions from their houses as they flee. Pregnant women and nursing mothers will have a hard time because their physical conditions will limit their mobility. Weather would make flight harder in the winter, and observant Jews would seek to discourage travel on the Sabbath.

---

[136] (Constable, 2003)

...Jesus explained the reason for such hasty retreat. A tribulation much greater than any the world had ever seen or would ever see would be about to break on the Jews. This description fits the Old Testament pictures of the Great Tribulation, the last three and a half years of the Tribulation (Rev. 11:2; 13:5). It is not a fitting description of the destruction of Jerusalem in 70 A.D., as bad as that was. Certainly the Nazi Holocaust in which an estimated 6,000,000 Jews perished and the Russian pogroms in which perhaps 20,000,000 died were worse times than the destruction of Jerusalem. Yet the Great Tribulation will be the worst of all times for the Jews. The coming distress would be unprecedented in its suffering (cf. Dan. 12:1; Rev. 7:14).

In a century that has seen two world wars, now lives under the threat of extinction by nuclear holocaust, and has had more Christian martyrs than in all the previous nineteen centuries put together, Jesus' prediction does not seem farfetched. But the age will not run its course; it will be cut short.

...Unless God ends (Gr. *ekolobothesan*, "to terminate or cut off") the Tribulation, no living thing will remain alive.[137]

This does not mean that the period will be less than three-and-a-half years, but that it will be definitely terminated suddenly by the second coming of Christ.[138]

As you consider the verses below, you should have an idea of what people are referring to as the "Rapture."

1st Thessalonians 4:15–17

15 *For this we say to you by the word of the Lord, that we who are alive and remain **until the coming** of the Lord, will not precede those who have fallen asleep.*

---

[137] (Carson, 1984)

[138] (Constable, 2003)

16 *For the Lord Himself will descend from heaven with a shout, with the voice of the archangel and with the trumpet of God, and the dead in Christ will rise first.*
17 *Then we who are alive and remain <u>**will be caught up together with them in the clouds to meet the Lord in the air,**</u> and so we shall always be with the Lord.*

"The dead in Christ will rise first." Hal Lindsey said that is because they are six feet below us. I am sure he was joking, but I think it is a valid point. We will all be caught up together with them in the clouds.

1st Corinthians 15:51–52
51 *Behold, I tell you a mystery; we will not all sleep, but we will all be changed,*
52 *in a moment, in the twinkling of an eye, <u>**at the last trumpet; for the trumpet will sound, and the dead will be raised imperishable, and we will be changed**</u>.*

The word "rapture" comes from the Latin verb *rapere*, meaning to transport from one place to another or to be caught up. This word never occurs anywhere in the entire Bible. This word has become very popular in the last 100 years. If it is such an important doctrine, why isn't it found much before 1900? The teaching of the rapture as a pre-tribulation event has caused many to cling to it as their hope instead of the kingdom.

> Early in the twentieth century, some held the pretribulational rapture to be central to the faith. Great controversy followed, but eventually most Bible believers realized the issue was not worthy of such contention.[139]

I debated putting anything in this book about the "Rapture" because I agree this issue is not that important. I finally decided to add this

---

[139] (Cabal & Cabal T, 2007)

chapter because many evangelicals have never looked at the rapture in any other way except pre-tribulation.

I think it's important to consider that the rapture may happen after the tribulation, because if it does, I don't want you to be upset if you find yourself facing trials that you did not expect to endure. If I am wrong, I will be pleasantly surprised.

We have seen so many warnings about overcoming and enduring until the end. If tribulations arise and it is obvious the end times are near, could someone lose faith, give in, and accept the mark of the beast? If we at least consider the possibility, perhaps we can be better prepared mentally to trust the Holy Spirit to get us through any tribulations that arise.

Matthew 24:36–44

36 *"But of that day and hour **no one knows, not even the angels of heaven, nor the Son**, but the Father alone.*

37 *For the coming of the Son of Man will be just like the days of Noah.*

38 *For as in those days before the flood they were eating and drinking, marrying and giving in marriage, until the day that Noah entered the ark,*

39 *and they did not understand until the flood came and took them all away; **so will the coming of the Son of Man be**.*

40 *Then there will be two men in the field; one will be taken and one will be left.*

41 *Two women will be grinding at the mill; one will be taken and one will be left.*

42 *Therefore be on the alert, for you do not know which day your Lord is coming.*

43 *But be sure of this, that if the head of the house had known at what time of the night the thief was coming,*

he would have been on the alert and would not have allowed his house to be broken into.
44 *For this reason you also must be ready; for __the Son of Man is coming at an hour when you do not think He will__."*

When God used a flood to purge the earth, He did not zap the believers out of the world, but He gave them a way to get through it. He didn't wave a magic wand and present a pre-built ark to Noah, but Noah had to spend years building the ark. If we do have to go through tribulation—and many of us will in life, even if it is not "*the* Tribulation"—we need to be prepared and have decided in our mind how we will react. The answer is to completely rely on God, but in times of stress, that is not always our first reaction.

> Believers will most likely be here on earth during the tribulation, but under the loving care of God. Perhaps some will suffer during this time, but if so, it will come from the people on earth, not from God. Rabid persecution will more than likely be prevalent during this time. That trial about to come upon the whole habitable world is brought about by God to "try them that dwell upon the earth."
>
> The words **trial** and **test** come from the same Greek word, *peirazo*. The trial is also the test. This test, or trial, will be done to sift the wheat from the chaff, or the believers from the unbelievers.
>
> Jesus also taught about this time in the parable about the wheat and the tares. He said to let them grow together until the judgment came, and they would be separated. Nothing will prove the truth of a confession to God more than persecution. If people remain faithful through persecution, their faith is well grounded upon the knowledge of God's grace and truth.[140]

---

[140] (Kenison F., The Apocalypse of Revelations, 1996)

This may seem strange, but a study on the word "trumpet" led me to this conclusion. In the Old Testament, the trumpet was used to summon battle and to call people to worship.

Numbers 10:1–10

1 *The LORD spoke further to Moses, saying,*

2 *"Make yourself two trumpets of silver, of hammered work you shall make them; and **you shall use them for summoning the congregation** and for having the camps set out.*

3 *When both are blown, all the congregation shall gather themselves to you at the doorway of the tent of meeting.*

4 *Yet if only one is blown, then the leaders, the heads of the divisions of Israel, shall assemble before you.*

5 *But when you blow an alarm, the camps that are pitched on the east side shall set out.*

6 *When you blow an alarm the second time, the camps that are pitched on the south side shall set out; an alarm is to be blown for them to set out.*

7 *When convening the assembly, however, you shall blow without sounding an alarm.*

8 *The priestly sons of Aaron, moreover, shall blow the trumpets; and **this shall be for you a perpetual statute throughout your generations.***

9 *When you go to war in your land against the adversary who attacks you, then you shall sound an alarm with the trumpets, that you may be remembered before the LORD your God, and be saved from your enemies.*

10 *Also in the day of your gladness and in your appointed feasts, and on the first days of your months, you shall blow the trumpets over your burnt offerings, and over the sacrifices of your peace offerings; and*

*they shall be as a reminder of you before your God. I
am the LORD your God."*

Isaiah 27:12–13

12 *In that day the LORD will start His threshing from
the flowing stream of the Euphrates to the brook of
Egypt, and you will be gathered up one by one, O
sons of Israel.*

13 *It will come about also in that day that a great
trumpet will be blown, and those who were perishing
in the land of Assyria and who were scattered in the
land of Egypt will come and worship the LORD in the
holy mountain at Jerusalem.*

Matthew 24:29–31

29 *"But **immediately after the tribulation** of those
days THE SUN WILL BE DARKENED, AND THE MOON WILL NOT
GIVE ITS LIGHT, AND THE STARS WILL FALL from the sky, and
the powers of the heavens will be shaken.*

30 *And then the sign of the Son of Man will appear in
the sky, and then all the tribes of the earth will mourn,
and they will see the SON OF MAN COMING ON THE CLOUDS
OF THE SKY with power and great glory.*

31 *And **He will send forth His angels with A GREAT
TRUMPET and THEY WILL GATHER TOGETHER His elect
from the four winds, from one end of the sky to the
other**."*

Look again at the first words in verse 29 above. When does it say
when the Son of Man (Jesus) will gather His elect? Immediately **after**
the tribulation!

Now, let's take a good look at 1st Thessalonians 4:16, which says the
Lord will descend from heaven *"with the voice of the archangel, and
with the sound of the trumpet of God."* At the sound of the trumpet,

the rapture occurs. The elect are gathered when they see the Son of Man coming in the clouds in power and glory. The resurrection and the rapture occur at the last trumpet of God.

In **1st Corinthians 15:52**, it is written, "...***at the last trumpet***; *for the trumpet will sound, and the dead will be raised imperishable, and we will be changed.*" You will notice it says the **last** trumpet. How many trumpets will sound at the end of the age? According to Revelation, there will be seven trumpets, and the seventh out of seven is the last.

> ### Revelation 8:2
> *And I saw the seven angels who stand before God, and **seven trumpets were given to them**.*

> ### Revelation 8:6
> *And the seven angels who had the seven trumpets prepared themselves to sound them.*

> ### Revelation 10:7
> *...but in the days of the voice of the **seventh angel**, when he is about to sound, then the mystery of God is finished, as He preached to His servants the prophets.*

> ### Revelation 11:15
> *Then the **seventh angel sounded**; and there were loud voices in heaven, saying,*
> *"The kingdom of the world has become the kingdom of our Lord and of His Christ; and He will reign forever and ever."*

This was the seventh, and the last, trumpet! This is when the kingdom starts! This is when "*the dead will be raised imperishable, and we will be changed.*" This is when the rapture will occur. This is after the tribulation.

No place in the Bible says the Lord comes three times. If He came and raptured us up, and we met Him in the air, that would be a "coming" (*parousia* or παρουσία). Then, the end of the great tribulation would be a third coming. Why do we refer to it as the second coming?

1st Thessalonians 4:15

For	this	we	say	to	you	by	the	word	of	the	Lord	,	that		we	who
γὰρ	τοῦτο	→	λέγομεν	→	ὑμῖν	ἐν	→	λόγῳ	→	→	κυρίου		ὅτι		ἡμεῖς	οἱ
gar	touto		legomen		hymin	en		logō			kyriou		hoti		hēmeis	hoi

are	alive	and	•	remain	until	the	coming	of	the	Lord	,	will
→	ζῶντες	•	οἱ	περιλειπόμενοι	εἰς	τὴν	παρουσίαν		τοῦ	κυρίου		
	zōntes		hoi	perileipomenoi	eis	tēn	parousian		tou	kyriou		

not	precede		those	who	have	fallen	asleep	.
οὐ μὴ	φθάσωμεν		τοὺς	←	→	κοιμηθέντας	←	
ou mē	phthasōmen		tous			koimēthentas		

The above shows the English and Greek interlinear text and the direct English translation of the original Greek word for word. Note that the word used here for coming is παρουσία (*parousia*). Also please note the definite article "ὁ" (the) placed in front of the word *parousia*. This means that this verse is referring to "**THE** Coming."

> The word παρουσια [*parousia*] was the technical word "for the **arrival** or visit of the king or emperor" and can be traced from the Ptolemaic period into the second century A.D.[141]

> (παρουσίᾳ). Literally *presence*. So 2nd Cor. 10:10. Hence, **the presence of one *coming***, and so *coming*, especially in the New Testament, of the future, visible return of our Lord to raise the dead, judge the world, and finally establish the kingdom of God.[142]

---

[141] (Robertson A. T., 1933)
[142] (Vincent, 1887)

If "**The Coming**," or "**The Presence**," is when we are caught up in the air to meet the Lord, then it makes me think that this "rapture" does not occur until the Lord returns.

For the next reason why I believe the rapture follows the tribulation, we need to start with one of the parables of Jesus. He explains the meaning later, so bear with me. The parable is in regard to what He calls "tares and wheat."

Matthew 13:24–30

24 *Jesus presented another parable to them, saying, "The kingdom of heaven may be compared to a man who sowed good seed in his field.*
25 *But while his men were sleeping, his enemy came and sowed tares among the wheat, and went away.*
26 *But when the wheat sprouted and bore grain, then the tares became evident also.*
27 *The slaves of the landowner came and said to him, 'Sir, did you not sow good seed in your field? How then does it have tares?'*
28 *And he said to them, 'An enemy has done this!' The slaves said to him, 'Do you want us, then, to go and gather them up?'*
29 *But he said, 'No; for while you are gathering up the tares, you may uproot the wheat with them.*
30 *Allow both to grow together __until the harvest; and in the time of the harvest I will say to the reapers__, "First gather up the tares and bind them in bundles to burn them up; but gather the wheat into my barn."'"*

Tares are weeds that look very much like wheat, until the wheat is ripe. That is why the landowner said that he doesn't want to chance losing any wheat. We shouldn't try to tear out suspected tares now; we should wait for the harvest. It is apparent to me that this parable is making an analogy of putting the wheat in the barn as allowing the saints to enter into the Kingdom. At the same time, the tares are burned up.

Joel 3:12–17

12 *"...I will sit to judge all the surrounding nations.*
13 ***Put in the sickle, for the harvest is ripe***. *Come, tread, for the wine press is full; the vats overflow, for their wickedness is great.*
14 *Multitudes, multitudes in the valley of decision! For the day of the LORD is near in the valley of decision.*
15 *The sun and moon grow dark and the stars lose their brightness.*
16 *The LORD roars from Zion and utters His voice from Jerusalem, and the heavens and the earth tremble. But the LORD is a refuge for His people and a stronghold to the sons of Israel.*
17 *Then you will know that I am the LORD your God, dwelling in Zion, My holy mountain. So Jerusalem will be holy, and strangers will pass through it no more."*

Revelation 14:14–20

14 *Then I looked, and behold, a white cloud, and sitting on the cloud was **one like a son of man, having a golden crown on His head and a sharp sickle in His hand.***
15 *And another angel came out of the temple, crying out with a loud voice to Him who sat on the cloud, "Put in your sickle and reap, for the hour to reap has come, because the harvest of the earth is ripe."*
16 *Then He who sat on the cloud swung His sickle over the earth, and the earth was reaped.*

17 *And another angel came out of the temple which is in heaven, and he also had a sharp sickle.*

18 *Then another angel, the one who has power over fire, came out from the altar; and he called with a loud voice to him who had the sharp sickle, saying, "Put in your sharp sickle and gather the clusters from the vine of the earth, because her grapes are ripe."*

19 *So the angel swung his sickle to the earth and gathered the clusters from the vine of the earth, and threw them into the great wine press of the wrath of God.*

20 *And the wine press was trodden outside the city, and blood came out from the wine press, up to the horses' bridles, for a distance of two hundred miles."*

Verses 14 through 16 refer to the harvest of Christians, or the rapture. The Lord Jesus does the reaping. Verses 17 through 20 refer to the harvesting of the enemies of God by another angel. This all occurs in the same time frame.

Now six verses later, the disciples ask Jesus to what the parable of tares and wheat referred:

Matthew 13:36–43

36 *Then He left the crowds and went into the house. And His disciples came to Him and said, "Explain to us the parable of the tares of the field."*

37 *And He said, "__The one who sows the good seed is the Son of Man__,*

38 *and the field is the world; and as for __the good seed, these are the sons of the kingdom; and the tares are the sons of the evil one;__*

39 *and the enemy who sowed them is the devil, and __the harvest is the end of the age;__ and the reapers are angels.*

40 *So just as the tares are gathered up and burned with fire, so shall it be at the end of the age.*
41 *The Son of Man will send forth His angels, and they will gather out of His kingdom all stumbling blocks, and those who commit lawlessness,*
42 *and will throw them into the furnace of fire; in that place there will be weeping and gnashing of teeth.*
43 *Then* THE RIGHTEOUS WILL SHINE FORTH AS THE SUN *in the kingdom of their Father. He who has ears, let him hear."*

With all of the arguments presented here, I am convinced that the "rapture" is after the tribulation, or more specifically at the coming of Christ. We will meet Him in the air, but as the crowd went out of the gates of Jerusalem to greet and return with Christ on Palm Sunday, we will greet Christ and return with Him at the second coming.

However you choose to believe, at least consider the possibility of the post-tribulation rapture so you will be pleasantly surprised if the rapture occurs before the tribulation. At least you will have considered the possibility that you may have to endure persecution and tribulation, but know that the Lord can give you the strength to persevere.

Many saints throughout history have had to suffer tremendous torture and mistreatment due to their faith in Christ. May the Lord give us the strength and the faith to endure it, whether the "great tribulation" or just local persecution.

21

OUR RESURRECTION

According to First Kings 17:17–23, Elijah went to the town of Zarephath and met a widow who was starving and about to make a loaf of bread with the last of her supplies. Elijah told her that the Lord God of Israel would keep her bowl of flour and jar of oil full. That miracle kept her and her family alive until the famine was over. A little while later, her son became ill and died. Elijah prayed to God and the child was revived. This was the first time recorded in the Bible that someone was brought back from the dead.

2nd Kings 4:16–38 describes how Elijah's successor, Elisha, was used by God to restore the Shunnamite woman's son back to life. He had been dead for a while and his body was cold, but after Elisha lay on top of him, he sneezed seven times and opened his eyes. 2nd Kings 31 tells us that later, after Elisha had died and was buried, another man was about to be buried. When the group burying him spied a band of men coming, they threw his body into the sepulcher of Elisha. **When the dead man's body touched Elisha's bones**, he was brought back to life and stood up on his feet.

The New Testament Scriptures tell us of three different occurrences when Jesus brought people back to life after they had died. The widow of Nain' son **was already in the coffin**, and Jesus brought him back to life.

Luke 7:12–15

12 *Now as He approached the gate of the city, a dead man was being carried out, the only son of his mother, and she was a widow; and a sizeable crowd from the city was with her.*

13 *When the Lord saw her, He felt compassion for her, and said to her, "Do not weep."*

14 *And He came up and touched the coffin; and the bearers came to a halt. And He said, "Young man, I say to you, arise!"*

15 *The dead man sat up and began to speak. And Jesus gave him back to his mother.*

A synagogue official named Jairus was asking Jesus to come and heal his twelve-year-old daughter when news came that his daughter had died. Jesus brought her back to life as well.

Mark 5:38–42

38 *They came to the house of the synagogue official; and He saw a commotion, and people loudly weeping and wailing.*

39 *And entering in, He said to them, "Why make a commotion and weep? The child has not died, but is asleep."*

40 *They began laughing at Him. But putting them all out, He took along the child's father and mother and His own companions, and entered the room where the child was.*

41 *Taking the child by the hand, He said to her, "Talitha kum!" (which translated means, "Little girl, I say to you, get up!").*

42 *Immediately the girl got up and began to walk, for she was twelve years old. And immediately they were completely astounded.*

For some reason, the story of Lazarus, Mary and Martha's brother, is more popular than the ones above. He had been dead for four days, and his body was already starting to smell. I enjoy the way the KJV translates what Martha said: *"Lord, by this time he **stinketh**: for he hath been dead four days."*

John 11:38–44

38 *So Jesus, again being deeply moved within, came to the tomb. Now it was a cave, and a stone was lying against it.*

39 *Jesus said, "Remove the stone." Martha, the sister of the deceased, said to Him, "Lord, by this time there will be a stench, for he has been dead four days."*

40 *Jesus said to her, "Did I not say to you that if you believe, you will see the glory of God?"*

41 *So they removed the stone. Then Jesus raised His eyes, and said, "Father, I thank You that You have heard Me.*

42 *I knew that You always hear Me; but because of the people standing around I said it, so that they may believe that You sent Me."*

43 *When He had said these things, He cried out with a loud voice, "Lazarus, come forth."*

44 *The man who had died came forth, bound hand and foot with wrappings, and his face was wrapped around with a cloth. Jesus said to them, "Unbind him, and let him go."*

Though all of these people had been made alive after death, they still eventually died. Physical death is a certainty; however, one can also be spiritually dead. The Scriptures describe those who are spiritually dead while they are physically alive.

"Death" is more than a biological concept. Death speaks of the spiritual state of human beings as separated from

283

God, and morally warped. The spiritually dead lie under God's condemnation and have no way to win His favor. Only the gift of life through Jesus Christ can counteract the death which holds humankind in a firm grip. See John 5:16–26.[143]

John 5:24–29

24 *"Truly, truly, I say to you, he who hears My word, and believes Him who sent Me, has eternal life, and does not come into judgment, but has passed out of death into life.*

25 *Truly, truly, I say to you, an hour is coming and now is, when the dead will hear the voice of the Son of God, and those who hear will live.*

26 *For just as the Father has life in Himself, even so He gave to the Son also to have life in Himself;*

27 *and He gave Him authority to execute judgment, because He is the Son of Man.*

28 *Do not marvel at this; for an hour is coming, in which **all who are in the tombs** will hear His voice,*

29 *and will come forth; those who did the **good deeds to a resurrection of life,** those who committed the **evil deeds to a resurrection of judgment**."*

All of the dead will come forth: those who performed good deeds to a resurrection of life, and those who committed evil deeds to a resurrection of judgment. Paul said in **Acts 24:15** *"that there shall certainly be a resurrection of both the righteous and the wicked."* There is only one resurrection.

All will be resurrected, but those who are Christ's are resurrected to an immortal spiritual body (like Christ had after He was resurrected), and the others are resurrected to a corruptible body.

---

[143] (Richards L. &., 1987)

Daniel also saw the resurrection as one event, with two aspects: everlasting life, and disgrace or everlasting contempt.

Daniel 12:2
Many of those who sleep in the dust of the ground will awake, these to everlasting life, but the others to disgrace and everlasting contempt.

In **Acts 24:16**, Paul said, *"And herein do I exercise myself, to have always a conscience void of offence toward God, and toward men."*

Why did Paul add this thought? He not only taught one resurrection with two aspects, but he also based his obedience on this view of the resurrection. He wanted to be accounted worthy of obtaining the life to come.[144]

Luke 20:35
*"...but those who are considered worthy **to attain to that age** and the resurrection from the dead..."*

Jesus said that those who are worthy to attain to that age. The Greek word that is translated "to attain to" is τυχεῖν *(tuchein)*, which means *to obtain, to receive, to attain, to experience,* or *to hit the mark.*

The target is the Kingdom. Jesus is saying **you must be on target to get into the Kingdom**.

Later in this book, I will address this topic in more detail; however, I want to make this clear. It may take you a while to understand this concept, but many Christians think that since Christ died for their sins, they will automatically get into the Kingdom. Not true. Sin has been dealt with, and no one will ever be judged again for sins! Entrance into the Kingdom is based only on a relationship with Jesus, which can only come from believing in what Christ did for you at the Cross.

---

[144] (Kenison F., 1999)

Matthew 7:20–23

20 *"So then, you will **know them by their fruits**.*

21 *Not everyone who says to Me, 'Lord, Lord,' will enter the kingdom of heaven, but he who does the will of My Father who is in heaven will enter.*

22 *Many will say to Me on that day, 'Lord, Lord, did we not prophesy in Your name, and in Your name cast out demons, and in Your name perform many miracles?'*

23 *And then I will declare to them, '**I never knew you; DEPART FROM ME, YOU WHO PRACTICE LAWLESSNESS**.'"*

How does one know that they will enter the Kingdom? Even Paul was not certain, but it was his hope.

> The resurrection is with Paul not simply an objective event, a destiny to be looked for, a new condition to be anticipated, but an *attainment*, an object of aspiration and strenuous moral endeavour, to be reached only by suffering loss, by being found in Christ, by knowing Him in the power which He has over us and in us in virtue of His resurrection, by partnership with Him in suffering, by becoming conformed unto His death and dying as He died unto sin.[145]

Philippians 3:8–14

8 *I count all things to be loss in view of the surpassing value of knowing Christ Jesus my Lord, for whom I have suffered the loss of all things, and count them but rubbish so that I may gain Christ,*

9 *and be found in him, not having a righteousness of mine own, even that which is of the law, but that which is through faith in Christ, the righteousness which is from God by faith:*

---

[145] (Salmond, 1897)

10 *that I may know him, and the power of his resurrection, and the fellowship of his sufferings, becoming conformed unto his death;*
11 *if by any means I may attain unto the resurrection from the dead.*
12 *Not that I have already obtained, or am already made perfect: but I press on,* if so be that I may lay hold on that for which also I was laid hold on by Christ Jesus.
13 Brethren, I count not myself yet to have laid hold: *but one thing I do, forgetting the things which are behind, and stretching forward to the things which are before,*
14 *I press on toward the goal unto the prize of the high calling of God in Christ Jesus.*

Revelations 20:4–6

4 *Then I saw thrones, and they sat on them, and judgment was given to them. And I saw the souls of those who had been beheaded because of their testimony of Jesus and because of the word of God, and those who had not worshiped the beast or his image, and had not received the mark on their forehead and on their hand; and they came to life and reigned with Christ for a thousand years.*
5 *The rest of the dead did not come to life until the thousand years were completed. This is the first resurrection.*
6 *Blessed and holy is the one who has a part in the first resurrection; over these the second death has no power, but they will be priests of God and of Christ and will reign with Him for a thousand years.*

Verse 5 says that the rest of the dead did not come to life until the thousand years were completed. This is the first resurrection.

It reads as if the first resurrection comes after the thousand years. Here is a good example of why studying with help from the original Koine Greek can be beneficial. In Greek, the first Resurrection is ἡ ἀνάστασις ἡ πρώτη (anastasis prōtē), or "the resurrection the primary." The definite article is used with both words, expressing an emphasis as the main resurrection.

> Prote (or πρώτη from the root word πρῶτος) - means "the first," developed along three lines: **a**. spatially "the front"; this meaning became less common later; **b**. the first in time and number, **c**. the first in rank and value, "the most eminent, important."[146]

If the first resurrection came after the thousand years, how did the people in verse 4 come to life? Verse 6 says that those who have a part in the first resurrection are blessed and holy. Yet, many interpret this verse extremely out of context, reading that the people resurrected after the thousand years are the wicked and evil people.

Going back to verse 5, the word that is translated as "come to life" is οὐκ ἔζησαν (*ouk anezesan*). *Ouk is "not." Anezesan* is a compound word formed from *ana* ("again") and *zoe* (spiritual life). This is saying that the rest of the dead "lived not again" until the thousand years were completed. The statement "this is the first resurrection" is referring to verse 4, the primary resurrection. Then, verse 6 confirms this by saying that the people in the primary resurrection reigned for 1,000 years.

All are resurrected at the return of Christ, but some are resurrected to spiritual bodies and others are resurrected to bodies as they have now.

> Observe here,

> [1.] That there shall be a resurrection of the dead, the dead bodies of men, of all men from the beginning to the end

---

[146] (Kittel G. B., 1964)

of time. It is certain, not only that the soul does not die with the body, but that the body itself shall live again; we have not only another life to live when our present life is at an end, but there is to be another world, which shall commence when this world is at an end, into which all the children of men must enter at once by a resurrection from the dead, as they entered into this, one after another, by their birth.

[2.] It shall be a resurrection *both of the just and of the unjust,* the sanctified and the unsanctified, of those that did well, and to them our Saviour has told us that it will be a *resurrection of life;* and of those that did evil, and to them that it will be a resurrection of condemnation, Jn. 5:29. See Dan. 12:2. This implies that it will be a resurrection to a final judgment, by which all the children of men will be determined to everlasting happiness or misery in a world of retribution, according to what they were and what they did in this state of probation and preparation. The just shall rise by virtue of their union with Christ as their head; the unjust shall rise by virtue of Christ's dominion over them as their Judge.

[3.] God is to be depended upon for the resurrection of the dead: I have *hope towards God,* and in God, that there shall be a resurrection; it shall be effected by the almighty power of God, in performance of the word which God hath spoken; so that those who doubt of it betray their ignorance both of the scriptures and of the power of God, Mt. 22:29.

[4.] The resurrection of the dead is a fundamental article of our creed, as it was also of that of the Jewish church. It is what *they themselves also allow;* nay, it was the expectation of the ancient patriarchs, witness Job's confession of his faith; but it is more clearly revealed and more fully confirmed by the gospel, and therefore those who believed it should have been thankful to the preachers of the gospel for their explications and proofs of it, instead of opposing them.

[5.] In all our religion we ought to have an eye to the other world, and to serve God in all instances with a confidence in him *that there will be a resurrection of the dead*, doing all in preparation for that, and expecting our recompense in that.[147]

Matthew 22:23–32

23 *On that day some Sadducees (who say there is no resurrection) came to Jesus and questioned Him,*

24 *asking, "Teacher, Moses said, 'If a man dies having no children, his brother as next of kin shall marry his wife, and raise up children for his brother.'*

25 *Now there were seven brothers with us; and the first married and died, and having no children left his wife to his brother;*

26 *so also the second, and the third, down to the seventh.*

27 *Last of all, the woman died.*

28 *In the resurrection, therefore, whose wife of the seven will she be? For they all had married her."*

29 *But Jesus answered and said to them, "You are mistaken, not understanding the Scriptures nor the power of God.*

30 *For in the resurrection they neither marry nor are given in marriage, but are like angels in heaven.*

31 *But regarding the resurrection of the dead, have you not read what was spoken to you by God:*

32 *'I AM THE GOD OF ABRAHAM, AND THE GOD OF ISAAC, AND THE GOD OF JACOB'?* ***He is not the God of the dead but of the living.***"

---

[147] (Henry, 1996, c 1991)

Hebrews 11:35–40

35 *Women received back their dead by resurrection; and others were tortured, not accepting their release, so that they might obtain **a better resurrection**;*

36 *and others experienced mockings and scourgings, yes, also chains and imprisonment.*

37 *They were stoned, they were sawn in two, they were tempted, they were put to death with the sword; they went about in sheepskins, in goatskins, being destitute, afflicted, ill-treated*

38 *(men of whom the world was not worthy), wandering in deserts and mountains and caves and holes in the ground.*

39 *And all these, having gained approval through their faith, did not receive what was promised,*

40 *because God had provided something better for us, so that apart from us they would not be made perfect.*

John 5:24–29

24 *"Truly, truly, I say to you, he who hears My word, and believes Him who sent Me, has eternal life, and does not come into judgment, but has passed out of death into life.*

25 *Truly, truly, I say to you, an hour is coming and now is, when the dead will hear the voice of the Son of God, and those who hear will live.*

26 *For just as the Father has life in Himself, even so He gave to the Son also to have life in Himself;*

27 *and He gave Him authority to execute judgment, because He is the Son of Man.*

28 *Do not marvel at this; for an hour is coming, in which all who are in the tombs will hear His voice,*

29 *and will come forth; those who did the good deeds to a resurrection of life, those who committed the evil deeds to a resurrection of judgment."*

John 11:21–27

21 *Martha then said to Jesus, "Lord, if You had been here, my brother would not have died.*

22 *Even now I know that whatever You ask of God, God will give You."*

23 *Jesus said to her, "Your brother will rise again."*

24 *Martha said to Him, "<u>__I know that he will rise__</u> <u>__again in the resurrection on the last day.__</u>"*

25 *Jesus said to her, "I am the resurrection and the life; he who believes in Me will live even if he dies,*

26 *and everyone who lives and believes in Me will never die. Do you believe this?"*

27 *She said to Him, "Yes, Lord; I have believed that You are the Christ, the Son of God, even He who comes into the world."*

22

OUTER DARKNESS

First, the term "outer darkness" does not mean hell and is not eternal; it only lasts 1,000 years. Some pastors, for whom I have the utmost respect, teach that the outer darkness is just for "unfaithful Christians." I understand where they get that concept, but I am not inclined to agree with them. I believe that "outer darkness" occurs at the same time the 1,000 year Kingdom occurs, and that it is the abode of the resurrected "dead ones" that were resurrected into bodies of corruption (like those we have now). Those in the Kingdom will "rule and reign" over those in Outer Darkness.

Matthew is the only book that uses the exact phrase "outer darkness." He uses the words *skotos* and *exoteros*. *Skotos* is defined as darkness, the opposite of light. *Exoteros* means outer, furthest out, or outside.

> The whole phrase is "τὸ σκότος τὸ ἐξώτερον: (an idiom, literally 'the outer darkness') a place or region which is both dark and removed (presumably from the abode of the righteous) and serving as the abode of evil spirits and devils—'outer darkness, darkness outside.' ἐκβληθήσονται εἰς τὸ σκότος τὸ ἐξώτερον 'they will be thrown into outer darkness' Mt 8:12. In a number of languages this

expression in Mt 8:12 must be rendered as 'they will be thrown outside where it is dark.'"[148]

In the original Greek, the definite article is used for both *skotos* and *exoteros*. The Greek language does not have an indefinite article as English does. We use "the" as a definite article and "an" as an indefinite article. In the Greek, if they use the article τò, it designates a specific topic. This requires that the English translation say **the** outer darkness.

> The article is never meaningless in Greek, though it often fails to correspond with the English idiom...Its free use leads to exactness and finesse.[149]

> In the least, we cannot treat it lightly, for its presence or absence is the crucial element to unlocking the meaning of scores of passages in the NT.

> In short, there is no more important aspect of Greek grammar than the article to help shape our understanding of the thought and theology of the NT writers.[150]

This is a specific place or position, not just outside in the dark.

If some are to rule and reign, then there must be subjects under this reign. The Kingdom will be based in the Promised Land of Israel, but the rest of the world will be populated. During the millennium, there will be a place that Matthew calls the outer darkness. Anyone in the outer darkness will be weeping and gnashing their teeth. Let's look at some of the things that Jesus said in regard to this outer darkness which occurs at the same time as His reign.

---

[148] (Louw, 1996)

[149] (Robertson)

[150] (Wallace, 1999)

Matthew 8:11–12

11 *"I say to you that many will come from east and west, and recline at the table with Abraham, Isaac and Jacob in the kingdom of heaven;*

12 *but the sons of the kingdom will be cast out into __the outer darkness; in that place there will be weeping and gnashing of teeth.__"*

Matthew 22:2–3

2 *"The kingdom of heaven may be compared to a king who gave a wedding feast for his son.*

3 *"And he sent out his slaves to call those who had been invited to the wedding feast, and they were unwilling to come."*

Although this is a parable, it can be understood that the Jews are the ones who had been invited but did not want to come. They had the right to come as children of Israel, but they rejected the bridegroom. The sons of the Kingdom are the Jews who did not accept Jesus as the Messiah.

Matthew 22:4–14

4 *"Again he sent out other slaves saying, 'Tell those who have been invited, "Behold, I have prepared my dinner; my oxen and my fattened livestock are all butchered and everything is ready; come to the wedding feast."'*

5 *But they paid no attention and went their way, one to his own farm, another to his business,*

6 *and the rest seized his slaves and mistreated them and killed them.*

7 *But the king was enraged, and he sent his armies and destroyed those murderers and set their city on fire.*

8 Then he said to his slaves, 'The wedding is ready, but those who were invited were not worthy.

9 Go therefore to the main highways, and as many as you find there, invite to the wedding feast.'

10 Those slaves went out into the streets and gathered together all they found, both evil and good; and the wedding hall was filled with dinner guests.

11 But when the king came in to look over the dinner guests, he saw a man there who was not dressed in wedding clothes,

12 and he said to him, 'Friend, how did you come in here without wedding clothes?' And the man was speechless.

*13 Then the king said to the servants, '**Bind him hand and foot, and throw him into the outer darkness; in that place there will be weeping and gnashing of teeth**.'*

14 For many are called, but few are chosen."

Those clothed with the wedding clothes will be left in the Kingdom; the ones without wedding clothes will be thrown into the outer darkness. Note that even though they invited both the "evil and good," it does not say the man was thrown out because he was evil. Therefore, the wedding clothes must be a key. The wedding clothes are synonymous with the white robes found in Revelation 7:13–14.

Revelation 7:9–14

*9 After these things I looked, and behold, a great multitude which no one could count, from every nation and all tribes and peoples and tongues, standing before the throne and before the Lamb, **clothed in white robes**, and palm branches were in their hands;*

10 and they cry out with a loud voice, saying, "Salvation to our God who sits on the throne, and to the Lamb."

11 And all the angels were standing around the throne and around the elders and the four living creatures; and they fell on their faces before the throne and worshiped God,

12 saying, "Amen, blessing and glory and wisdom and thanksgiving and honor and power and might, be to our God forever and ever. Amen."

13 Then one of the elders answered, saying to me, **_"These who are clothed in the white robes, who are they, and where have they come from?"_**

14 I said to him, "My lord, you know." And he said to me, **_"These are the ones who come out of the great tribulation, and they have washed their robes and made them white in the blood of the Lamb."_**

The parable in Matthew 22 is a story and not a literal description, but the wedding clothes are related to being clothed in righteousness, washed in the blood of the lamb. Those who have not put on the righteousness of Christ will be cast into outer darkness.

Matthew 25:30–34

30 "Throw out the worthless slave into **_the outer darkness; in that place there will be weeping and gnashing of teeth_**.

31 But when the Son of Man comes in His glory, and all the angels with Him, then He will sit on His glorious throne.

32 All the nations will be gathered before Him; and He will separate them from one another, as the shepherd separates the sheep from the goats;

33 and He will put the sheep on His right, and the goats on the left.

34 Then the King will say to those on His right, 'Come, you who are blessed of My Father, inherit the kingdom prepared for you from the foundation of the world.'"

When those who see the Kingdom and how wonderful it is realize that they are not going to take part in it, but could have, they will weep and gnash their teeth. Imagine being invited to a great celebration and the guests include many of your friends and celebrities; it is the party of the year. You received an invitation, but you are asked to please RSVP so they can order enough food. You meant to RSVP, but got sidetracked and just didn't get to it. The night of the party, you put on your best clothes, and go to the hall but they won't let you in. You are outside in the dark. You can smell the wonderful food, hear the live band, and hear all of your friends laughing and having a great time. You really wish you could be there. Now picture that feeling magnified to the point that you start weeping when you realize that you will be out there in the dark, for perhaps a thousand years.

Matthew 24:48–51

"If that evil slave says in his heart, 'My Master is not coming for a long time, 'and shall begin to beat his fellow slaves and eat and drink with drunkards, the master of that slave will come on a day when he does not expect him and cut him to pieces and assign him a place with the hypocrites; weeping shall be there and gnashing of teeth."

The above knew him as Master, yet made a deliberate decision to go against Him.

> Theologians of Arminian and semi-Arminian tendencies have extended the time of probation beyond the grave, and taught that those who have never heard of Christ in this life will be given an opportunity of repentance and faith in the life to come.[151]

Jesus wants all to be saved, and this is the second chance. I firmly believe that everyone will enter into the Kingdom, some in glorified

---

[151] (Brown, 1919)

bodies and some in bodies of corruption. Those in Outer Darkness may or may not be there for the entire 1,000 years.

BALAAM

Balaam was not an Israelite, but he had a reputation as a bona fide prophet whose curses always came true. Apparently, he had a relationship with the God of Israel. Archeologists have discovered some ancient writings from around 700 BC that refer to Balaam as a "seer of the gods."

The Israelites were almost finished with their 40-year trek in the wilderness and had just defeated the armies of the Amorites and the King of Bashan (Numbers 21 and 22). Moses then led his people to camp in the plains of Moab near Jericho. Balak, King of Moab, was aware of how the Israelites had destroyed the other armies, and he was afraid that they would defeat him as well. He knew of Balaam's reputation as a prophet and sent for him to come and curse Israel. Balak believed that if Balaam were to curse Israel, he would be able to defeat them in battle.

Numbers 22:5–6

5 *So he sent messengers to Balaam the son of Beor, at Pethor, which is near the River, in the land of the sons of his people, to call him, saying, "Behold, a people came out of Egypt; behold, they cover the surface of the land, and they are living opposite me.*
6 *Now, therefore, please come, curse this people for me since they are too mighty for me; perhaps I may be able to defeat them and drive them out of the land.*

For I know that he whom you bless is blessed, and he whom you curse is cursed."

Balaam, however, was warned by the Lord that he should not go to Moab. The king of Moab would not accept Balaam's refusal and sent his royal messengers back with offers of greater wealth and honor. Balaam revealed an inner lust for wealth and position by returning to the Lord to ask whether he should go. His words to the messengers, however, were very pious: *"Though Balak were to give me his house full of silver and gold, I could not go beyond the command of the Lord my God, to do less or more"* (Nm. 22:18). Although Balaam would do only what the Lord allowed, he became a prime example of someone who does the right thing for the wrong reason.[152]

God told Balaam to go to Balak, but to only say the words that God would put into his mouth. As Balaam was riding his donkey to get to Balaam's camp, the Lord (still angry) sent an angel to block his path. The donkey saw the angel with a sword and veered away so as not to get struck dead by the angel. The donkey tried three times to keep Balaam from getting killed by the angel, and the last time he lay down on the ground while Balaam was still sitting on top of him. Each time the donkey turned aside, Balaam struck him with a stick. The last time, the donkey actually spoke to Balaam asking him why he was hitting him. The Lord then allowed Balaam to see the angel with the sword, who told him that he was about to kill him, but the donkey had saved his life. Balaam then said, "If you don't want me to go, I will turn around."

One would think at this point that Balaam would have gotten the hint. First, God told him *no*, and then said go ahead and go, but then threatened to kill him—and he *still* wants to go. He really wanted that money. So, God again tells him to go ahead and go, but to only

---

[152] (Elwell, 1988)

say what He tells him to say. This reminds me of times when I wanted to go fishing and my wife didn't want me to go, but she (out of frustration and rather irritated) would tell me, "Go ahead and go."

When Balaam finally spoke to reveal what God told him to say, he blessed Israel three times. This really irritated Balak, but Balaam basically said, "I warned you that I could only say what God would tell me to say." Balaam must have then counseled Balak and the Midianites on what to do to hurt the Israelites. By luring them into sin with harlots and enticing them to eat food that was sacrificed to idols, God might turn His back on the Israelites.

Numbers 25:1–3

1 *While Israel remained at Shittim, the people began to play the harlot with the daughters of Moab.*

2 *For they invited the people to the sacrifices of their gods, and the people ate and bowed down to their gods.*

3 *So Israel joined themselves to Baal of Peor, and the LORD was angry against Israel.*

Numbers 31:16

Behold, these caused the sons of Israel, __*through the counsel of Balaam*__*, to trespass against the LORD in the matter of Peor, so the plague was among the congregation of the LORD.*

Deuteronomy 23:3–5

3 *No Ammonite or Moabite shall enter the assembly of the Lord; none of their descendants, even to the tenth generation, shall ever enter the assembly of the Lord,*

4 *because they did not meet you with food and water on the way when you came out of Egypt, and because they hired against you Balaam the son of Beor from Pethor of Mesopotamia, to curse you.*

5 *Nevertheless, the Lord your God was not willing to listen to Balaam, but the Lord your God turned the curse into a blessing for you because the Lord your God loves you.*

John was told in Revelation 2:12 to write to the angel of the church in Pergamum.

Revelation 2:14
But I have a few things against you, because <u>**you have there some who hold the teaching of Balaam, who kept teaching Balak to put a stumbling block before the sons of Israel, to eat things sacrificed to idols and to commit acts of immorality**</u>.

The church has often tolerated those who hold to false doctrines. In this instance, verse 2:14, it was the teaching of Balaam. God says here that the church should not tolerate those who *kratountas*, meaning **hold with great strength** to false doctrines. The teachings of Balaam were those of the earth goddess religion. Sex was not limited to marriage, but practiced with temple prostitutes. **Fornication** comes from *porneuo*, which means to prostitute your body to the lust of another. They also ate food sacrificed to idols. II Peter 2:9–22 describes several other characteristics of Balaam's followers: they pursued the **lust of the flesh**; they were **daring, self-willed,** and **spoke evil** of glories; they **loved the rewards of unrighteousness** and spoke great swelling **words of vanity**; they lured others with the **desires of the flesh** and promised them **freedom,** even though they themselves were in bondage to corruption.[153]

Therefore the teachers are just like Cain (the embodiment of violence, lust, greed, and rebellion against God in Jewish tradition), Balaam (who tried to make money by

---

[153] (Kenison F., The Apocalypse of Revelations, 1996)

leading people into sin, Nm. 31:16; Dt. 23:4), and Korah (who rebelled against God's authority in Moses, Nm. 16). They are also dangerous to the believers, for they are turning the meal which was part of the Eucharist into an orgy (cf 1st Cor. 11:20–22), and could corrupt the practice of the rest of the church. They care only for themselves and are devoid of real spiritual gifts from God (like waterless clouds or the dead trees of winter, Lk. 13:6–9), being ready for the second death (their fate is so sure that it is seen as having already happened).[154]

You may wonder why I am writing about Balaam in a book on the Kingdom of God, in the chapter on Outer Darkness. It is because Balaam and the false prophets who were enticing the church to stray into carnal sin will be in the Outer Darkness for the full 1,000 years.

2nd Peter 2:15–17

15 *...forsaking the right way, they have gone astray, having followed the way of Balaam, the son of Beor, who loved the wages of unrighteousness;*
16 *but he received a rebuke for his own transgression, for a mute donkey, speaking with a voice of a man, restrained the madness of the prophet.*
17 *These are springs without water and mists driven by a storm, **for whom the black darkness has been reserved**.*

Jude 11–13

11 *Woe to them! For they have gone the way of Cain, and for pay they have rushed headlong into the error of Balaam, and perished in the rebellion of Korah.*
12 *These are the men who are hidden reefs in your love feasts when they feast with you without fear, caring for themselves; clouds without water, carried*

---

[154] (Elwell, 1988)

along by winds; autumn trees without fruit, doubly dead, uprooted;
13 *wild waves of the sea, casting up their own shame like foam; wandering stars,* <u>**for whom the black darkness has been reserved forever.**</u>

Forever does not carry the same emphasis on length of time in Greek or Hebrew as in English. A better translation is usually until the end of the age. It means for a long time or until the end of that age, but not eternity. A longer time would be indicated by repeating the phrase, i.e. forever and forever.

23

THE JUDGMENT SEAT OF CHRIST

So many look at heaven as our final reward and where we will spend eternity, but they don't stop to think about what the scriptures say about judgment. I cannot find any place in the Bible that describes a judgment regarding entrance into heaven. The notion of St. Peter standing at the pearly gates of Heaven determining who enters and who does not is not Biblical. It does, however, set the stage for a lot of jokes. Most people envision that as soon as they die, they will go to judgment. This is not at all Scriptural.

The first judgment was against sin. Our sin is why Christ was crucified. The verdict for this judgment was death, and Christ paid the penalty. Since none of us were alive at that time, that payment had to cover all future sins. It is not our believing that brings forgiveness of sins that happened 2,000 years ago. The next judgment can no longer be in regard to sin, but it will be to determine if we believed that Christ paid the price for our sins. When someone says "Do you believe in Christ?" they are not asking if you believe He existed or was born on Christmas day, but if you believe that He was crucified on the Cross for your sins and was resurrected for your justification.

Romans 4:25
He who was delivered over because of our transgressions, and was raised because of our justification.

Christ is the shepherd, true believers are the sheep, and His sheep know His voice.

John 10:26–29

26 *"But you do not believe because you are not of My sheep.*

27 *My sheep hear My voice, and I know them, and they follow Me;*

28 *and I give eternal life to them, and they will never perish; and no one will snatch them out of My hand.*

29 *My Father, who has given them to Me, is greater than all; and no one is able to snatch them out of the Father's hand."*

Matthew 25:31–32

31 *"But when the Son of Man comes in His glory, and all the angels with Him, then He will sit on His glorious throne.*

32 *All the nations will be gathered before Him; and He will separate them from one another, as the shepherd separates the sheep from the goats..."*

When Christ returns to the earth to set up His Kingdom, He will determine who will enter into spiritual life *(a resurrection of life)* or remain spiritually dead. This is the separation of the sheep from the goats, the righteous from the unrighteous. Many people do not realize that Christ will judge us. They still perceive God as a judge with a big hammer ready to smash us because we are sinful. Even though these people have been forgiven, they do not believe in the atonement through Christ, and, therefore, do not receive the righteousness of Christ.

John 5:21–29

21 *"For just as the Father raises the dead and gives them life, even so the Son also gives life to whom He wishes.*

22 *For not even the Father judges anyone, but **He has given all judgment to the Son**,*

23 *so that all will honor the Son even as they honor the Father. He who does not honor the Son does not honor the Father who sent Him.*

24 *Truly, truly, I say to you, he who hears My word, and believes Him who sent Me, has eternal life, and does not come into judgment, but has passed out of death into life.*

25 *Truly, truly, I say to you, an hour is coming and now is, when the dead will hear the voice of the Son of God, and those who hear will live.*

26 *For just as the Father has life in Himself, even so He gave to the Son also to have life in Himself;*

27 *and He gave Him authority to execute judgment, because He is the Son of Man.*

28 *Do not marvel at this; for an hour is coming, in which all who are in the tombs will hear His voice,*

29 *and will come forth; those who did the good deeds to a resurrection of life, those who committed the evil deeds to a resurrection of judgment."*

2nd Corinthians 5:10

For we must all appear before the judgment seat of Christ, so that each one may be recompensed for his deeds in the body, according to what he has done, whether good or bad.

The judgment seat of the Christ (τοῦ βήματος τοῦ Χριστοῦ or *tou bēmatos tou Christou*) is referred to as the Bema seat from the Greek word *bēmatos*. The Faithlife Study Bible says:

Bēmatos is where a ruler would make civic decisions including criminal proceedings.[155]

---

[155] (Barry, 2012)

All will appear before Him; this is sometimes referred to as the judgment of the Lamb.

Acts 17:31

He has fixed a day in which He will judge the world in righteousness through a Man whom He has appointed, having furnished proof to all men by raising Him from the dead.

Acts 10:42

He has ordered us to preach to the people and solemnly to testify that this is the One who has been appointed by God to judge all of the living and the dead.

2nd Timothy 4:1

"I solemnly charge you in the presence of God and of Christ Jesus, who is to judge the living and the dead, and by His appearing and His kingdom..."

Soon—perhaps sooner than we think—we shall stand before the Bema, the judgment seat of Christ, to give an account of what we have done in the body, whether good or bad. What is our Lord going to say to us? Will it be "Well done, good and faithful servant" or "Shame on you, slothful servant!" A lot depends on our motivation for the ministry. God give every preacher the grace to be activated by the same hope, fear, and love that enabled the apostle to exclaim: "I am compelled to preach!" (1st Cor. 9:16).[156]

A great philosopher said, "I have spent my life laboriously doing nothing." A great emperor said, "I have tried everything and nothing is of any profit." Goethe, the great German poet, said, "My life has been a continual rolling of a stone uphill, which has continually rolled back."[157]

---

[156] (Mare)
[157] (Harris)

But Paul, the preacher, at the end of his life could say, "I have fought the good fight, I have finished the race, I have kept the faith. Finally, there is laid up for me the crown of righteousness, which the Lord, the righteous Judge, will give to me on that Day, and not to me only but also to all who have loved His appearing" (2nd Tim. 4:7–8, emphasis ours).[158]

When Jesus Christ comes and sits on the throne of judgment, what is the basis of His judgment?

Matthew 7:21–23

21*"Not everyone who says to Me, 'Lord, Lord,' will enter the kingdom of heaven, but he who does the will of My Father who is in heaven will enter.*

22 *Many will say to Me on that day, 'Lord, Lord, did we not prophesy in Your name, and in Your name cast out demons, and in Your name perform many miracles?'*

23 *And then I will declare to them, '__I never knew you; DEPART FROM ME, YOU WHO PRACTICE LAWLESSNESS.__"*

Luke conveys a very similar scenario.

Luke 13:24–29

24 *"Strive to enter through the narrow door; for many, I tell you, will seek to enter and will not be able.*

25 *Once the head of the house gets up and shuts the door, and you begin to stand outside and knock on the door, saying, 'Lord, open up to us!' then He will answer and say to you, 'I do not know where you are from.'*

26 *Then you will begin to say, 'We ate and drank in Your presence, and You taught in our streets';*

---

[158] (Olford, 1998)

27 *and He will say, 'I tell you, I do not know where you are from; DEPART FROM ME, ALL YOU EVILDOERS.'*
28 ***In that place there will be weeping and gnashing of teeth when you see Abraham and Isaac and Jacob and all the prophets in the kingdom of God, but yourselves being thrown out***.
29 *And they will come from east and west and from north and south, and will recline at the table in the kingdom of God."*

You can legitimately draw some parallels between the concept of entering into the Kingdom and the history regarding the children of Israel entering the Promised Land. The generation of Israelites that Moses led out of Egypt was not allowed to enter into the Promised Land. Moses was also denied entrance due to his failure to completely obey God.

Numbers 14:26–30

26 *The LORD spoke to Moses and Aaron, saying,*
27 *"How long shall I bear with this evil congregation who are grumbling against Me? I have heard the complaints of the sons of Israel, which they are making against Me.*
28 *Say to them, 'As I live,' says the LORD, 'just as you have spoken in My hearing, so I will surely do to you;*
29 ***your corpses will fall in this wilderness, even all your numbered men, according to your complete number from twenty years old and upward, who have grumbled against Me.***
30 ***'Surely you shall not come into the land in which I swore to settle you***, *except Caleb the son of Jephunneh and Joshua the son of Nun."*

Numbers 20:8–13

8 *"Take the rod; and you and your brother Aaron assemble the congregation and **speak to the rock***

__before their eyes, that it may yield its water__. You shall thus bring forth water for them out of the rock and let the congregation and their beasts drink."

__9__ So Moses took the rod from before the LORD, just as He had commanded him;

__10__ and Moses and Aaron gathered the assembly before the rock. And he said to them, "Listen now, you rebels; shall we bring forth water for you out of this rock?"

__11__ Then Moses lifted up his hand and __struck the rock twice with his rod__; and water came forth abundantly, and the congregation and their beasts drank.

__12__ But the LORD said to Moses and Aaron, "__Because you have not believed Me, to treat Me as holy in the sight of the sons of Israel, therefore you shall not bring this assembly into the land which I have given them__."

__13__ Those were the waters of Meribah, because the sons of Israel contended with the LORD, and He proved Himself holy among them.

How could God be so harsh, that after all that Moses had done for forty years as a servant of God and a leader of God's people, he was not allowed to enter the Promised Land because he hit a rock twice instead of speaking to it?

> The nature of the sin is not clear, but Moses and Aaron were apparently taking to themselves honor that belonged to God alone. Because of the sin they were denied the privilege of leading the Israelites into the Promised Land. The punishment may seem too severe for the sin, but it shows that the privileged role of leadership given to Moses and Aaron carried with it an unusual measure of responsibility.[159]

---

[159] (Elwell, 1988)

We scarcely perceive anything reprehensible in this matter, yet, since God declares that the fall of Moses displeased Him, we must abide by His decision rather than our own. And hence, too, let us learn that our works, on the surface of which nothing but virtue is apparent, are often abounding in secret defects, which escape the eyes of men, but are manifest to God alone.[160]

It does seem harsh, but we do know that Moses will be in the Kingdom. The shadow of the cross falls both forward into the future and into the past to those who believe. We know Moses will be in the Kingdom because Peter, John, and James witnessed Moses and Elijah appearing in glory with Christ as He will be in the Kingdom. How can I say that this is a preview of the Kingdom? Look at what Jesus said before Peter, John, and James went up on the mountain and saw this.

Luke 9:26–31

26 *"For whoever is ashamed of Me and My words, the Son of Man will be ashamed of him when He comes in His glory, and the glory of the Father and of the holy angels.*

27 *But I say to you truthfully,* ***there are some of those standing here who will not taste death until they see the kingdom of God."***

28 *Some eight days after these sayings, He took along Peter and John and James, and went up on the mountain to pray.*

29 *And while He was praying, the appearance of His face became different, and* ***His clothing became white and gleaming***.

30 *And behold, two men were talking with Him; and they were* ***Moses and Elijah***,

---

31 *<u>who, appearing in glory, were speaking of His</u>* *<u>departure which He was about to accomplish at</u>* *<u>Jerusalem</u>*.

The writer of Hebrews uses what happened to that generation of Israelites as an example to Christians that they may not fall away.

Hebrews 3:7–19

7 *Therefore, just as the Holy Spirit says,*
"Today if you hear His voice,
8 *Do not harden your hearts as when they provoked Me,*
As in the day of trial in the wilderness,
9 *Where your fathers tried Me by testing Me,*
And saw My works for forty years.
10 *Therefore I was angry with this generation,*
And said, 'They always go astray in their heart,
And they did not know My ways';
11 *As I swore in My wrath,*
'They shall not enter My rest.'"
12 *Take care, brethren, that there not be in any one of you an evil, unbelieving heart that falls away from the living God.* [He says "falls away from the living God"]
13 *But encourage one another day after day, as long as it is still called "Today," so that none of you will be hardened by the deceitfulness of sin.* ["Hardened by the deceitfulness of sin": That is what sin does to you. It causes you to forget that you are forgiven, and you then fall away from God.]
14 *For we have become partakers of Christ, <u>if we</u>* *<u>hold fast the beginning of our assurance firm until</u>* *<u>the end</u>,* [We are constantly being encouraged to hold fast, endure until the end,]
15 *while it is said,*
"Today if you hear His voice,
Do not harden your hearts, as when they provoked Me."

16 *For who provoked Him when they had heard? Indeed, did not all those who came out of Egypt led by Moses?*

17 *And with whom was He angry for forty years? Was it not with those who sinned, whose bodies fell in the wilderness?*

18 *And to whom did He swear that they would not enter His rest, but to those who were disobedient?*

19 *So we see that they were **not able to enter because of unbelief**.* [It does not say because of sin, but unbelief.]

As I have been saying, good works and righteous deeds cannot be done in the power of the flesh. They have to be a result of being led by the Holy Spirit, which only happens to those who are focused on the love of God and their relationship with Him. The Bible is full of warnings to those who try to do works under their own power, and that is folly—or, more than folly, an outright offense to the Lord.

Romans 10:9–10

9 *...that if you confess with your mouth Jesus as Lord, and believe in your heart that God raised Him from the dead, you will be saved;*

10 *for **<u>with the heart a person believes, resulting in righteousness</u>**, and with the mouth he confesses, resulting in salvation.*

Romans 8:1–11

1 *Therefore there is now no condemnation for those who are in Christ Jesus.*

2 *For the law of the Spirit of life in Christ Jesus has set you free from the law of sin and of death.*

3 *For what the Law could not do, weak as it was through the flesh, God did: sending His own Son in*

*the likeness of sinful flesh and as an offering for sin,
He condemned sin in the flesh,*

4 *so that **the requirement of the Law might be
fulfilled in us, who do not walk according to the
flesh but according to the Spirit**.*

5 *For those who are according to the flesh set their
minds on the things of the flesh, but those who are
according to the Spirit, the things of the Spirit.*

6 *For the mind set on the flesh is death, but **the mind
set on the Spirit is life and peace**,*

7 *because the mind set on the flesh is hostile toward
God; for it does not subject itself to the law of God,
for it is not even able to do so,*

8 *and **those who are in the flesh cannot please God**.*

9 *However, you are not in the flesh but in the Spirit, if
indeed the Spirit of God dwells in you. But if anyone
does not have the Spirit of Christ, he does not belong
to Him.*

10 *If Christ is in you, though the body is dead because
of sin, yet the spirit is alive because of righteousness.*

11 *But if the Spirit of Him who raised Jesus from the
dead dwells in you, He who raised Christ Jesus from
the dead **will also give life to your mortal bodies**
through His Spirit who dwells in you.*

The Law is not just the Ten Commandments and the other laws in the
Old Testament; it is all of those "do and don'ts" that those "according
to the flesh" try to get you to set your mind on. That is death (verse 6)!
It amazes me how many "church people" push this message of law.

Matthew 23:3–6

3 *"...therefore all that they tell you, do and observe,
but do not do according to their deeds; for they say
things and do not do them.*

4 They tie up heavy burdens and lay them on men's shoulders, but they themselves are unwilling to move them with so much as a finger.

5 But they do all their deeds to be noticed by men; for they broaden their phylacteries and lengthen the tassels of their garments.

6 They love the place of honor at banquets and the chief seats in the synagogues..."

"Bear one another's burdens, and so fulfill the law of Christ". The legalist is not interested in lifting burdens. Instead, he *adds* to the burdens of others (Acts 15:10). This was one of the sins that the Master severely condemned: "They [the Pharisees] bind heavy burdens, hard to bear, and lay them on men's shoulders; but they themselves will not move them with one of their fingers" (Matt. 23:4).

Paul uses the word *burdens* to show the subtlety and cruelty of legalism. In fact, legalists exacerbate the problems of those who are already weighed down.

By way of contrast, he who is Spirit-filled has a releasing ministry. In love he wants to see his brother set free for service (5:13)![161]

1st Corinthians 3:13

...each man's work will become evident; for the day will show it, because it is to be revealed with fire; and the fire itself will test the quality of each man's work.

<u>Works do not justify, they testify!</u> They testify to what is in our hearts. Works are a response to what Christ has done for us. Good works testify of one submitting to the Holy Spirit, but evil deeds testify of one living by the flesh. If we try to live the Christian life by

---

[161] (Olford, 1998)

the power of the flesh, we strengthen the flesh, and the spirit grows weaker and atrophies. Like a muscle, the more you use the flesh, the stronger it becomes, and when the flesh wants to carry out its desires, we have no strength in spirit do overcome it.

I have heard it said that if you want to know what kind of person someone is, see what they do when they are alone and away from everyone that they know. Children are molested, women are raped, adultery is rampant, and on and on. These are sins that are covered by the blood of Christ, and one can always return to the Lord in repentance, but to go on sinning willfully means they are not in a relationship with Christ.

1st Corinthians 6:9–20

9 *Or do you not know that t__he unrighteous will not inherit the kingdom of God?__ Do not be deceived; neither fornicators, nor idolaters, nor adulterers, nor effeminate, nor homosexuals,*

10 *nor thieves, __nor the covetous,__ nor drunkards, nor revilers, nor swindlers, __will inherit the kingdom of God__.*

11 *Such were some of you; but you were washed, but you were sanctified, but you were justified in the name of the Lord Jesus Christ and in the Spirit of our God.*

12 *All things are lawful for me, but not all things are profitable. All things are lawful for me, but I will not be mastered by anything.*

13 *Food is for the stomach and the stomach is for food, but God will do away with both of them. __Yet the body is not for__ immorality, __but for the Lord__, and the Lord is for the body.*

14 *Now God has not only raised the Lord, but will also raise us up through His power.*

15 *Do you not know that your bodies are members of Christ? Shall I then take away the members of*

Christ and make them members of a prostitute? May it never be!

16 *Or do you not know that the one who joins himself to a prostitute is one body with her? For He says, "THE TWO SHALL BECOME ONE FLESH."*

17 *But the one who joins himself to the Lord is one spirit with Him.*

18 *Flee immorality. Every other sin that a man commits is outside the body, but the immoral man sins against his own body.*

19 *Or do you not know that your body is a temple of the Holy Spirit who is in you, whom you have from God, and that you are not your own?*

20 *For you have been bought with a price: therefore glorify God in your body.*

As Christians, we have to be very careful how we use this message. This message is used by so many Christians to condemn homosexuality and condemn homosexuals to hell. In my mind, that is disobeying the greatest commandment to love our neighbor as ourselves. We do not know what the motives are in a person or what their relationship with God is like. It is not our job to condemn others; we have enough difficulties in the flesh ourselves.

> Jesus says regarding judging—*don't*. The average Christian is the most penetratingly critical individual. Criticism is a part of the ordinary faculty of man; but in the spiritual domain nothing is accomplished by criticism. The effect of criticism is a dividing up of the powers of the one criticized; the Holy Ghost is the One in the true position to criticize, He alone is able to show what is wrong without hurting and wounding. It is impossible to enter into communion with God when you are in a critical temper; it makes you hard and vindictive and cruel, and leaves you with the flattering unction that you are a superior person. Jesus says, as a disciple, cultivate the

uncritical temper. It is not done once and for all. Beware of anything that puts you in the superior person's place.

There is no getting away from the penetration of Jesus. If I see the mote in your eye, it means I have a beam in my own. Every wrong thing that I see in you, God locates in me. Every time I judge, I condemn myself (see Romans 2:17–20). Stop having a measuring rod for other people. There is always one fact more in every man's case about which we know nothing. The first thing God does is to give us a spiritual spring-cleaning; there is no possibility of pride left in a man after that. I have never met the man I could despair of after discerning what lies in me apart from the grace of God.[162]

James 4:11–12

11 *Do not speak against one another, brethren. He who speaks against a brother or judges his brother, speaks against the law and judges the law; but if you judge the law, you are not a doer of the law but a judge of it.* **12** *There is only one Lawgiver and Judge, the One who is able to save and to destroy; but who are you who judge your neighbor?*

In each of these passages, "judging" carries quasi-legal meanings. The choices or the motives of others are called into question, and a condemning verdict is passed in each. Each part of this process is ruled out by the above Scripture passages. Human beings are not competent to call another's motives or practices into question. Even when actions are clearly wrong, forgiveness, not condemnation, is the appropriate response. A judgmental attitude and punitive attempts are both wrong. We are to draw back, remembering that God alone is competent to judge, and to stop judging others.[163]

---

[162] (Chambers, 1986)
[163] (Richards L. O., 1999)

Matthew 12:36–37

36 *"But I tell you that every careless word that people speak, they shall give an accounting for it in the Day of Judgment.*
37 *For by your words you will be justified, and by your words you will be condemned."*

Even our words are important. I am terribly guilty of this, and I really pray that I will get better. Not just swearing, but being critical of other drivers, newscasters, bosses, and public servants. None of this is something I want to do, but find myself doing it anyway.

Romans 7:15–8:1

15 *For what I am doing, I do not understand; for **I am not practicing what I would like to do, but I am doing the very thing I hate**.*
16 *But if I do the very thing I do not want to do, I agree with the Law, confessing that the Law is good.*
17 *So now, no longer am I the one doing it, but sin which dwells in me.*
18 *For I know that nothing good dwells in me, that is, in my flesh; for the willing is present in me, but the doing of the good is not.*
19 *For **the good that I want, I do not do, but I practice the very evil that I do not want**.*
20 *But if I am doing the very thing I do not want, I am no longer the one doing it, but sin which dwells in me.*
21 *I find then the principle that evil is present in me, the one who wants to do good.*
22 *For I joyfully concur with the law of God in the inner man,*
23 *but I see a different law in the members of my body, waging war against the law of my mind and making me a prisoner of the law of sin which is in my members.*

24 *Wretched man that I am!* **_Who will set me free_**
from the body of this death?
25 *Thanks be to God through* **_Jesus Christ our Lord!_**
So then, on the one hand I myself with my mind am
serving the law of God, but on the other, with my flesh
the law of sin.
8:1 *Therefore there is now no condemnation for those*
who are in Christ Jesus. [Note: Paul did not separate
this letter by chapter and verse.]

The eternal Judge has declared us pardoned, justified, and
righteous. No one, human or satanic, can condemn us or
permanently lay any charge against us (vv. 33–34).

The extent of this forgiveness is literally mind-boggling.
God says, "Their sin I will remember no more" (Jer. 31:34).
David wrote, "As far as the east is from the west, so far
has He removed our transgressions from us" (Ps. 103:12).
And Isaiah gives the reason: "The Lord has caused the
iniquity of us all to fall on Him [Christ]" (Isa. 53:6; cf. 1st
Peter 2:24).[164]

Grace is defined simply as 'unmerited favour' or
'undeserved benefit'. Christians should never look at non-
Christians with a spirit of contempt.[165]

Love, of course, is the key. Love is the great commandment. Love
is what fulfills the Law. God is love. The way that is written in the
Greek is similar to an equal sign: God *is* love; therefore, love *is* God.
The word for love here is ἀγάπη (*agape*). Agape love is defined in
1st Corinthians 13 and it is the love that says, "I will put your needs
before mine and I would die for you." Since this love can only come
from God, it cannot be manifested by non-believers. The only way
we can have Agape is as a response to believing that God first loved

---

[164] (MacArthur J., 1997)
[165] (Sproul, The Purpose of God: Ephesians, 1994)

us. This is Agape love, not brotherly love, or romantic love, or even the love a parent has for their child. Agape love manifests itself undeniably in our works.

Matthew 25:34–40

34 *"Then the King will say to those on His right, 'Come, you who are blessed of My Father, inherit the kingdom prepared for you from the foundation of the world.*

35 *For I was hungry, and you gave Me something to eat; I was thirsty, and you gave Me something to drink; I was a stranger, and you invited Me in;*

36 *naked, and you clothed Me; I was sick, and you visited Me; I was in prison, and you came to Me.'*

37 *Then the righteous will answer Him, 'Lord, when did we see You hungry, and feed You, or thirsty, and give You something to drink?*

38 *And when did we see You a stranger, and invite You in, or naked, and clothe You?*

39 *When did we see You sick, or in prison, and come to You?'*

40 *The King will answer and say to them, 'Truly I say to you, to the extent that you did it to one of these brothers of Mine, even the least of them, you did it to Me.'"*

1st John 4:16–21

16 *We have come to know and **have believed the love which God has for us**. God is love, and the one who abides in love abides in God, and God abides in him.*

17 *By this, **love is perfected with us, so that we may have confidence in the day of judgment**; because as He is, so also are we in this world.*

18 *There is no fear in love; but perfect love casts out fear, because fear involves punishment, and the one who fears is not perfected in love.*

19 ***We love, because He first loved us.***

20 *If someone says, "I love God," and hates his brother, he is a liar; for the one who does not love his brother whom he has seen, cannot love God whom he has not seen.*

21 *And this commandment we have from Him, that the one who loves God should love his brother also.*

1st John 2:28

*Now, little children, **abide in Him**, so that when He appears, we may have confidence and not shrink away from Him in shame at His coming.*

Have I made this decision about sin—that it must be killed right out in me? It takes a long time to come to a moral decision about sin, but it is the great moment in my life when I do decide that just as Jesus Christ died for the sin of the world, so sin must die out in me, not be curbed or suppressed or counteracted, but crucified. No one can bring any one else to this decision. We may be earnestly convinced, and religiously convinced, but what we need to do is to come to the decision which Paul forces here.

Haul yourself up, take a time alone with God, make the moral decision and say—'Lord, identify me with Thy death until I know that sin is dead in me.' Make the moral decision that sin in you must be put to death.

It was not a divine anticipation on the part of Paul, but a very radical and definite experience. Am I prepared to let the Spirit of God search me until I know what the disposition of sin is—the thing that lusts against the Spirit

323

of God in me? Then if so, will I agree with God's verdict on that disposition of sin—that it should be identified with the death of Jesus? I cannot reckon myself "dead indeed unto sin" unless I have been through this radical issue of will before God.

Have I entered into the glorious privilege of being crucified with Christ until all that is left is the life of Christ in my flesh and blood? "I am crucified with Christ; nevertheless I live; yet not I, but Christ liveth in me.[166]

Unrepentant sin is trampling the blood of Christ.

Hebrews 10:26–27

26 *For if we go on sinning willfully after receiving the knowledge of the truth, there no longer remains a sacrifice for sins,*
27 *but a terrifying expectation of judgment and* THE FURY OF A FIRE WHICH WILL CONSUME THE ADVERSARIES.

The word *"wilfully"* stands in contrast with sins of weakness, ignorance and error in (Hebrews) 5:2. If the writer meant to say that, after the commission of wilful and heinous sins, "there remaineth no more sacrifice for sins," this would not only be the most terrible passage in Scripture, but would do away with the very object of Redemption, and the possibility of any Forgiveness of Sins. It would, as Kurtz says, "be in its consequences truly subversive and destructive of the whole Christian soteriology (study of salvation)." But the meaning rather is, *"If we are willing sinners,"* "if *we are in a state of* deliberate and voluntary defiance to the will of God." He is alluding not only to those sins which the Jews described as being committed presumptuously "with uplifted hand" (Num. 15:30; Ps. 19:13; see 6:4–8, 12:16, 17), but to the

---

[166] (Chambers, 1986)

deliberate continuity of such sins as a self-chosen law of life; as for instance when a man has closed against himself the door of repentance and said "Evil, be thou my good." Such a state is glanced at in 2 Pet. 2:20, 21; Matt. 12:43–45.[167]

"The full *knowledge of the truth."* Something more is meant than mere historical knowledge. He is contemplating Christians who have made some real advance, and then have relapsed into "desperation or the wretchlessness of unclean living."

"...no sacrifice for sins is any longer left for them." They have rejected the work of Christ, and it cannot be done for them over again. There is one atoning sacrifice, and that they have repudiated. He does not say that they have exhausted the infinite mercy of God, nor can we justly assert that he held such a conclusion; he only says that they have, *so long as they continue in such a state*, put themselves out of God's covenant, and that there are no other covenanted means of grace. For they have trampled underfoot the offer of mercy in Christ and there is no salvation in any other (Acts 4:12).[168]

After a willful sin has been committed, nothing you can do will cause God to forgive you, because He already has! Your conscience may need to be cleansed by asking your Father in heaven to forgive you, but judicially as a judge, you have been forgiven, not by anything you did or didn't do, but by the atoning work of Christ.

Hebrews 10:28–39

28 *Anyone who has set aside the Law of Moses dies without mercy on the testimony of two or three witnesses.*

---

[167] (Farrar, 1893)
[168] (Farrar, 1893)

29 How much severer punishment do you think he will deserve who has trampled underfoot the Son of God, and has regarded as unclean the blood of the covenant by which he was sanctified, __and has insulted the Spirit of grace__?

30 For we know Him who said, "VENGEANCE IS MINE, I WILL REPAY." And again, "THE LORD WILL JUDGE HIS PEOPLE."

31 It is a terrifying thing to fall into the hands of the living God.

32 But remember the former days, when, after being enlightened, you endured a great conflict of sufferings,

33 partly by being made a public spectacle through reproaches and tribulations, and partly by becoming sharers with those who were so treated.

34 For you showed sympathy to the prisoners and accepted joyfully the seizure of your property, knowing that you have for yourselves a better possession and a lasting one.

35 Therefore, do not throw away your confidence, which has a great reward.

36 For __you have need of endurance, so that when you have done the will of God, you may receive what was promised.__

37 FOR YET IN A VERY LITTLE WHILE, HE WHO IS COMING WILL COME, AND WILL NOT DELAY.

38 BUT MY RIGHTEOUS ONE SHALL LIVE BY FAITH; AND IF HE SHRINKS BACK, MY SOUL HAS NO PLEASURE IN HIM.

39 But we are not of those who shrink back to destruction, but of those who have faith to the preserving of the soul.

If we forget the sacrifice that Christ has made for that sin, then we tend to make sin a pattern for our lives, eventually turning our backs on God. But we must endure, keep on repenting, and turning back to God, because He has made the ultimate sacrifice. No matter how often we slip and willfully sin, don't shrink back but continue living in the faith that Christ has died for all of our sins.

Galatians 5:19–25

19 *Now the deeds of the flesh are evident, which are: immorality, impurity, sensuality,*

20 *idolatry, sorcery, enmities, strife, jealousy, outbursts of anger, disputes, dissensions, factions,*

21 *envying, drunkenness, carousing, and things like these, of which I forewarn you, just as I have forewarned you, that **those who practice such things will not inherit the kingdom of God**.*

22 *But the fruit of the Spirit is love, joy, peace, patience, kindness, goodness, faithfulness,*

23 *gentleness, self-control; against such things there is no law.*

24 *Now **those who belong to Christ Jesus have crucified the flesh with its passions and desires**.*

25 ***If we live by the Spirit, let us also walk by the Spirit**.*

This may be depressing, but finish Paul's thought:

1st Corinthians 6:11

And such were some of you; but you were washed, but you were sanctified, but you were justified in the name of the Lord Jesus Christ and in the Spirit of God.

Victory is for those who overcome (Revelation 2:7, 11, 17). Overcomers are conquerors. To overcome, one must fight. We battle best as we pray most. The secret of victory lies in Christ's power alone.[169]

---

[169] (Stone, 1995)

Overcoming is not accomplished by fleshly self-discipline, strength of character, or willpower. It **does not mean that you try to stop sinning**! It means that you **stay in the relationship** with God through what Christ did at the Cross. That will cause you to change your mind about sin, which is what repentance means. Romans 2:4 says that the *"kindness of God leads you to repentance."* The Greek word for repentance is μετάνοιά (*metanoia*).

> ...to change one's way of life as the result of a complete change of thought and attitude with regard to sin and righteousness—'to repent, to change one's way, repentance...[170]

In response to God's love and kindness, your desires will change and you will only want to live a life that is pleasing to Him. You will want to allow the Holy Spirit to guide you and that will enable you to sin less and less. The longer and more consistently you walk with Him, the closer you will come to complete sanctification. It is hard to cheat on your spouse when you are holding their hand; it is hard to sin when you are walking with God.

> "Overcometh" is nikaō (νικαω), "to carry off the victory, come off victorious." The verb implies a battle. Here the forces of the world-system of evil, the flesh (totally depraved nature), the devil, and the pernicious age-system (zeitgeist German) with which the saint is surrounded, are all engaged in a battle against the saint, carrying on an incessant warfare, the purpose of which is to ruin his Christian life and testimony. The verb is in the present tense, "is constantly overcoming the world." It is a habit of life with the saint to gain victory over the world. To go down in defeat is the exception, not the rule.[171]

---

[170] (Louw, 1996)
[171] (Wuest, 1997, c1984)

In Revelations, John was told to write a letter to seven different churches.

> **Revelation 1:10–11**
>
> **10** *I was in the Spirit on the Lord's day, and I heard behind me a loud voice like the sound of a trumpet,* **11** *saying, "Write in a book what you see, and send it to the seven churches: to Ephesus and to Smyrna and to Pergamum and to Thyatira and to Sardis and to Philadelphia and to Laodicea."*

The following verses are written to the seven churches. These seven letters to seven churches represent the totality of all churches. All churches can examine what is written in these prophecies and find application for their own use.

The seven churches listed were: Ephesus, located in what is now Turkey; Smyrna, several miles to the north; Pergamos, about 55 miles northeast of Smyrna; Thyatira, 40 miles southeast of Pergamos; Sardis, 30 miles southeast of Thyatira; Philadelphia, 28 miles southeast of Sardis; and, finally, Laodicea, about 40 miles southeast of Philadelphia. These cities were located in a rough triangular shape on the map, and none of the seven cities was more than 125 miles from any other.

All Seven Churches

> **Revelation 2:7**
>
> *"To him who overcomes, I will grant to eat of the tree of life, which is in the Paradise of God."*

Smyrna

> **Revelation 2:11**
>
> *"He who overcomes shall not be hurt by the second death."*

Pergamum

Revelation 2:17

"He who has an ear, let him hear what the Spirit says to the churches. To him who overcomes, to him I will give some of the hidden manna, and I will give him a white stone, and a new name written on the stone which no one knows but he who receives it."

Thyatira

Revelation 2:26

"He who overcomes and he who keeps My deeds until the end, to him I will give authority over the nations."

Sardis

Revelation 3:5

"He who overcomes shall thus be clothed in white garments; and I will not erase his name from the book of life, and I will confess his name before My Father, and before His angels."

Philadelphia

Revelation 3:12

"He who overcomes, I will make him a pillar in the temple of God..."

Laodicea

Revelation 3:21

"He who overcomes, I will grant to him to sit down with Me on My throne, as I also overcame and sat down with My Father on His throne."

How do you overcome?

1st John 5:4–5

4 *For whatever is born of God overcomes the world and this is the victory that has overcome the world— our faith.*

5 *And who is the one who overcomes the world, but he who believes that Jesus is the Son of God?*

Overcoming is similar to enduring until the end.

Matthew 10:16–23

16 *"Behold, I send you out as sheep in the midst of wolves; so be shrewd as serpents and innocent as doves.*

17 *But beware of men, for they will hand you over to the courts and scourge you in their synagogues;*

18 *and you will even be brought before governors and kings for My sake, as a testimony to them and to the Gentiles.*

19 *But when they hand you over, do not worry about how or what you are to say; for it will be given you in that hour what you are to say.*

20 *For it is not you who speak, but it is the Spirit of your Father who speaks in you.*

21 *Brother will betray brother to death, and a father his child; and children will rise up against parents and cause them to be put to death.*

22 *You will be hated by all because of My name, __but it is the one who has endured to the end who will be saved__.*

23 *But whenever they persecute you in one city, flee to the next; for truly I say to you, you will not finish going through the cities of Israel until the Son of Man comes."*

Sin causes us to stray from God, and if we don't continually come back into His presence, we will not overcome or endure until the end. It is never too late; God will always welcome you back with open arms. The prodigal son has returned. You don't have to do anything but believe that you are forgiven. Start praying and praising.

Let's look at who will enter into the Kingdom and what they exhibited in their lives.

> **Revelation 20:4**
> *And I saw thrones, and they that sat upon them, and judgment was given to them. And I saw the souls of those who had been **beheaded because of the testimony of Jesus** and because of the word of God, and **those who had not worshipped the beast or his image, and had not received the mark upon their forehead and upon their hand**; and they came to life and reigned with Christ for a thousand years.*

Martyrs, those who had been beheaded for Christ, have a sure ticket to the Kingdom. Don't ever worship the beast or take a mark on your hand or forehead, or you will miss the kingdom.

If you parallel the exodus from Egypt to the believer's walk today (the Passover parallels the cross, the trek in the wilderness parallels our walk, and the entrance into the promised land parallels the entrance into the kingdom), then worshipping the beast really parallels the main reason they didn't enter into the land, which was that they worshipped other gods and idols, one of the most common sins of the nation of Israel.

So how do we enter into the Kingdom? One way is to become as children.

Matthew 18:1–6

*...at that time the disciples came to Jesus, saying, "Who then is the greatest in the kingdom of Heaven?" and He called a child to himself and set him before them and said "Truly I say to you, **unless you are converted and become like children, you shall not enter the kingdom of heaven**. And whoever receives one such child in My name receives Me; but whoever causes one of these little ones to stumble, it is better for him that a heavy millstone be hung around his neck, and that he be drowned in the depth of the sea."*

Children are trusting and open-minded. Children are loving, not prejudiced, and hug easily. Children believe readily. They are not cynical or condemning, and they smile a lot.

Doing the will of God will get you into the Kingdom.

Matthew 7:21

"Not everyone who says to Me 'Lord, Lord' will enter the kingdom of heaven; but he who does the will of My Father who is in heaven."

John 3:16

"For God so loved the world, that He gave His only begotten Son, that whoever believes in Him should not perish, but have eternal life."

Eternal does not mean eternity as we think of it, though the concept still applies. The emphasis, however, is on the quality of life rather than the length of time. Eternal life also refers to the Kingdom. In the verse above, the word "believes" is in the present tense, which indicates continuous action. Believe and continue to believe. As you believe, you have an eternal quality of life.

Sins are forgiven, but to continue in unrepentant sin is trampling the blood of Christ. When we do sin, we should repent and confess it to get back into fellowship with God as a Father. When we finally give up and quit repenting, deciding to go on sinning willfully and not repent, we are choosing to give up the Kingdom.

One way to be sure to miss the Kingdom is by denying Christ.

Matthew 10:33
"Whoever shall deny Me before men, I will also deny him before My Father who is in heaven."

2nd Timothy 2:12
If we endure, we shall also reign with Him; if we deny Him, He will also deny us…

2nd Peter 2:1
But false prophets also rose among the people, just as there will also be false teachers among you, who will secretly introduce destructive heresies, even denying the Master who bought them, bringing swift destruction upon themselves.

Jude 4
For certain persons have crept in unnoticed, those who were long before hand marked out for this condemnation, ungodly persons who turn the grace of our God into licentiousness and deny our only Master and Lord, Jesus Christ.

Revelation 3:8
"I know your deeds. Behold, I have put before you an open door which no man can shut, because you have a little power, and have kept My word, and have not denied My name."

Remember, Peter denied Christ. He said he did not know Him. However, Peter did not let the guilt for that drive him away from God. The Lord used him in a tremendous way. He was forgiven, just as you are forgiven. Not just as you "*can*" be forgiven, because that would mean Christ did not accomplish it all at the cross. You are forgiven. If you continue to deny Christ, then you will not have a relationship with Him, and He will say, "Depart from me, I never knew you."

Who else won't enter? Hypocrites:

Matthew 23:13
"But woe to you scribes and Pharisees, hypocrites, because you shut off the kingdom from men; for you do not enter in yourselves, nor do you allow those who are entering to go in."

Those who seek justification by their own flesh trying to obey the law and putting others under that law as well:

Galatians 5:4
*You have been **severed** from Christ, you who are seeking to be justified by law; you have fallen from grace.*

1st Timothy 6:9–21
But those who want to get rich fall into temptation and a snare and many foolish and harmful desires which plunge men into ruin and destruction. For the love of money is a root of all sorts of evil, and some by longing for it have wandered away from the faith, and pierced themselves with many a pang...I charge you keep the commandment without stain or reproach until the appearing of our Lord Jesus Christ.

The love of money can choke out the word of the Kingdom. It is not that we can point fingers at the wealthy and accuse them of suffering from the love of money; we don't know their hearts. A poor man can also want to get rich and fall into temptation, perhaps as often as or more often than a wealthy man. Don't pursue riches, but seek first the kingdom of God.

The commandment Paul charges Timothy with is a singular commandment. I trust that he meant the one commandment Christ gave in **Matthew 22:36–40**: *"You shall love the Lord your God with all your heart, and with all your soul, and with all your mind...and you shall love your neighbor as yourself."*

Revelation 14:9–12

If anyone worships the beast and his image, and receives a mark on his forehead or upon his hand, he also will drink of the wine of the wrath of God, which is mixed in full strength in the cup of His anger; and he will be tormented with fire and brimstone in the presence of the holy angels and in the presence of the Lamb. And the smoke of their torment goes up forever and ever; and they have no rest day and night, those who worship the beast and his image, and whoever receives the mark of his name.

"I think of praying at all times as living in continual God-consciousness, where everything we see and experience becomes a kind of prayer, lived in deep awareness of and surrender to our Heavenly Father. It is something I share with my Best Friend—something I instantly communicate with God. To obey this exhortation means that, when we are tempted, we hold the temptation before God and ask for His help. When we experience something good and beautiful, we immediately thank the Lord for it. When we see evil around us, we ask God to make it right and to allow us to help accomplish that, if it is according to His will. When we meet someone who does not know Christ, we pray for God to draw that person to Himself and to use us to be a faithful witness. When we encounter trouble, we turn to God as our Deliverer."[172]

Now, after having explained that the thought of occasional sin in the life of a child of God is not to be entertained for a moment, because the believer's slavery has been transferred from one master, Satan, to another Master, even the Lord Jesus, and this, because the believer has had the power of the indwelling sinful nature broken and the divine nature implanted, Paul proceeds to show the attitude which the believer should be careful to maintain with reference to his change of masters. Paul apologizes for using such a human illustration as slavery to explain one's former relationship to Satan and one's present relationship to God. But he says that he finds it necessary to do so because of their defective spiritual insight which in turn is due to certain moral defects. The translation reads: "I am using a human term of speech because of the weakness of your flesh, for even as ye put your members as slaves at the service of uncleanness and lawlessness resulting in an abiding state of lawlessness, so now put your members once for all as slaves at the service of righteousness resulting in holiness."

One might ask at this point why such an exhortation is necessary if the power of the evil nature has been broken and the divine nature implanted, resulting in a transfer of affection to another Master, even the Lord Jesus? Why is it necessary for Paul to exhort believers to put themselves at the service of Christ, when they have a nature that impels them to do so? The answer is that the will of the believer, even though it is inclined in regeneration towards Christ and the doing of good, still has a certain bent at times to the doing of evil, the result of the habitual and constant

---

[172] (MacArthur J. F., 1995)

inclination it had towards evil before grace did its work. The habits formed by years of sin must be overcome. That moral twist must be unbent. *The only way to do this is to form new habits of the will by keeping our choices inclined towards obedience to our new Master, Christ. The divine nature is there to keep our choices in line with the Word of God as we yield to the ministry of the Holy Spirit and trust Him to work in us, but we must ever be on the alert lest those habits formed by years of choosing the wrong, lead us to render obedience to our old master, Satan. As we establish new habits of choice, gradually our renewed wills are bent more and more in the direction of the good, and it becomes increasingly easier to do the right and increasingly harder to do the wrong.*

Then Paul reminds the believer of the wasted years spent in sin, with their evil consequences. "For when ye were slaves of sin, ye were free with respect to righteousness." That is, in our unsaved state, there was no restraint put upon sin in our lives by any righteousness we might have had, for we had none. And because there was no check upon sin that would restrain evil in our lives, sin ran rampant. The apostle reminds the believer: "Therefore what fruit were ye constantly having at that time? of which things now ye are ashamed? For the end of those things is death." Thus another reason is presented why the believer does not want even to provide for an occasional sin in his life. He is ashamed of the years which he spent in sin, and of the corruption it bred. And so Paul concludes his argument with the words: "But now having been made free from sin and having become bondslaves of God, ye are having your fruit resulting in holiness, and the end, eternal life. For the pay which sin doles out is death, but the free gift of God is life eternal in Jesus Christ our Lord."

Thus Paul answers the second question: "What then? shall we sin occasionally because we are not under law but under grace?" by asserting that that cannot be the desire of a child of God and cannot be a fact in his life, and for the reason that he has had his slavery transferred from Satan to the Lord Jesus, this act of transference having been accomplished by the breaking of the power of the evil nature, which nature caused the person to love to serve the Devil, and by the impartation of the divine nature which impels the believer to serve the Lord Jesus.

Thus God's grace not only justifies the believer (that is, takes away the guilt and penalty of sin and bestows a positive righteousness)—even the Lord Jesus Himself in whom the believer stands perfectly righteous for time and eternity, but it sanctifies him, in that it breaks the power of sin in his life, and produces in him a life which glorifies God.

Dear Christian reader, if you have not been obtaining consistent victory over sin, will you not let this study of Romans VI point the way to the victorious life? There is victory for you when you understand and follow God's directions with regard to the correct technique of how to gain this victory.[173]

---

[173] (Wuest, 1997, c1984)

24

WHAT WILL THE KINGDOM BE LIKE?

No one today really knows what the Kingdom will be like and what we will do when we are there, but we do have some descriptions from Isaiah. Many times when the Kingdom is mentioned as a hope, it says that the elect will be a Kingdom of priests and they will reign along with Christ.

> This priestly role was first given to Israel, who defaulted; was then given to the Levites, whose performance was less than memorable; and finally has been given to the Gentiles. Now, it is the duty of both the Jews and the Gentiles, whom God has reconciled unto himself as one.
>
> God no longer makes any differentiation between Jews and Gentiles; both are in one tree, the good olive tree. God has not cast away the Jewish people, but has engrafted the Gentiles into the tree along with the remnant of the Jews who remained in the tree. The Jews will be grafted in again at some future time, and will bring forth the desired fruit.[174]

---

[174] (Kenison F., The Truth Revealed in Romans, 1999)

> The choice of Israel had nothing to do with their goodness or fitness to serve. They were chosen because of the promises to Abraham, Isaac, and Jacob.[175]

These promises extend to believers. Trust God when He says He loves you and has forgiven your sins and evil deeds. I see this phrase so many times that I have to wonder what it implies. The Bible never says that we will sit around and watch large screen television, or that the Kingdom life is similar to how I picture retirement. I think if you would ask a priest of the Catholic Church what his work was like, many of them would tell you that they enjoy serving the Lord and it does not seem like work to them, but I would also think that they are very busy.

Being a priest and "reigning" indicates responsibility. Today, any job or position in a company that has responsibility requires a lot of work. These people can really enjoy their jobs. To them it is not work, and they are compensated quite well because of the value they provide to their employers. A priest in the Kingdom will probably not be paid but will receive additional blessings the more they share the love of God. This is true even today. If you want more blessings, concentrate on being a servant, or even a slave, to the Lord and let Him use you to minister to those around us. If you do that, you will be a priest in the Kingdom. As "priests to our God," we worship Him, but we also share His love and Grace with others.

This raises the question, if we are to be priests and reign upon the earth, then who are we reigning over? Could it be the ones who are resurrected at the return of Christ, but who are not resurrected out from among the dead ones? These would be those who would be resurrected to a perishable body. If these people are alive, then they might continue to have children and live in the world as they do today, only under the rule of Christ.

---

[175] (Kenison F., 1999)

Isaiah 2:2–4

2 *Now it will come about that*
In the last days,
The mountain of the house of the Lord
Will be established as the chief of the mountains,
And will be raised above the hills;
And all the nations will stream to it.
And many peoples will come and say, "Come, let us
go up to the mountain of the Lord,
3 *To the house of the God of Jacob;*
That He may teach us concerning His ways,
And that we may walk in His paths."
For the law will go forth from Zion,
And the word of the Lord from Jerusalem.
4 *And He will judge between the nations,*
And will render decisions for many peoples;
And they will hammer their swords into plowshares,
and their spears into pruning hooks.
Nation will not lift up sword against nation,
And never again will they learn war.

Isaiah 11:1–10

1 *Then a shoot will spring from the stem of Jesse,*
And a branch from his roots will bear fruit.
2 *And the Spirit of the Lord will rest on Him,*
The spirit of wisdom and understanding,
The spirit of counsel and strength,
The spirit of knowledge and the fear of the Lord.
3 *And He will delight in the fear of the Lord,*
And He will not judge by what His eyes see,
Nor make a decision by what His ears hear;
4 *But with righteousness He will judge the poor,*
And decide with fairness for the afflicted of the earth;
And He will strike the earth with the rod of His mouth,

And with the breath of His lips He will slay the wicked.
5 Also righteousness will be the belt about His loins,
And faithfulness the belt about His waist.
6 And the wolf will dwell with the lamb,
And the leopard will lie down with the kid,
And the calf and the young lion and the fatling together;
And a little boy will lead them.
7 Also the cow and the bear will graze;
Their young will lie down together;
And the lion will eat straw like the ox.
8 And the nursing child will play by the hole of the cobra,
And the weaned child will put his hand on the viper's den.
9 They will not hurt or destroy in all My holy mountain,
For the earth will be full of the knowledge of the Lord
As the waters cover the sea.
10 Then it will come about in that day that the nations will resort to the root of Jesse, who will stand as a signal for the peoples; and His resting place will be glorious.

Nature or the creation can be cruel and harsh. We see predators kill defenseless animals for food. They attack and kill the weak, even amongst their own breed, and pose a threat to humans. Plants can poison us or stick us with harmful needles. Insects can sting, spread disease, and destroy our homes and crops. Food spoils. Bacteria infect us and make us sick. Ask a farmer how easy it is to make a living from the land. It was not supposed to be that way, and it was not that way in the Garden of Eden. When Adam was evicted from the Garden, God did not curse him; He cursed the ground.

Genesis 3:17–19

17 *Then to Adam He said, "Because you have listened to the voice of your wife, and have eaten from the tree about which I commanded you, saying, 'You shall not eat from it'; cursed is the ground because of you; in toil you will eat of it all the days of your life.*

18 *Both thorns and thistles it shall grow for you; and you will eat the plants of the field;*

19 *By the sweat of your face you will eat bread, till you return to the ground, because from it you were taken; for you are dust, and to dust you shall return."*

Even nature suffered from man's disobedience to God. Man's sinful state of rebellion against God has caused creation to suffer. Man was created to have dominion over the creation; now he is enslaved to it. It takes a lot of hard work and sweat to get the ground to cooperate enough to provide food. God cursed the ground. In the Kingdom, it will be returned to its original glory and believers will be revealed as the sons of God.

Romans 8:19–22

19 *For the anxious longing of the creation waits eagerly for the revealing of the sons of God.*

20 *For the creation was subjected to futility, not willingly, but because of Him who subjected it, in hope*

21 *that the creation itself also will be set free from its slavery to corruption into the freedom of the glory of the children of God.*

22 *For we know that the whole creation groans and suffers the pains of childbirth together until now.*

This is a hope that will impact one's daily walk with God, a hope that is real and a comfort to those who are suffering. It is something to cling to when undergoing persecution or experiencing the death of a loved one. Believers feel sorrow, but not like those who have no hope. Since people must be resurrected to enter into this Kingdom, they will enjoy the benefits of a resurrected body. They will be able to pass through walls, appear and disappear at will, and will not suffer any of the afflictions that the human body suffers from today. These are the things that Jesus was able to do after He had been resurrected.

Resurrected bodies can be difficult to comprehend. What will these bodies be like? Will they look the same as they do now? How can fleshly bodies, which will have rotted away or scattered as ashes, come back to life? Resurrected bodies will be just like the body Christ exhibited after He was resurrected. He could eat, Thomas could feel the wounds in His hands, and they recognized Him. Paul addresses these very questions in his letter to the church of Corinth.

1st Corinthians 15:35–44

35 *But someone will say, "How are the dead raised? And with what kind of body do they come?"*

36 *You fool! That which you sow does not come to life unless it dies;*

37 *and that which you sow, you do not sow the body which is to be, but a bare grain, perhaps of wheat or of something else.*

38 *But God gives it a body just as He wished, and to each of the seeds a body of its own.*

39 *All flesh is not the same flesh, but there is one flesh of men, and another flesh of beasts, and another flesh of birds, and another of fish.*

40 *There are also heavenly bodies and earthly bodies, but the glory of the heavenly is one, and the glory of the earthly is another.*

41 *There is one glory of the sun, and another glory of the moon, and another glory of the stars; for star differs from star in glory.*

42 So also is the resurrection of the dead. It is sown a perishable body, it is raised an imperishable body; 43 it is sown in dishonor, it is raised in glory; it is sown in weakness, it is raised in power; 44 it is sown a natural body, it is raised a spiritual body. If there is a natural body, there is also a spiritual body.

They who inherit the Kingdom will rule and reign along with Jesus in this Kingdom. They will not be sitting on clouds and playing harps, but will have a responsibility to judge the nations.

Revelation 20:6
...they will be priests of God and of Christ and will reign with Him for a thousand years.

Revelation 5:9–10
9 ...they sang a new song, saying, "Worthy are You to take the book and to break its seals; for You were slain, and purchased for God with Your blood men from every tribe and tongue and people and nation. 10 You have made them to be a kingdom and priests to our God; and they will reign upon the earth."

Isaiah 33:24
*And **no resident will say, "I am sick"**; The people who dwell there will be forgiven their iniquity.*

Isaiah 35:4–10
4 Say to those with anxious heart, "Take courage, fear not. Behold, your God will come with vengeance; The recompense of God will come, But He will save you."

5 Then the eyes of the blind will be opened,
And the ears of the deaf will be unstopped.
6 Then the lame will leap like a deer,
And the tongue of the dumb will shout for joy.
For waters will break forth in the wilderness
And streams in the Arabah.
7 And the scorched land will become a pool,
And the thirsty ground springs of water;
In the haunt of jackals, its resting place,
Grass becomes reeds and rushes.
8 And a highway will be there, a roadway,
And it will be called the Highway of Holiness.
The unclean will not travel on it,
But it will be for him who walks that way,
And fools will not wander on it.
9 No lion will be there,
Nor will any vicious beast go up on it;
These will not be found there.
But the redeemed will walk there,
10 And the ransomed of the Lord will return,
And come with joyful shouting to Zion,
With everlasting joy upon their heads.
They will find gladness and joy,
And sorrow and sighing will flee away.

Highlights regarding what it will be like from the preceding scriptures from Isaiah are:

- Nations will still exist, and they will want to go to the mountain of the Lord to be taught how to walk in His paths.
- They will hammer their swords into plowshares…Does that mean they still have to plow?
- There will be no more war.
- The "wolf will dwell with the lamb…"

- You "will joyously draw water from the springs of salvation." Today, when we really get emotional about the joy of our salvation, it is a foretaste of what we will feel all the time in the Kingdom as we joyously draw water from the springs of salvation.
- The "eyes of the blind will be opened."
- The "lame will leap like a deer."
- The "highway of holiness will be there."
- The "ransomed of the Lord will return …with everlasting joy upon their heads."

Other prophets offer a similar preview:

Joel 3:18
And in that day
The mountains will drip with sweet wine,
And the hills will flow with milk,
And all the brooks of Judah will flow with water;
And a spring will go out from the house of the Lord
To water the valley of Shittim.

Micah 4:6–7
6 *"In that day," declares the Lord,*
"I will assemble the lame
And gather the outcasts,
Even those whom I have afflicted.
7 *"I will make the lame a remnant*
And the outcasts a strong nation,
And the Lord will reign over them in Mount Zion
From now on and forever.

Revelation 21:4
…and He will wipe away every tear from their eyes;
and there will no longer be any death; there will no

longer be any mourning, or crying, or pain; the first things have passed away.

1st Corinthians 15:35–58

35 *But someone will say, "How are the dead raised? And with what kind of body do they come?"*

36 *You fool! That which you sow does not come to life unless it dies;*

37 *and that which you sow, you do not sow the body which is to be, but a bare grain, perhaps of wheat or of something else.*

38 *But God gives it a body just as He wished, and to each of the seeds a body of its own.*

39 *All flesh is not the same flesh, but there is one flesh of men, and another flesh of beasts, and another flesh of birds, and another of fish.*

40 ***There are also heavenly bodies and earthly bodies, but the glory of the heavenly is one, and the glory of the earthly is another.***

41 *There is one glory of the sun, and another glory of the moon, and another glory of the stars; for star differs from star in glory.*

42 ***So also is the resurrection of the dead. It is sown a perishable body, it is raised an imperishable body;***

43 *it is sown in dishonor, it is raised in glory; it is sown in weakness, it is raised in power;*

44 *it is sown a natural body, it is raised a spiritual body. If there is a natural body, there is also a spiritual body.*

45 *So also it is written, "The first man, Adam, became a living soul." The last Adam became a life-giving spirit.*

46 *However, the spiritual is not first, **but the natural; then the spiritual**.*

47 *The first man is from the earth, earthy; the second man is from heaven.*

48 *As is the earthy, so also are those who are earthy; and as is the heavenly, so also are those who are heavenly.*

49 *Just as we have borne the image of the earthy, we will also bear the image of the heavenly.*

50 *Now I say this, brethren, that flesh and blood cannot inherit the kingdom of God; nor does the perishable inherit the imperishable.*

51 *Behold, I tell you a mystery; we will not all sleep, but we will all be changed,*

52 *in a moment, in the twinkling of an eye, at the last trumpet; for the trumpet will sound, and the dead will be raised imperishable, and we will be changed.*

53 ___For this perishable must put on the imperishable, and this mortal must put on immortality___.

54 *But when this perishable will have put on the imperishable, and this mortal will have put on immortality, then will come about the saying that is written, "___Death is swallowed up in victory___.*

55 *O death, where is your victory? O death, where is your sting?"*

56 *The sting of death is sin, and the power of sin is the law;*

57 *but thanks be to God, who gives us the victory through our Lord Jesus Christ.*

58 *Therefore, my beloved brethren, be steadfast, immovable, always abounding in the work of the Lord, knowing that your toil is not in vain in the Lord.*

Whatever our existence in the Kingdom will be like, whatever Christians will do while there, I can guarantee that it will be wonderful. It is the first step to getting all of creation and mankind into the relationship that God intended us to have from the beginning. He had to let us see how we could handle life on our own. Now those who have realized that we cannot make it on our own will be ministering to those who thought they could. When they physically see Christ as King and they observe others receiving the blessings they could have had if they had accepted Christ, they will also be willing to enter into the perfect fellowship with Him. It may take some the full 1,000 years to come to this point. Those who never do will be terminated.

> The messianic reign thus culminates God's historical kingdom purpose. Destined to rule the earth for God (Gen. 1:26–28; Ps 8; Heb. 2:6ff.), man failed through sin, but God will triumph over failure through his own Son, Christ the God-Man, who will bring his kingdom on earth as it is in heaven (Matt. 6:10). When this is accomplished, the Son gives up the kingdom to the Father and this inaugurates the eternal state (1 Cor. 15:24ff.).[176]

---

[176] (Saucy, 1979)

25

THE GREAT WHITE THRONE JUDGMENT

The Kingdom will be a millennial Kingdom, a 1,000-year period. During that time, Christ will rule the earth from His throne in Jerusalem, along with His resurrected saints. Other people who will be resurrected back into similar bodies as they have now, along with their offspring, will be the ones ruled over. Satan will be bound for the 1,000-year reign, but those who have mortal bodies will still have a sinful nature. The "outer darkness" will exist so those living in it can be ministered to and develop a relationship with God through Jesus Christ.

His rule will be characterized by peace, prosperity, and righteousness. It will be a time of unprecedented physical and spiritual blessing throughout the world. It is clear from Isaiah 11 that the curse on the earth will be lifted, for "the wolf will live with the lamb...the cow will feed with the bear...and the lion will eat straw like the ox" (vv. 6–7).

But even in this environment, with Satan bound, man will still show himself to be a sinner. And when Satan is loosed once more, many will follow him in rebellion against Christ. This event will occur after the end of the Millennium and will lead to the final judgment at the "great white throne" (Rev. 20:11). The wicked will be cast into the lake of fire, but a new heaven and a new earth will be prepared for the righteous (Rev. 21:1–22:5).[177]

Revelation 20:7–10

7 *When the thousand years are completed, Satan will be released from his prison,*

8 *and will come out to deceive the nations which are in the four corners of the earth, Gog and Magog, to gather them together for the war; the number of them is like the sand of the seashore.*

9 *And they came up on the broad plain of the earth and surrounded the camp of the saints and the beloved city, and fire came down from heaven and devoured them.*

10 *And the devil who deceived them was thrown into the lake of fire and brimstone, where the beast and the false prophet are also; and they will be tormented day and night forever and ever.*

The greatest harvest of souls this earth has ever seen will come during the Millennium. Our Lord will rule as earth dictator. There will be universal righteousness, peace, and prosperity. Satan and his demons will be in the bottomless pit, the nation of Israel will be saved, and only true doctrine will be preached. But despite all this, there will be masses of humanity still unsaved at the end of the thousand years. To these the final judgment of The Great White Throne and the earth-conflagration will come as a surprise.[178]

After the 1,000-year reign of Christ on earth, another judgment will take place. This is referred to in Scripture as the Great White Throne

---

[177] (Hardman, 1996)
[178] (Wuest, 1997, c1984)

Judgment. This judgment does not include those who were in the Kingdom with Christ; it is only for those who do not have spiritual bodies.

Revelation 20:11–15

11 *Then I saw a great white throne and Him who sat upon it, from whose presence earth and heaven fled away, and no place was found for them.*

12 *And I saw the dead, the great and the small, standing before the throne, and **books were opened; and another book was opened, which is the book of life; and the dead were judged from the things which were written in the books, according to their deeds**.*

13 *And the sea gave up the dead which were in it, and death and Hades gave up the dead which were in them; and they were judged, every one of them according to their deeds.*

14 *Then death and Hades were thrown into the lake of fire. This is the second death, the lake of fire.*

15 *And if anyone's name was not found **written in the book of life**, he was thrown into the lake of fire.*

Verse 20:12 continues John's description of the final judgment of mankind as they stand before God. Notice that they are "the dead." If they are dead, how did they stand? Surely, John meant they were spiritually dead.

And to show that God is no respecter of persons, John declared that "small and great" stand before God. A person's status in the secular world will have no influence on this final judgment.

The "open books" indicate that this judgment is just, and without error. Every deed will be brought into judgment to reveal whether or not those deeds were based upon a faith and love of God.

The "book of life" contained the names of those who did not recant their faith, or follow the anti-christ religion, but instead followed the one true God. The book of life contains not only the overcomers from the age of grace in which we now live, but also those of the age as well. Perhaps it could be considered the roster of the heavenly church.[179]

It is important to note here that the Greek word "Hades" (ᾅδης) refers to the Hebrew word שְׁאוֹל (Sheol), which simply means *grave*. Unfortunately, the King James Version translated it as hell, and thus a new doctrine was born.

> **HADES** — that which is out of sight, a Greek word used to denote the state or place of the dead. All the dead alike go into this place. To be buried, to go down to the grave, to descend into hades, are equivalent expressions. In the LXX. this word is the usual rendering of the Hebrew sheol, the common receptacle of the departed.[180]

This passage in Revelation 20:11–15 causes all premillennial theologians difficulties regarding its literal interpretation, which seems to conflict with the rest of the verses in the Bible regarding the second coming and the Judgments. Most premillennialists place the Great White Throne Judgment at the end of the 1,000-year millennial reign. The resurrection of both the just and the unjust occurs at the beginning of the millennium. However, verses 12 and 13 seem to be out of sequence with what I have just stated. I have not been able to find any satisfactory explanation in my research, and it proves that this is not an easy concept to understand. Much of Revelations is not sequential, but to use that excuse here is not acceptable to me at this time.

One thing that is clear is that death and the grave will be cast into the lake of fire. If the grave is the place where the dead ones go, then the grave

---

[179]

[180] (Easton, 1893)

will no longer be needed and death will be done away with as well. This is the destruction of death and the grave. They both will cease to exist.

Now, anyone whose name is not found in the book of life will also be thrown into the lake of fire. Scriptures never talk about anyone's name being added to the book of life, but only erased or blotted out. From what I can gather, that means that before the foundation of the world, names were in the book of life. Rejecting Christ, accepting the mark of the beast, or rebelling against Christ after 1,000 years of living under His reign will cause your name to be blotted out or erased. It will no longer be found there. It appears that those who take the mark of the beast did not have their names in the book of life from the foundation of the world.

How many chances are we given? I cannot imagine anyone passing on all of those chances, but I also cannot imagine how men can walk into a school and kill innocent children. How can they become suicide bombers to kill innocent people—not as an act of war, but just as an act of pure hatred and rebellion against even their own religion?

Psalms 69:26–28
26 *For they have persecuted him whom You Yourself have smitten,*
And they tell of the pain of those whom You have wounded.
27 *Add iniquity to their iniquity,*
And may they not come into Your righteousness.
28 *May they be **blotted out of the book of life***
And may they not be recorded with the righteous.

Philippians 4:3
*Indeed, true companion, I ask you also to help these women who have shared my struggle in the cause of the gospel, together with Clement also and the rest of my fellow workers, whose **names are in the book of life**.*

Revelation 3:5
*"He who overcomes will thus be clothed in white garments; and I will not **erase his name from the book of life**, and I will confess his name before My Father and before His angels."*

Revelation 13:8
All who dwell on the earth will worship him, everyone whose name has not been written from the foundation of the world in the book of life of the Lamb who has been slain.

This verse indicates that the names of those who worship the beast were not written in the book of life before the foundation of the world.

The "Lake of Fire" appears to be the result of the last judgment. It appears to be final. However, I know many people who believe that the Lake of Fire is another purification process, because the Greek word for fire is πυρὸς (*puros*), which they say means *purify*. While the concept appeals to me, I cannot believe it since it would be a violation of one of my rules of interpretation laid out in the second chapter of this book: "The obvious meaning is true." I cannot switch rules to make a doctrine fit.

"Lake of fire" is an:

> ...idiom, literally 'lake of fire (and sulfur),' occurring in some slightly different forms six times in Revelation, three times with the addition of θεῖον 'sulfur') a place of eternal punishment and destruction—'lake of fire, hell.' καὶ ὁ διάβολος ὁ πλανῶν αὐτοὺς ἐβλήθη εἰς τὴν λίμνην τοῦ πυρὸς καὶ θείου 'then the Devil, who deceived them, was thrown into the lake of fire and sulfur' Re 20:10.[181]

---

[181] (Louw, 1996)

Who else will be thrown into the Lake of Fire? According to the following, the "Beast and the False Prophet."

Revelation 19:20

And the beast was seized, and with him the false prophet who performed the signs in his presence, by which he deceived those who had received the mark of the beast and those who worshiped his image; these two were thrown alive into the lake of fire which burns with brimstone.

The beast and the false prophet are the only ones thrown into the lake of fire at this point in time. Satan is cast into the pit for a thousand years, and then he will be released for a short time, and then he will be cast into the lake of fire after the Great White Throne Judgment which occurs at the end of 1,000 years.

The Deceiver or the "Divider"

Daimonios is a noun while all the derivatives of *diabolos* are adjectives and are only descriptive of some thing or someone. Why the KJV translated it as "devil" is truly puzzling. The word *diabolos* is composed of two Greek words: *dia*, **through**, and *balloo*, **thrust** or **cast**. Thus, the word means to thrust through, or to divide. If we translated the adjective *diabolos* as a noun, it should be as "a divider," or "a dividing person."[182]

Revelation 20:10

And the devil who deceived them was thrown into the lake of fire and brimstone, where the beast and the false prophet are also; and they will be tormented day and night forever and ever.

---

[182] (Kenison F., 1999)

Others

Revelation 21:8

But for the cowardly and unbelieving and abominable and murderers and immoral persons and sorcerers and idolaters and all liars, their part will be in the lake that burns with fire and brimstone, which is the second death.

We have heard that before. Who is not immoral or a liar?

1st Corinthians 6:11

Such were some of you; but you were washed, but you were sanctified, but you were justified in the name of the Lord Jesus Christ and in the Spirit of our God.

John saw this destruction of death that Paul wrote about. He also saw the destruction of the grave at the same time. When death is overcome, there will be no need for hell, at least in terms of the grave, because men will no longer suffer physical death. But there will still be a need for hell as a place for the spiritually dead. Therefore, they were cast into the lake of fire, which is the "second death."

So far, the false christ, the false prophet, the devil, and now death and the grave have all been cast into the lake of fire. They have all been destroyed. After this time, there will be no need of death and, therefore, no need of an earthly grave. Whenever those who have opposed God are cast into the second death it is the end of the road for all their aspirations which were contrary to God. The "lake of fire" now becomes the abode of the wicked dead.[183]

---

[183] (Kenison F., The Apocalypse of Revelations, 1996)

Isaiah 66:18–24

18 *"For I know their works and their thoughts; the time is coming to gather all nations and tongues. And they shall come and see My glory.*

19 *I will set a sign among them and will send survivors from them to the nations: Tarshish, Put, Lud, Meshech, Tubal and Javan, to the distant coastlands that have neither heard My fame nor seen My glory. And they will declare My glory among the nations.*

20 *Then they shall bring all your brethren from all the nations as a grain offering to the* LORD, *on horses, in chariots, in litters, on mules and on camels, to My holy mountain Jerusalem," says the* LORD, *"just as the sons of Israel bring their grain offering in a clean vessel to the house of the* LORD.

21 *I will also take some of them for priests and for Levites," says the* LORD.

22 *"For just as the new heavens and the new earth Which I make will endure before Me," declares the* LORD,
"So your offspring and your name will endure.

23 *And it shall be from new moon to new moon And from sabbath to sabbath,
All mankind will come to bow down before Me," says the* LORD.

24 *"Then they will go forth and look
On the corpses of the men
Who have transgressed against Me.
For their worm will not die
And their fire will not be quenched;
And they will be an abhorrence to all mankind."*

Abhorrence means an abomination, revulsion, or disgust.

Verse 24 above mentions that the worm will not die, and the fire will not be quenched. Mark quotes this verse in Mark 9:

Mark 9:43–48

43 *"If your hand causes you to stumble, cut it off; it is better for you to enter life crippled, than, having your two hands, to go into hell, into the unquenchable fire,*
44 *[where* THEIR WORM DOES NOT DIE, AND THE FIRE IS NOT QUENCHED.*]*
45 *"If your foot causes you to stumble, cut it off; it is better for you to enter life lame, than, having your two feet, to be cast into hell,*
46 *[where* THEIR WORM DOES NOT DIE, AND THE FIRE IS NOT QUENCHED.*]*
47 *"If your eye causes you to stumble, throw it out; it is better for you to enter the kingdom of God with one eye, than, having two eyes, to be cast into hell,*
48 *where* THEIR WORM DOES NOT DIE, AND THE FIRE IS NOT QUENCHED.*"*

The quotation goes with γέεννα (Geheena—The trash pit outside of Jerusalem) and is designed to characterize eschatological hell. Since we find in contemporary Judaism both the idea of the annihilation of the damned and also that of their unceasing punishment both interpretations are possible here, too, according to the wording. Exegetes refer the non-dying of the worm either to full destruction, the definitive loss of life or to unremitting corruption, eternal torment. In view of τὸ πῦρ τὸ ἄσβεστον (fire unquenchable) in verse 43 the latter interpretation is to be preferred. There is no suggestion that the worm and fire are to be related separately to soul and body along the line of gnawings of conscience and physical pain. In the first instance both terms describe the destruction of corpses and they are then used figuratively for the punishment of hell which affects the whole man.[184]

Revelation 21:1–3

1 *Then I saw a new heaven and a new earth; for the first heaven and the first earth passed away, and there is no longer any sea.*

2 *And I saw the holy city, new Jerusalem, coming down out of heaven from God, made ready as a bride adorned for her husband.*

3 *And I heard a loud voice from the throne, saying, "Behold, the tabernacle of God is among men, and He will dwell among them, and they shall be His people, and God Himself will be among them..."*

The Greek language has two words that are translated as "new" in the New Testament. They are καινός (*kainó*) and νέος (*néos*). *Néos* means new as we use it today in English: "fresh," or as in "new" converts. *Kainós*, on the other hand, means new in nature. The *new* earth refers to a "renewed," or even "remodeled," earth.

KAINOS (Greek). kye-noss.

Greek word for "new" (2nd Corinthians 5:17). It expresses a newness in quality more than in time; neos suggests new in time.[185]

Theological Data. kainós denotes the new and miraculous thing that the age of salvation brings. It is thus a key theological term in eschatological promise: the new heaven and earth in Rev. 21:1; 2 Pet. 3:13, the new Jerusalem in Rev. 3:12; 21:2[186]

---

[184] (Kittel G. B., 1964)
[185] (Standard Bible Dictionary, 2006)
[186] (Kittel G. F., 1985)

A new heaven, a new earth, and a new Jerusalem. As I understand it, after the Great White Throne Judgment, the Kingdom continues, but everything on heaven and earth is renewed. Jesus will turn everything over to God the Father.

1st Corinthians 15:24–28

24 *...then comes the end, when **He hands over the kingdom to the God and Father**, when He has abolished all rule and all authority and power.*

25 *For He must reign until He has put all His enemies under His feet.*

26 *The last enemy that will be abolished is death.*

27 *For* HE HAS PUT ALL THINGS IN SUBJECTION UNDER HIS FEET. *But when He says, "All things are put in subjection," it is evident that He is excepted who put all things in subjection to Him.*

28 *When all things are subjected to Him, then **the Son Himself also will be subjected to the One who subjected all things to Him, so that God may be all in all**."*

"Behold, I am making all things new" (Rev. 21:5). With these words, biblical eschatology attains its goal. The creation of new heavens and new earth completes the divine regeneration of all things spoiled through sin. Begun in the microcosmos of individual hearts during the present age, the process will not be complete until the macrocosmos of the universe is made new. From a regenerate heart to a glorified body at the first resurrection and the lifting of the curse of nature during the millennium, each phase of the eschatological drama is a step toward this final goal. In this final act, the very structure of the universe is transformed. The old will be disrupted to make room for the new. "The heavens will disappear with a roar; the elements will be destroyed by fire, and the earth and everything in it will be laid bare" (2nd Peter 3:10; cf. Isa.

34:4; 51:6). This must not be interpreted as an annihilation. Rather, as in all of God's regenerative acts, the old must die to be created anew, but continuity is retained.

The picture of this final state is one of sublime perfection. While it is frequently spoken of as heaven, in reality the heavenly comes down to earth. In the final vision of the Apocalypse John says, "I saw the Holy City, the new Jerusalem, coming down out of heaven from God, prepared as a bride beautifully dressed for her husband. And I heard a loud voice from the throne saying, 'Now the dwelling of God is with men, and he will live with them. They will be his people, and God himself will be with them and be their God' " (Rev. 21:2, 3). There will yet be the new heavens above the earth and God will still be transcendent over the earth and will therefore be the God of heaven. But heaven is more than a place beyond the earth; it is the abode of God. Thus the heavenly realm comes to earth. What was formerly described as the "heavenly Jerusalem" (Heb. 12:22) becomes the "new Jerusalem" of the new earth.

Three characteristics stand out in John's description of the eternal abode of God's people. While the apostle's description of the city as being made of pure gold, as pure as glass, with walls of jasper and gates made of single pearls (Rev. 21:18–21) is probably symbolical, it is without question intended to reveal a place of exquisite beauty. "It shone with the glory of God, and its brilliance was like that of a very precious jewel, like a jasper, clear as crystal" (Rev. 21:11).

It is also a place of fullness of life. With all sin and death forever banished (Rev. 20:10 ff., 21:8; 22:3), it is "Paradise regained." The "river of the water of life," with the "tree of life" on each side, flows in "the middle of the great street of the city" depicting the plenitude of eternal life enjoyed by all (Rev. 22:1, 2; cf. Ps. 46:4, Zech. 14:8). It is the "Sabbath-rest" of God (Heb. 4:9) with release from all burdensome toil (Rev. 14:13), but filled with the joyful activity of loving worship and service (Rev. 5:8, 9; 7:15; 22:3).

Above all, and at the foundation of all its beauty and perfection of life, the final abode brings perfect fellowship with God. In the first phase of the realized eschatology of this age, we enjoy the presence of the indwelling Holy Spirit. When Christ returns, we will be with him, but in the new creation, God's redemptive plan will be complete and we will be forever in the presence of the fullness of the revelation of the triune God. Of this day John writes, "The throne of God and of the Lamb will be in the city, and his servants will serve him. They will see his face, and his name will be on their foreheads" (Rev. 22:3, 4). While biblical eschatology holds forth the new creation with all of its glories as the inheritance of the saints, it is ultimately the inheritance of God himself that brings perfection. Long ago, the heart of the psalmist was fixed on this hope: "The Lord is the portion of my inheritance and my cup.... Indeed, my heritage is beautiful to me" (Ps. 16:5, 6).[187]

---

[187] (Saucy, 1979)

26

THE TIMELINE OF THE KINGDOM

The chronological order of the eschatological events is as follows:

- The Return Of Christ
- The Defeat Of The Antichrist
- The Binding Of Satan
- The First Resurrection
- The Judgment by Christ
- The Millennium
- The Release Of Satan
- The Last Judgment
- Death and Hades are thrown into the Lake of Fire with Satan and all of his followers
- The New Heavens And Earth

The figure featured later in this chapter is my interpretation of the timeline. I have researched it enough to know that I am not the only one who sees it this way, but it is only an illustration of what I have been discussing. It is not critical in any way that you believe this way, only that you walk with Christ.

The final sign of the end times will be the "Abomination of Desolation."

Mark 13:14–23

14 *"But **when you see the abomination of desolation standing where it should not be (let the reader understand)**, then those who are in Judea must flee to the mountains.*

15 *The one who is on the housetop must not go down, or go in to get anything out of his house;*

16 *and the one who is in the field must not turn back to get his coat.*

17 *But woe to those who are pregnant and to those who are nursing babies in those days!*

18 *But pray that it may not happen in the winter.*

19 *For those days will be a time of tribulation such as has not occurred since the beginning of the creation which God created until now, and never will.*

20 *Unless the Lord had shortened those days, no life would have been saved; but for the sake of the elect, whom He chose, He shortened the days.*

21 *And then if anyone says to you, 'Behold, here is the Christ'; or, 'Behold, He is there'; do not believe him;*

22 *for false Christs and false prophets will arise, and will show signs and wonders, in order to lead astray, if possible, the elect.*

23 *But take heed; behold, I have told you everything in advance."*

The term was first used by Daniel in the Old Testament. Some people think that "the Abomination of Desolation" is a person or the antichrist.

Daniel 11:31

And forces from him [the king of the North, verses 2–30] *will arise, desecrate the sanctuary fortress, and **do away with the regular sacrifice**. And they will set up the **abomination of desolation**. And by* *smooth words he will turn to godlessness those who act wickedly toward the covenant, but the people who know their God will display strength and take action.*

Daniel 12:11

*And from the time that the regular sacrifice is abolished, and **the abomination of desolation** is set up, there will be 1,290 days.*

The Abomination of Desolation was a detestable object of pagan idolatry so loathsome to God that his people would feel desolate and devastated in its presence…In another vision of coming abomination, a detestable object would be set up in the temple in Jerusalem (Dn. 11:31) 1,290 days after the beginning of a period of sacrilege (Dn. 12:11), thus destroying the temple's holiness and rendering it unclean by ceremonial and ethical standards.[188]

This term was not entirely unknown to the Jews living during the time of Jesus. Their history taught that during the Maccabean times about 200 years earlier the king of Syria, Antiochus Epiphanes IV, sent his general "Apollonius, with twenty thousand troops under orders to seize Jerusalem on a Sabbath. There he erected an idol of Zeus and desecrated the altar by offering swine on it. This idol became known to the Jews as 'the abomination of desolation' (*hassiqqus mesomem*, 11:31), which served as a type of a future abomination that will be set up in the Jerusalem sanctuary to be built in the last days (cf. Christ's prediction in Matt 24:15)." [189]

Realize that this is the **sign of the end times**. The Antichrist will set up or perform this despicable object or act of vile rebellion against the sacred worship of God, and I believe it will be in the newly rebuilt Temple in Jerusalem.

---

[188] (Elwell, 1988)
[189] (Constable, 2003)

2nd Thessalonians 2:3–4

3 *Let no one in any way deceive you, for **it will not come unless the apostasy comes first**, and the man of lawlessness is revealed, the son of destruction,*
4 *who opposes and exalts himself above every so-called god or object of worship, so that he takes his seat in the temple of God, displaying himself as being God.*

I am convinced that the apostasy is the act of placing the "Abomination of Desolation" in the temple. The Greek word for apostasy (ἀποστασία or apostasia) means "to rise up in open defiance of authority, with the presumed intention to overthrow it or to act in complete opposition to its demands—'to rebel against, to revolt, to engage in insurrection, rebellion.'"[190]

After this sign or act, the great tribulation starts. According to a literal interpretation of the weeks in Daniel, this is the seventieth week of years, or seven years.

Daniel 9:24–27

24 *Seventy weeks have been decreed for your people and your holy city, to finish the transgression, to make an end of sin, to make atonement for iniquity, to bring in everlasting righteousness, to seal up vision and prophecy and to anoint the most holy place.*
25 *So you are to know and discern that **from the issuing of a decree to restore and rebuild Jerusalem until Messiah the Prince there will be seven weeks and sixty-two weeks**; it will be built again, with plaza and moat, even in times of distress.*
26 *Then after the sixty-two weeks the Messiah will be cut off and have nothing, and the people of the prince who is to come will destroy the city and the sanctuary.*

---

[190] (Louw, 1996)

And its end will come with a flood; even to the end there will be war; desolations are determined.
27 And he will make a firm covenant with the many for one week, but in the middle of the week he will put a stop to sacrifice and grain offering; and on the wing of abominations will come one who makes desolate, even until a complete destruction, one that is decreed, is poured out on the one who makes desolate.

Seventy weeks, or most likely weeks (period of a group of seven) of years, are to take place from the issuing of the decree to rebuild Jerusalem until the holy place is anointed. Seventy times seven equals 490 years. The first portion of the seventy weeks is assumed to be seven weeks (49 years) for the rebuilding of Jerusalem after the Babylonian captivity. The next period is the 62 weeks (434 years) after which the Messiah will be cut off. This is assumed to be when Christ was crucified. All of this totaled 483 years from the decree to rebuild the city of Jerusalem until the death of Christ. The exact timing of this prophecy is debated, but certainly it is in regards to the coming of Christ the Messiah. The time between the death of Christ and the seventieth week is not mentioned. This is how the idea of a seven year tribulation has been derived.

Whenever one considers the timing of the return of Christ, the following passage has to be considered.

1st Thessalonians 5:1–11

1 Now as to the times and the epochs, brethren, you have no need of anything to be written to you.
*2 For you yourselves know full well that **the day of the Lord will come just like a thief in the night**.*
*3 While they are saying, "Peace and safety!" then **destruction will come upon them suddenly like labor pains upon a woman with child, and they will not escape**.*
*4 **But you, brethren, are not in darkness, that the day would overtake you like a thief**;*

5 for you are all sons of light and sons of day. We are not of night nor of darkness;

6 so then let us not sleep as others do, but let us be alert and sober.

7 For those who sleep do their sleeping at night, and those who get drunk get drunk at night.

8 But since we are of the day, let us be sober, having put on the breastplate of faith and love, and as a helmet, the hope of salvation.

9 For God has not destined us for wrath, but for obtaining salvation through our Lord Jesus Christ,

10 who died for us, so that whether we are awake or asleep, we will live together with Him.

11 Therefore encourage one another and build up one another, just as you also are doing.

One of the main arguments for the Pre-Tribulation rapture is found in verse 2 above. Those who believe in the Pre-Tribulation rapture argue that He cannot surprise the believers as a thief in the night if we have any expectation that He is about to arrive. If we are to pass through the tribulation for seven years, we would expect His return to happen at the end of those seven years.

The next verse and the rest of this chapter seem to answer that objection. After the world is fat, dumb, and happy with their new leader, the Anti-Christ, they will be saying, "Peace and safety." Destruction coming as a surprise indicates, at least to me, that they will be suddenly hit with the "Day of the Lord." However, we who are not in darkness will not be overtaken by surprise like a thief in the night, but will instead be alert, putting on the breastplate (armor) of faith and love and as a helmet the hope of salvation (future tense or the Kingdom). I see nowhere in this passage that makes a case for a pre-tribulation escape of the believers.

I make no attempt to try and explain who or what the Anti-Christ or the beast is. Volumes have been written on this subject, and I believe

371

they are only speculation. It could be a man, a government, or some kind of an organization. Be on the alert for anything that has any kind of appearance of the descriptions in the Word.

I am concerned with all of the problems with credit card and identity theft, and that a solution may end up being a mark of a number of some kind, without which we will not be able to buy or sell. If one has to pay homage or forsake one's faith in any way to receive this mark, I would really be in prayer about it for a long time.

In the chapter on why I believe in the post-tribulation rapture, I talk about the last trumpet, and that at that point we will be caught up in the air or clouds to meet with Christ while He is on His way down to earth. In that moment, in the twinkling of an eye, we will be changed and thus we will be with the Lord forever.

> **Matthew 24:29–31**
> **29** *"But immediately **after the tribulation** of those days* THE SUN WILL BE DARKENED, AND THE MOON WILL NOT GIVE ITS LIGHT, AND THE STARS WILL FALL *from the sky, and the powers of the heavens will be shaken.*
> **30** *And then the sign of the Son of Man will appear in the sky, and then all the tribes of the earth will mourn, and they will see the* SON OF MAN COMING ON THE CLOUDS OF THE SKY *with power and great glory.*
> **31** *And **He will send forth His angels with** A GREAT TRUMPET **and** THEY WILL GATHER TOGETHER **His elect from the four winds, from one end of the sky to the other**."*

> **1st Corinthians 15:51–58**
> **51** *Behold, I tell you a mystery; we will not all sleep, but we will all be changed,*
> **52** *in a moment, in the twinkling of an eye, at the last trumpet; for the trumpet will sound, and the dead will be raised imperishable, and we will be changed.*

53 For this perishable must put on the imperishable, and this mortal must put on immortality.

54 But when this perishable will have put on the imperishable, and this mortal will have put on immortality, then will come about the saying that is written, "DEATH IS SWALLOWED UP in victory.

55 "O DEATH, WHERE IS YOUR VICTORY? O DEATH, WHERE IS YOUR STING?"

56 The sting of death is sin, and the power of sin is the law;

57 but thanks be to God, who gives us the victory through our Lord Jesus Christ.

58 Therefore, my beloved brethren, be steadfast, immovable, always abounding in the work of the Lord, knowing that your toil is not in vain in the Lord."

After Christ returns to the earth, Satan is thrown into the abyss, and bound for a thousand years, or until the end of the millennium. I asked an amillennialist once if Satan was bound and this was the Kingdom, then why did Satan still seem to have so much influence on people. In all seriousness, he told me that they believe he is on a long chain.

Revelation 20:1–3

1 Then I saw an angel coming down from heaven, holding the key of the abyss and a great chain in his hand.

2 And he laid hold of the dragon, the serpent of old, who is the devil and Satan, and bound him for a thousand years;

3 and he threw him into the abyss, and shut it and sealed it over him, so that he would not deceive the nations any longer, until the thousand years were completed; after these things he must be released for a short time.

The Timeline below shows all of this graphically as I interpret prophecy.

Fig. 6 Timeline for the Kingdom

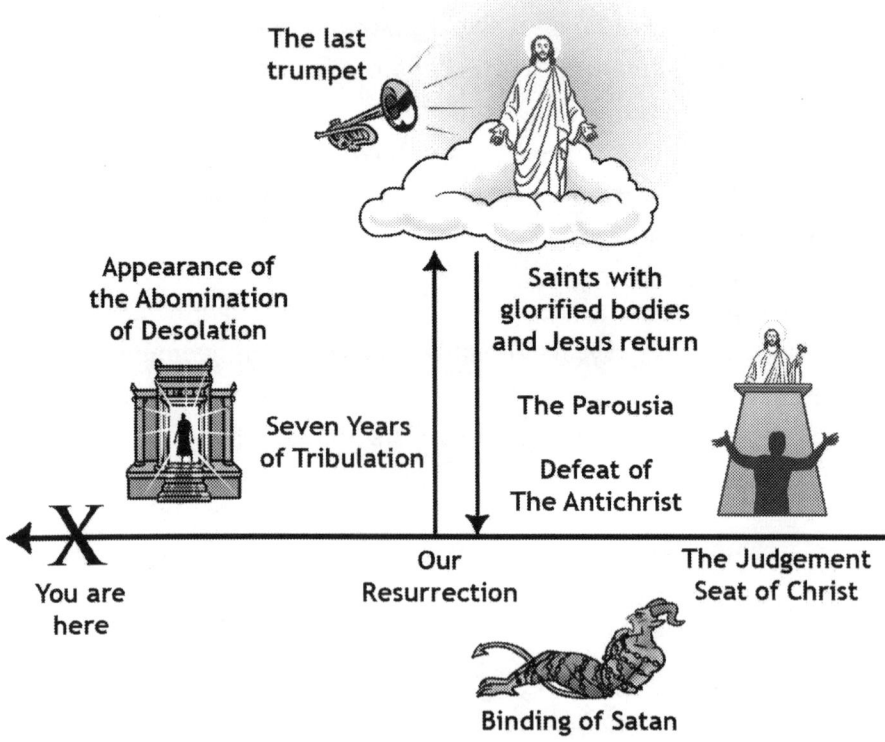

374

Rev. 20: 7-9

Fire came down
from heaven to
devour them

New Heaven
and New Earth

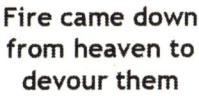

Release of Satan:
He gathers
the nations
for war

Great White
Throne
Judgement

Tree
of Life

Millennial Reign
of Christ
1000 years

I believe that millions
will become followers of
Christ during this time

New
Jerusalem

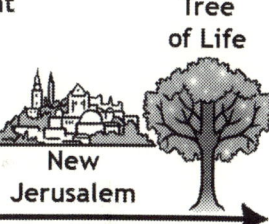

The Devil, Death,
and Hades will be
cast into the Lake
of Fire

Outer Darkness

1st Thessalonians 4:13–18

13 *But we do not want you to be uninformed, brethren, about those who are asleep, so that you will not grieve as do the rest who have no hope.*

14 *For if we believe that Jesus died and rose again, even so God will bring with Him those who have fallen asleep in Jesus.*

15 *For this we say to you by the word of the Lord, that we who are alive and remain until the coming of the Lord, will not precede those who have fallen asleep.*

16 *For the Lord Himself will descend from heaven with a shout, with the voice of the archangel and with the trumpet of God, and the dead in Christ will rise first.*

17 *Then we who are alive and remain will be caught up together with them in the clouds to meet the Lord in the air, and so we shall always be with the Lord.*

18 *Therefore comfort one another with these words.*

Revelation 20:7–11

7 *When the thousand years are completed, Satan will be released from his prison,*

8 *and will come out to deceive the nations which are in the four corners of the earth, Gog and Magog, to gather them together for the war; the number of them is like the sand of the seashore.*

9 *And they came up on the broad plain of the earth and surrounded the camp of the saints and the beloved city, and fire came down from heaven and devoured them.*

10 *And the devil who deceived them was thrown into the lake of fire and brimstone, where the beast and the false prophet are also; and they will be tormented day and night forever and ever.*

11 *Then I saw a great white throne and Him who sat upon it, from whose presence earth and heaven fled away, and no place was found for them.*

Above, I said that I believe millions will become followers of Christ during the outer darkness. Where do I get the idea that millions will be saved? It is true that Scripture never says those words. In the passage below, you will see that Israel had a partial hardening so that the Gentiles could be saved (future tense) into the Kingdom.

Romans 11:25–26

25 *For I do not want you, brethren, to be uninformed of this mystery—so that you will not be wise in your own estimation—that a partial hardening has happened to Israel until the fullness of the Gentiles has come in;*
26 ___and so all Israel will be saved___*; just as it is written, "The Deliverer will come from Zion, He will remove ungodliness from Jacob."*

Matthew 8:12

...but the sons of the kingdom will be cast out into the outer darkness; in that place there will be weeping and gnashing of teeth.

The sons of the Kingdom, who are the physical descendants of Abraham, will be cast into outer darkness. However, when they see that Jesus is the Messiah and realize that the Kingdom is present, I am convinced that they will become followers of Christ very quickly. "All of Israel" that will be saved, including the more than six million Jews who were slaughtered by the Nazis during World War II.

At the close of the millennium, Satan will be released to lead those whose hearts have not been changed (identified as Gog and Magog) in one final rebellion against "the camp of God's people, the city he loves" (Rev 20:7, 8; cf. Ezek. 38–39). The final manifestation of sin on the earth will be crushed by supernatural fire from heaven and the devil will be consigned to his final destiny, the lake of fire, to be followed shortly by his followers' receiving the sentence of the "second death" at the great white throne judgment that takes place at the close of the millennium (Rev 20:10–15).[191]

On the timeline shown, Revelation 20:7–8 says that Satan will deceive Gog and Magog. Most people today do not understand what that means. Gog was the prince in the land called Magog. He was a mortal enemy of Israel.

Ezekiel 38:2

Son of man, set your face toward Gog of the land of Magog, the prince of Rosh, Meshech and Tubal, and prophesy against him...

In John's imagery, though, Gog and Magog represented all the nations of the earth who had turned against the rule of Jesus, the Christ, and *The God*.

> Everyone who has ever lived is now on earth, and they are either for or against God and his Christ. There were still so many people against God that John said the number of them was "as the sand of the sea." They were called to participate in the battle of Armageddon, which will be the final battle that men will ever be allowed to wage against God. Those who do not wish to follow God will gather for this last battle, and they will be defeated.[192]

> Here, it indicates that those people, who have answered the call to fight against Jesus Christ and his saints, are streaming together from throughout the entire earth.

---

[191] (Saucy, 1979)

[192] (Kenison F., The Apocalypse of Revelations, 1996)

This is amazing! This horde of people coming to fight against God has lived under the law of God for 1,000 years, while being ministered to by the glorified saints. Yet, when given the opportunity, they again choose to establish the rule of man, the old Adamic nature. It is puzzling why so many will still refuse the love of God, and why they believe they can be victorious over God.

John saw the camp of the saints set apart from the beloved city, or Jerusalem. The "camp" could mean all the land that God had promised Abraham. This land was given to Israel again at the coming of the Lord, and it was to be divided among the New Israel.

This Promised Land and its boundaries, which include much of what we call the Middle East, will be the location for the physical aspects of the kingdom of God on earth. The glorified saints will go forth from this area, at the instructions of Jesus, the Christ, to bring order out of the chaos created on earth by the anti-christ government. The rule of Jesus from the Promised Land will extend over the whole earth and he will be the king of kings.

"Fire" from God refers to God's righteous judgment, which is for the purpose of the reuniting men with himself. Since the fire devoured them, this sounds like a great doom, and it is! But, here again, this was a spiritual battle, not a physical one.

This fire from heaven and its purpose was often misunderstood, even by the disciples. For example...

Luke 9:54–56

"And when his disciples James and John saw this, they said, Lord, wilt though that we call fire down from heaven as did Elias, and consume them? But, he turned, and rebuked them, and said, Ye know not

what manner of spirit ye are of. For the son of Man is not come to destroy men's lives, but to save them."

...The disciples had not yet realized that they were to act in love through the spirit. Jesus rebuked them because they still considered those who were out of the way as enemies, not people to whom they should demonstrate the love of God.[193]

Finally, after the 1,000-year reign is over, Satan is defeated and cast into fire and the final Great White Throne Judgment has taken place.

Revelation 21:1–2

1 *Then I saw a new heaven and a new earth; for the first heaven and the first earth passed away, and there is no longer any sea.*
2 *And I saw the holy city, new Jerusalem, coming down out of heaven from God, made ready as a bride adorned for her husband.*

According to Matthew's parable of the marriage feast, the king's son represented Jesus Christ, who was betrothed to the kingdom of God. John now saw the consummation of that parable. The kingdom of God, once a new creation of its own, has now been turned into a new heaven and a new earth. The kingdom of God has now reached its final stage of fulfillment, seen by John as the New Jerusalem coming down out of heaven, prepared as a bride for her husband.[194]

Revelation 21:3–8

3 *And I heard a loud voice from the throne, saying, "Behold, the tabernacle of God is among men, and He will dwell among them, and they shall be His people, and God Himself will be among them,*

---

[193] (Kenison F., The Apocalypse of Revelations, 1996)
[194] (Kenison F., The Apocalypse of Revelations, 1996)

4 and He will wipe away every tear from their eyes; and there will no longer be any death; there will no longer be any mourning, or crying, or pain; the first things have passed away."

5 And He who sits on the throne said, "Behold, I am making all things new." And He said, "Write, for these words are faithful and true."

6 Then He said to me, "It is done. I am the Alpha and the Omega, the beginning and the end. I will give to the one who thirsts from the spring of the water of life without cost.

7 He who overcomes will inherit these things, and I will be his God and he will be My son.

8 But for the cowardly and unbelieving and abominable and murderers and immoral persons and sorcerers and idolaters and all liars, their part will be in the lake that burns with fire and brimstone, which is the second death."

The Kingdom of our Lord Jesus Christ is over and eternity begins with the presence of God the Father. This is still physical on the new earth, but also eternal.

Revelation 22:1–3

1 Then he showed me a river of the water of life, clear as crystal, coming from the throne of God and of the Lamb,

2 in the middle of its street. On either side of the river was the tree of life, bearing twelve kinds of fruit, yielding its fruit every month; and the leaves of the tree were for the healing of the nations.

3 There will no longer be any curse; and the throne of God and of the Lamb will be in it, and His bond-servants will serve Him...

27

EPILOGUE

I have presented what I believe to be the Hope of mankind, the fulfilment of prophecy, and the reconciliation of man to God. That reconciliation was only made possible by the blood of Christ at the Cross. Nothing else. Learning of this reconciliation should elicit a response in us allowing that sacrifice to cleanse our conscience and instill in us a strong desire to yield our lives to the Holy Spirit. This is yielding to the Faith that God has given us.

I hope that the reader now has an understanding of the concept of salvation — not from sin, as that has already happened, but to enter Into the Kingdom. This requires a relationship with Him. We struggle with a guilty conscience that instills fear in us. Fear causes us to avoid entering into the presence of God and enjoying fellowship with Him. Understanding what Christ did at the cross enables us to overcome that evil conscience and the fear of God's displeasure or disappointment in us. God is never disappointed with us because we sin. When we know His unconditional love and forgiveness, we should respond by wanting to please Him. Loving others, putting their needs before your own, is pleasing to God.

What does it take to enter into the Kingdom? It requires that we yield to the leading of the Holy Spirit, allowing him to use us to His glory.

Christ will judge us by our relationship with Him and our works, which are motivated by His love. These are not works that are of our efforts, but works that come from dying to self and walking in the power of the Holy Spirit.

I once asked Sterling Lands, a wonderful friend and counselor of mine, "How do you have such a strong walk with God and completely dedicate yourself to Him?" His answer was so simple, yet so profound, that it affected my entire concept of living the Christian life and what I believe allows one to enter into the Kingdom. His answer was "*Just do it!*" I walked away thinking, "How can I do that? How can it be so simple? This pointed out to me that I was avoiding *just doing it* because I was not really ready to die to self and to live completely for God. I still had hopes of climbing the corporate ladder, of making more money, of making something of myself.

> *Man's* hope must be destroyed, that *God's* hope may be built upon its ruins. The human is swept away only that the divine may come in its stead. The temporal is in mercy wrested from our grasp, that the eternal may be our portion and inheritance.

> There is, then, that which God calls "the BETTER hope,"—a hope full of immortality; a hope which God Himself gives, and of which no man can rob us. It is divine and everlasting. It brings with it the peace which passeth all understanding; and it contains in it the joy unspeakable and full of glory. No disappointment in it, and no mockery! It is sure and glorious, like Him from whom it comes to us. It is connected with a crown, with an inheritance, with a kingdom, with a glory which fadeth not away, with an eternity of joy such as eye hath not seen, nor ear heard.

> The hope which God sets before us is no doubtful thing, but sure and glorious. It rests upon His gospel, in believing which we become men of hope.[195]

---

[195] (Bonar, 1881)

Yes; and he that believeth enters into a new life, and begins a holy walk,—a life and a walk corresponding to the faith which realizes both the grace of the Cross and the glory of the kingdom. "If any man be in Christ, he is a new creature;" and that same Holy Spirit who drew him to the Cross, is given him that he may follow Christ, and be holy as He was holy.[196]

Our desire should be to pray every moment of our life something like this:

"Father, help me to put my needs and desires behind and let Your love shine through me in my service to them. Enable me to love all who I meet with Your love. Let them see You in my actions, and let my actions bring glory to You and Your Son. Keep me from becoming proud for Your actions.

Allow me to yield to the Holy Spirit and guide my steps every moment today. Use me anyway You can. Make me a blessing to all I meet today."

I am blessed by the prayer of St. Francis:

> *Lord, make me an instrument of your peace,*
> *Where there is hatred, let me sow love;*
> *Where there is injury, pardon;*
> *Where there is doubt, faith;*
> *Where there is despair, hope;*
> *Where there is darkness, light;*
> *Where there is sadness, joy.*
> *O Divine Master,*
> *grant that I may not so much seek to be consoled, as to console;*
> *to be understood, as to understand;*

---

[196] (Bonar, 1881)

to be loved, as to love.
For it is in giving that we receive.
It is in pardoning that we are pardoned,
and it is in dying that we are born to Eternal Life.

I am convinced that God answers this kind of prayer when prayed in faith—faith that He loves all and faith that we are, indeed, forgiven; the faith that He desires to use us to glorify Him, as well as to show His love and glory to others.

I wondered why we have to pray for something more than once. Why should I have to pray every day for my children's health and safety? Why do we need to partition Him in prayer?

Then, I realized that God desires that I stay conscious of Him as much as possible, and prayer brings me in that relationship with Him that we need to walk the walk He wants of us. The more we are face to face with Him in prayer, the more apt we are to allow His Spirit and truth to control our actions.

It has been scientifically proven that the best way to engrain an action into someone or to train a dog is by intermittent reinforcement. This works better than constant reinforcement, where the subject is rewarded every time they perform the desired action.

Perhaps that is why the Lord does not always seem to answer prayers. He is not a genie to perform at our beck and call, but the creator of the universe and God almighty. As a loving Father, He answers prayers that are in line with His will, and, sometimes, He answers continual unceasing prayer and has been known to even change His mind, according to the Old Testament.

He wants us to constantly be in fellowship with Him and to depend on Him to live the life He desires for us. This is the life that will produce the works Christ would like to see that testify we know Him. This will also give you more joy in this present life than anything else this world can afford.

Jesus said,

> **Matthew 11:28–30**
> **28** *"Come to Me, all who are weary and heavy-laden, and I will give you rest.*
> **29** *Take My yoke upon you and learn from Me, for I am gentle and humble in heart, and* YOU WILL FIND REST FOR YOUR SOULS.
> **30** *For My yoke is easy and My burden is light."*

If it is hard, it is not Jesus; if you are trying to be a good Christian, you are going at it the wrong way. Allow the Holy Spirit to empower you to live your life; relax and just walk with Him. The result will amaze you.

God loves you and has given us the Holy Spirit to live the life He wants us to live. It is not because He demands us to be Holy just because He is Holy; it is because He loves us and the rest of the world so very much. Our walk in love with Him is such an enjoyable existence for us, and it bestows God's grace and love on those with whom we interact. We become the arms of God's love and our walk with Him benefits others.

> **Ephesians 6:23–24**
> **23** *Peace be to the brethren, and love with faith, from God the Father and the Lord Jesus Christ.*
> **24** *Grace be with all those who love our Lord Jesus Christ with incorruptible love.*

BIBLIOGRAPHY

Albert L. Winseman, D. M. (2004, May 24). *Eternal Destinations: Americans Believe in Heaven, Hell.* Retrieved from Gallup: http://www.gallup.com/poll/11770/Eternal-Destinations-Americans-Believe-Heaven-Hell.aspx

Archer, G. L. (1982). *Encyclopedia of Bible Difficulties.* Zondervan Publishing House.

Barry, J. D. (2012). *Faithlife Study Bible.* Bellingham, WA: Logos Bible Software.

Berry, E. (2003). *Second Coming IN (C.Brand, C. Draper, A. England, S. Bond, E.R. Clendenen & T. C. Butler, Eds.) Holman Illustrated Bible Dictionary.* Nashville, TN: Holman Bible Publishers.

Bonar, H. (1881). *How Shall I Go to God? And Other Readings.* London: The Religious Tract Society.

Boteler, M. M. (1915). *Sermon Notes from the Ministry of Jesus.* Cinncinatti, Oh: Standard.

Brown, W. A. (1919). *The Christian Hope: A Study in the Doctrine of Immortality.* New York: Charles Scribner's Sons.

Bullinter, E. (1898). *Figures of speech used in the Bible.* London; New York: Eyre & Spottiswoode: E.& J. B. Young & Co.

Cabal, J., & Cabal T, C. B. (2007). *How Should a Christian Understand the Age of the Earth Controversy? The Apologetics Study Bible: Real Questions, Straight Answers, Stonger Faith.* Nashville, TN: Holman Bible Publishers.

Calvin, J. &. (2010). *Commentaries on the Four Last Books of Moses Arranged in the Form of a Harmony (Vol 4, p 134).* Bellingham WA: Logos Bible Software.

Carpenter, E. &. (2000). *Holman Treasury of Key Bible Words: 200 Greek and 200 Hebrew Words Defined and Explained.* Nashville, TN: Broadman and Holman Publishers.

Carson, D. A. (1984). *The Expositor's Bible Commentary: Matthew, Mark, Luke.* Grand Rapids, MI: Zondervan Publishing House.

Cf. Council of Trent DS 1641. (n.d.). *Catechism of the Catholic Church - The Sacrement of the Eucharist.* Retrieved from Vatican VA: http://www.vatican.va/archive/ccc_css/archive/catechism/p2s2c1a3.htm

Chambers, O. (1986). *My Utmost for His Highest: Selections for the year.* Grand Rapids, MI: Oswald Chambers Publications; Marshall Pickering.

Constable, T. (2003). *Tom Constable's Expository Notes on the Bible.* Galaxie Software.

D. James Kennedy Ted Cabal et al. (2007). *"Christ: The fullfillment of Prophecy" The Apologetics Study Bilble: Real Questions, Straight Answers, Stronger Faith.* Nashville, TN: Holman Bible Publishers.

Easton, M. G. (1893). New York: Harper & Brothers.

Elwell, W. A. (1988). *Baker Encyclopedia of the Bible.* Grand Raids, MI: Baker Book House.

Fallon, G. A. (1967). *"Laymen as Good Stewards" Baker's Dictionary of Practical Theology.* Grand Rapids, MI: Baker Book House - ed. Ralph G. Turnbull.

Farrar, F. (1893). *The Epistle of Paul the Apostle to the Hebrews, With Notes and Introduction, Cambridge Greek Testament for Schools and Colleges.* Cambidge: Cambridge University Press.

Feinberg, C. (1986). *The Expositors Bible Commentary: Isaiah, Jeremiah, Lamentations, Ezekiel.* Grand Rapids, MI: Zondervan Publishing House.

Geisler, N. L. (1999). *Baker Encyclopedia of Christian apologetics.* Grand Rapids, MI: Baker Books.

Geisler, N. L. (2002). *Systematic Theology, Volume One: Introduction, Bible.* Minneapolis, MN: Bethany House.

Geisler, N. L. (2003). *Systematic Theology, Volume Two: God, Creation.* Minneapolis, MN: Bethany House.

Geisler, N. L. (2005). *Systematic Theology, Volume Four: Church, Last Things.* Minneapolis, MN: Bethany House.

Geoffrey W. Bromiley, e. (1979-1988). *The International Standard Bible Encyclopedia, Revised.* Wm. B. Eerdmans.

Hahn, S. (2012). *The Lexham Bible Dictionary.* Bellingham, WA: Logos Bible Software.

Hardman, S. G. (1996). *Meditations on the return of Christ and the end of the age: With an overview of future events.* Willow Grove, PA: Woodlawn Electronic Publishing.

Harris, S. (n.d.). *Quoted in Naismith 2400 Outlines.*

Henry, M. (1996, c 1991). Henrickson: Peabody.

Hobbs, H. H. (1990). *My Favorite Illustrations.* Naxhville, TN: Broadman Press.

Hodge, C. (1997, Originally published in 1872). Oak Harbor, WA: Logos Research Systems, Inc.

Jamieson, R. F. (1997). *A commentary, critical and explanatory, on the Old and New Testaments On Spine: Critical and explanatory commentary.* Oak Harbor, WA: Logos Research Systems, Inc.

Karleen, P. S. (1987). *The Handbood to Bible Study: With a Guide to the Scofield Study System.* New York: Oxford Universtiy Press.

Kenison, F. (1996). *The Apocalypse of Revelations.* Purkaitheion Press.

Kenison, F. (1999). *The Truth Revealed in Romans.* Iola, KS: Purkaitheion Press.

Kenison, F. (1999). *What Scriptures Say About Salvation.* Purkaitheion Press.

Kittel, G. B. (1964). *Theological dictionary of the New Testament.* Grand Rapids, MI: Eerdmans.

Kittel, G. F. (1985). *Theological Dictionary of the New Testament.* Grand Rapids, MI. W. B. Eerdmans.

Lange, J. P. (2008). *A Commentary on the Holy Scriptures: 1 Corinthians.* Bellingham, WA: Logos Bible Software.

Lange, J. P. (2008). *A commentary on the Holy Scriptures: Matthew.* Bellingham, WA: Logos Bible Software.

Levy, D. M. (1993). *The tavernacle shadows of the Messiah: sacrifices, and priesthood.* Bellmawr, NT: Friends of Israel Gospel Ministry.

Louw, J. P. (1996). *Greek English Lexicon of the New Testament: Based on semantic domains.* New York: United Bible Societies.

MacArthur, J. (1996). *The Glory of Heaven; The truth About Heaven, Angels, and Eternal Life.* Wheaton, Ill: Crossway Books.

MacArthur, J. (1997). *Heaven. John MacArthurs Bible Studies.* Chicago: Moody Press.

MacArthur, J. F. (1995). *Alone with God.* Wheaton, Il: Victor Books.

Manser, M. H. (2009). *Dictionary of Bible Themes: The Accesable and Comprehensive Tool for Topical Studies.* London: Martin Manser, Alister McGrath, J.I. PAcker, and Donald Wiseman.

Mare, T. b. (n.d.). *The Expositor's Bible Commentary, vol. 10, 243.*

Mauro, P. (1918). *After This or The Church, The Kingdom, and The Glory.* New York; Chicago; London; Edinburgh: Fleming H. Revell Company.

Meek, R. (2012). *Jeremiah, Book of Introduction To. In (J.D. Barry & L. Wentz, Eds)The Lexham Bible Dictionary.* Bellingham, W.A.: Logos Bible Software.

Meldau, F. J. (1988). *The prophets still speak: Messiah in both testaments.* Bellmawr, NJ: Friends of Israel Gospel Ministry.

Nash, R. H. (2007). *The Apologetics Study Bible: Real Questions, Straight Answers, Stronger Faith.* Nashville, TN: Holman Bible Publishers.

Olford, S. F. (1998). *Anointed Expository Preaching.* Nashville, TN: Broadman & Holman Publishers.

Peters, G. N. (1884). *The Theocratic Kingdom of our Lord Jesus, the Christ Vol. 2.* New York; London: Funk & Wagnalls.

Peters, G. N. (1884). *The Theocratic Kingdom of our Lord Jesus, the Christ Vol. I.* New York; London: Funk & Wagnalls.

Pierce, L. (n.d.). *Tense Voice Mood.* Bellingham, WA: Logo Bible Software.

Piper, J. (2006). *Fifty Reasons Why Jesus Came to Die.* Wheaton, Il: Crossway Books.

Reid, D. L. (1990). *In Dictionary of Christianity in America.* New York: United Bible Societies.

Richards, L. &. (1987). *The teachers commentary.* Wheaton, Il: Victor Books.

Richards, L. O. (1999). Grand Rapids, MI: Zondervan Publishing House.

Riley, W. B. (1913). *The Evolution of the Kingdom.* New York; London: Chas C. Cook; S.W. Partridge & Co.

Robertson. (n.d.). Grammar.

Robertson, A. T. (1933). *Word Pictures in the New Testament.* Nashville, TN: Broadman Press.

Sailhamer, J. H. (1990). *Genesis (F. E. Gaebelein, Ed.) The Expostor's Bible Commentary: Genesis, Exodus, Leviticus, Numbers.* Grand Rapids, Mi: Zondervan Publishing House.

Saldarini, A. J. (2011). New York: HarperCollins.

Salmond, S. D. (1897). *The Christian Doctrine of Immortatlity, Third Edition.* Edinburgh: T. & T. Clark.

Saucy, R. (1979). *The Eschatology of the Bible Article in The Expositor's Bible Commentary: Introductory Aticles Vol 1* (Vol. 1). (F. Gaebelein, Ed.) Grand Rapids, MI, USA: Zondervan Publishing House.

Schaff, P. &. (1997). *History of the Christian Church.* Oak Harbor, WA: Logos Research Systems, Inc.

Showers, R. (1990). *There really is a difference!: a comparison of covenant and dispensational theology.* Bellmawr, NJ: The Friends of Israel Gospel Ministry, Inc.

Sproul, R. C. (1994). *The Gospel of God: An Exposition of Romans.* Great Britain: Christian Focus Publications.

Sproul, R. C. (1994). *The Purpose of God: Ephesians.* Scotland: Christian Focus Publications.

Stacey, A. (2012, April 26th). *The religion of Islam.* Retrieved September 19, 2013, from http://www.islamreligion.com/articles/5214/#_ftn20138

Standard Bible Dictionary. (2006). Cincinnati, OH: Standard Publishing.

Stone, S. E. (1995). *Sermon Outlines on Galations, Ephesians, Philippians, Colossians (S. E. Stone, Ed.).* Cincinnati, OH: Standard.

Sussman, D. (2005, Dec 20). *Poll: Elbow Room No Problem in Heaven.* Retrieved from ABC NEWS: http://abcnews.go.com/US/Beliefs/story?id=1422658

Tan, P. L. (1996). *Encyclopedia of 7700 Illustrations: Signs of the Times.* Garland, TX: Bible Communications, Inc.

The International Preterist Association Website. (n.d.). *http://www.preterist.org/whatwebelieve.asp What is the preterist view of Bible Prophecy.*

Torrey, R. A. (1998). *The Return of the Lord Jesus: The key to the scripture, and solution of all our political and social problems.* Willow Grove, OA: Woodlawn Electronic Publishing.

Vincent, M. R. (1887). *Word Studies in the New Testament.* New York: Charles Scribner's Sons.

Wallace, D. B. (1999). *Greek Grammar Beyond the Basics - Exegetical Syntax of the New Testament.* Zondervan Publishing House and Galaxie Software.

Wood, C. R. (1994). *Sermon Outlines on Great Doctrinal Themes.* Grand Rapids, MI: Kregel Publications.

Wood, D. a. (1996). *New Bible Commentary.* Leicester, England; Downers Grove, IL: InterVarsity Press.

Wuest, K. S. (1997, c1984). Grand Rapids, MI: Eerdmans.

All quotes from *My Utmost for His Highest* by Oswald Chambers used with kind permission from the Oswald Chambers Publications Association.

INDEX OF SCRIPTURES

H

I

J

About the Author

Ken Stewart first attended the College of Emporia in Emporia, Kansas, where he became a Christian and was active in Campus Crusade for Christ. He started studying the Bible with a group of friends and felt inspired to write a book on the Kingdom. Forty-four years later, it is completed and you are holding it in your hands.

After four years in the Air Force and then operating Ken's TV Repair in Iola, Kansas. He eventually went on to earn a Bachelor of Science degree in Electronics Technology and a Master of Science degree in Plastics Engineering. For over 35 years, Ken has worked in the electronics and technology industry and currently works as a Sales Engineer. In his spare time, he enjoys fishing, playing guitar, and gardening. He especially enjoys studying the Bible. He currently lives in Hudson, Ohio with his wife, Sallie.